WANDERING WITH INTENT

Kim Mahood is a writer and artist who grew up in Central Australia and on Tanami Downs Station. She has worked closely with Aboriginal people across Australia's desert regions, maintains strong connections with Warlpiri and Walmajarri people, and has extensive experience in cultural and environmental mapping projects in the Tanami and Great Sandy Desert, western New South Wales, the Top End, Perth, Fremantle, and the Great Victoria Desert. She is the author of two previous nonfiction books, *Craft for a Dry Lake* (2000) and *Position Doubtful* (2016), and co-editor of *Desert Lake: art, science, and stories from Paruku* (CSIRO, 2013). Her work has received numerous awards, and is published in literary, art, and current affairs journals.

KIM MAHOOD

WANDERING WITH INTENT

ESSAYS FROM REMOTE AUSTRALIA

SCRIBE
Melbourne • London

Scribe Publications
18–20 Edward St, Brunswick, Victoria 3056, Australia
2 John St, Clerkenwell, London, WC1N 2ES, United Kingdom
3754 Pleasant Ave, Suite 100, Minneapolis, Minnesota 55409, USA

Published by Scribe in Australia and New Zealand 2022
Published in North America 2023

Excerpt from *The Night Parrot* by Dorothy Porter, 1984, used with
permission given by Andrea Goldsmith for the Estate of Dorothy Porter.

Every effort has been made to acknowledge and contact the copyright
holders for permission to reproduce material contained in this book.
Any copyright holders who have been inadvertently omitted from the
acknowledgements and credits should contact the publisher so that
omissions may be rectified in subsequent editions.

Typeset in Garamond Premium Pro by the publishers

Printed and bound in the UK by CPI Group (UK) Ltd, Croydon CR0 4YY

Scribe is committed to the sustainable use of natural resources and the use
of paper products made responsibly from those resources.

978 1 957363 28 8 (US edition)
978 1 925713 25 1 (Australian edition)
978 1 922586 65 0 (ebook)

scribepublications.com
scribepublications.com.au
scribepublications.co.uk

*For my mother, who began her writing career as Marie Healy,
expanded it under the pseudonym of Wanda Sterling,
and ended it as Marie Mahood.*

Contents

Previous publications

Earlier versions of nine essays in this collection have been published previously. 'Blow-ins on the cold desert wind' was first published in *Griffith Review 15: Divided Nation*, February 2007, and subsequently appeared in *The Best Australian Essays* 2007 (Black Inc., 2012). 'Kartiya are like Toyotas: white workers on Australia's cultural frontier' was first published in *Griffith Review 36: What Is Australia For?*, April 2012, and subsequently appeared in *The Best Australian Essays* 2012 (Black Inc., 2012). 'Country needs people' was first published in *The Monthly*, July 2017. 'Trapped in the gap' appeared as 'White Stigma' in *The Monthly*, August 2015. 'The seething landscape' was written for the National Museum of Australia exhibition catalogue *Songlines: tracking the Seven Sisters*, 2017. 'The man in the log' appeared in *The Monthly*, December 2018–January 2019. 'Lost and found in translation' was first published in *Griffith Review 63: Writing the Country*, February 2019. 'Flowers for Evelyn' was first published in *Chicago Quarterly Review 30: The Australian edition*, February 2020. A shorter version of 'The night parrot: it's a whitefella thing' appeared in the *Australian Book Review*, no. 415, October 2019.

Note on languages

Any inconsistences in the spelling of Aboriginal words are due to alternate spellings in the orthographies of the different languages. I have chosen to use the Warlpiri orthography for the word 'kardiya (kartiya)' because it is closer to the sound of the spoken word.

Preface

To essay means to try, to endeavour, to attempt. It implies risk and failure. It is also the only way to find out whether something is possible. These essays are a sort of written equivalent of hunting and gathering, of wandering with intent. They are the product of my own wandering among the conundrums and contradictions of the cross-cultural world I've chosen to inhabit, and of my intent to understand and honour it.

When I returned south in 2019, after the sixteenth consecutive year of working in the small desert community of Mulan in the southeast Kimberley, I found it almost impossible to write. The time I'd spent was wonderful, the project we'd worked on had been a success, my relationships with people had deepened and strengthened. The death or absence of the senior women I usually worked with had made space for the next generation to step up. The sadness of loss was compensated for by the participation of people who had been waiting on the sidelines. The times we'd shared had been hopeful, hilarious, challenging in all the best ways, and had banished the thoughts I'd harboured about whether it was time for me to move on. The Mulan mob were family, and the country was home. I would be coming back for as long as my health and my wits allowed.

But the edge I walked when writing about my interactions with the people and country that occupied such a significant place in my life was getting thinner and sharper. It had always been necessary to filter what I wrote through the lens of a white readership for whom the remote Indigenous world represented everything from a utopian idyll to a wretched dystopia, but so far I'd managed to meet my own standards of truth-telling. This was becoming more and more difficult to do.

The essays in this collection were written over a period of more than fifteen years, during which time the attitudes and sensitivities around who has the right to speak and write about Indigenous issues have become increasingly charged and complex. This has left me wondering about what the implications of cancel culture and identity politics might be for me. Some of the previously published essays would likely not make it into print in today's cultural climate, but I have chosen not to edit out what might now cause offence and attract criticism. To do so would be disingenuous, and a betrayal of my endeavour to understand and communicate, as honestly as I can, something of the unique cultural interface I've been enmeshed in and witness to for much of my life.

The zone between white and black has been part of my life for as long as I can remember. Since my early childhood in Central Australia, I have been entangled in particular Aboriginal families in multiple ways. My sense of the world has been constructed by that experience, my career has been directed by those relationships, and both have been the raw material of my creative work.

What compels me is watching relationships play out at the edge of cultural systems that baffle and subvert each other, where the frontier is still adaptive and resistant, the population is predominantly Aboriginal, and the land is a living entity that influences the lives of the human players. It is a dynamic and volatile world that has been impacted by colonialism but has retained its Indigenous character, much of which is interpreted by the white world as dysfunctional, but which continues to function with remarkable tenacity. I've spent years seeing the Indigenous people I know grow and change, take on responsibilities or avoid them, make choices about how to be the Indigenous player on someone else's agenda.

I write about what happens at the point of intersection, where traditional culture is still strong, where whites are in the minority but occupy most of the official positions, and where the unfolding narrative is complicated, nuanced, and evolving. I write to seduce my readers to travel with me to places they might otherwise never visit. I exercise my craft in the service of the things I'm passionate about — art, country, and the interface between Indigenous and non-Indigenous Australia.

That I exercise cultural privilege when writing about desert Aboriginal people is a given. The question is whether I exercise this privilege in a way that can be justified. I have been grappling with this conundrum since I began writing, and it never gets any easier.

My enduring aim is to maintain the trust I have established over the years — with the people I have lived with, worked with, and written about, and with the readers of my books.

1

Where words don't have edges

The Australian desert is a more complicated place than it used to be. There was a time when it functioned in the white Australian imagination more as a metaphor than as a real place, a negative space into which explorers, white children, and the occasional eccentric wanderer disappeared, leaving a frisson of existential anxiety and a satisfying conviction that the heart of the continent remained an impenetrable mystery. Its nomadic occupants, for the most part invisible, were thought to be Stone Age remnants: innocent, bloodthirsty, fabulous, and doomed. Until the last decades of the twentieth century, most of the words written about the desert and its occupants were written by white people — journalists, historians, anthropologists, novelists, settler wives — with varying degrees of insight, empathy, curiosity, patronage, incomprehension, and mythologising.

This solipsistic condition started to unravel with the emergence of the Western Desert painting movement in the 1970s and 1980s, which has in recent times effloresced into a cultural renaissance of astonishing vigour and originality. The iconic desert nomads, instead of fading discreetly into the mirage along with their obscure traditions, emerged in the vanguard of contemporary culture as charismatic individuals with rich and entertaining personal histories, as well as disturbing tales of displacement and murder. It turned out that they weren't even proper nomads, but the custodians of clearly defined tracts of land, the boundaries of which they transgressed at their peril. The desert — or deserts, for there are many different deserts in Australia, each of them with their own unique character — began to speak through the voices of the people who called them home.

The stories were encoded in the paintings, epics in which individual lives intersected with ancestral creation stories, and the beginnings of an understanding of the complexity of Aboriginal belief systems began to infiltrate the broader Australian culture. As the painting movement expanded, a more literal storytelling element emerged — of the frontier contact days, of growing up on the missions and cattle stations, of making the adaptations and adjustments necessary to the changes in their world.

Recognising that the desert is rich with stories of real people and particular places has not displaced the metaphoric space it occupies in our cultural imagination, but it has destabilised it, opened it up to challenge and reinterpretation. Painting, sculpture, dance, oral histories, and, more recently, film and virtual reality have all gone a long way towards weaving strands of brilliant colour through a once monochromatic fabric.

When Terri-ann White, the then director of UWA Publishing, contacted me about co-ordinating a writing workshop in the remote Aboriginal community of Mulan, I assumed she meant the sort of event to which would-be writers fly or drive at great expense, to experience the glamour of the desert along with the stimulus of a professional workshop. So I was intrigued when Terri-ann revealed that the model she had in mind was to draw on writing from the place itself. I wondered how that would work when much of the local population was not literate, and when those who did have competent literacy skills were more likely to be asked to translate the mysteries of a Centrelink form than to write an account of a personal experience.

It would be necessary to stretch the definition of 'writing' to include the oral traditions of the desert mob, and to allow for a spectrum of storytelling models. Having facilitated various workshops and meetings over the past decade, I wasn't about to make promises I couldn't keep. I told Terri-ann I'd do my best, but that I couldn't guarantee the outcomes. On the other hand, I knew that people were generally responsive to projects that involved storytelling and country. We could involve the schoolkids through the language-and-literacy program, and the older people were always happy to tell their stories. And there were bound to be a few whitefellas I could rope in.

Once I'd established that people were keen to participate, I gave Terri-ann the thumbs-up. I was filling in as co-ordinator for the Indigenous Protected Area, and, since I preferred my spartan two-room donga, I offered Terri-ann accommodation in the co-ordinator's demountable. For someone used to five-star hotels around the world, she earned her stripes in Mulan. We were in the throes of a plague of small, smelly flying beetles that found their way through gaps in the floor of the demountable and woke Terri-ann by dive-bombing her bedsheets in the early hours of the morning. She never complained, and I hope has since dined out on the story.

We spent a day in the school, adapting a model to suit the senior kids, the middle-school kids, and the little ones. They were full of enthusiasm, the paramount story being a hunting adventure they'd had on the previous weekend in which a dog brought down a kangaroo. Some wrote their own stories, while others dictated to the teachers, who honoured the poetics of the Aboriginal English spoken by the children. This was an excursion into literature, not grammar, and it was the authenticity of the kids' voices that needed to be on the page.

Another day was dedicated to local adults, who told stories I knew from many tellings. It reminded me of my childhood, listening to the adults around me tell their signature tales over and over, laying in a template of storytelling I still love, of incidents honed almost to the shape of a parable.

My friend Sam Togni was visiting the nearby community of Balgo, and I asked her to bring some of the Balgo mob over for a writing session. Sam arrived in a troop carrier loaded with a dozen people, including three white women, who were working or volunteering in the art centre and the women's culture centre. The group represented a spectrum of literacy I could not have assembled by design, ranging from a Queensland university undergraduate studying contemporary literature to an elderly Kukatja artist lifted by helicopter from the desert as a malnourished child.

People who could write transcribed for those who could not. The whitefellas wrote about the challenges they experienced as remote-area nurses, art centre managers, blow-ins and volunteers. The Aboriginal stories were testimonials: this is my place, this is my genealogy, this is who I am. Or they were existential: a desert childhood disrupted by a helicopter flight and a sudden transition from one reality into another; the interactions between traditional life and growing up in the Mission dormitories under a regime of God and cleanliness and obedience; encounters with featherfoot men and wild bush women.

Editing the stories for publication was a challenge. Translating the performed word into something that worked on the page was best approached as a form of poetry, keeping the rhythms and cadences of Aboriginal English and the style of individual voices. The genealogies and other iterations of belonging went through without change. For some people, this was the only story that mattered, especially if there was some challenge to its validity. I had learned to leave such things alone.

A year later, I took published copies of *Desert Writing: stories from country* back to Balgo and Mulan, and distributed them to everyone who had contributed. The kids saw their own words in print, read them aloud to their teachers and families, and critiqued their spelling and grammar in the light of a year's advancement.

Some of the kids would go south to boarding school for their secondary education, and some would suffer from homesickness so acute that they would abandon school and come home to stay. Some would make it through, and be equipped with greater choices, though many of them would also return home. I wondered if any of them would find solace in books, would discover that reading is an antidote to loneliness, and that the imagination thrives on solitude. And then, as readers often do, would they go on to write their own stories, transforming the stuff of their own imagination and experience into literature?

'Reading and writing change people and change societies,' claims the poet and classical scholar Anne Carson, in *Eros the Bittersweet*. Carson tells us that the word for 'word' in Homer also means speech, tale, song, line of verse, epic poetry as a whole. This conflation of meanings exists in many languages, including Australian Indigenous languages. People who moved carried their knowledge with them in songs and poetry. Words didn't exist as independent objects. They were the sounds that humans strung together to create meaning and to communicate with one another. Before writing usurped memory and the oral cultures that preserved it, minstrels and singers recounted narrative epics to an audience. Listening was shared, story was collective, and so to a great extent was memory.

Oral cultures are sensory, Carson says. The senses are open to the environment, absorbing the messages it carries from the human and non-human world. In oral cultures, the human self is not differentiated from the environment, or from other humans in the way that literate cultures have evolved. 'To close off the senses would be counterproductive to life and thought,' she writes.

As words were written down, they developed edges. In the Western world, somewhere between the emergence of the alphabet, the development of agriculture, and the invention of lyric poetry, writing harnessed the seduction of story, broke it down into words constructed from vowels and consonants, and organised the words into lines of text. And somewhere in this process, humans also developed edges. The 'I' stepped out from the cluster of sounds, capitalised itself, and spoke back to the mind that wrote it. Thus began the conversation with the self, and with it the process of increasing individuation, introspection, and self-awareness. As the solitary act of writing replaced the shared experience of memorising as a means of passing on knowledge, the concept of loneliness entered the human vocabulary.

The 'I' of Tim Leura Tjapaltjarri's painting *Spirit Dreaming through Napperby Country* (see colour section) is embedded in the web of beings that populate the story: ancestral forces that give the land form and meaning, a kinship that contains not just humans, but plants and animals and birds and insects and reptiles. The 'I' is shared with his brother Tjapaltjarris, designating his relationships with all others in his kin group, and beyond his country to all Tjapaltjarris or their equivalent, and their kin, throughout the desert. Tim Leura was assisted by his half-brother Clifford Possum to paint this monumental narrative, a statement of belonging and displacement, of the journey of his spirit through the lands to which he held ancestral title. The 'I' that inhabits this painting is inclusive, but it is also self-aware and individual. Geoffrey Bardon said of *Spirit Dreaming through Napperby Country*, which was completed in 1980:

It is an extraordinary work because it is the first painting in which a Western Desert artist stands aside from his tribal context and comments, quite self-consciously, on his art, his Dreamings and himself ... The Great Painting is a simple and brooding repudiation by him of his white masters. He apparently felt that his life's journey, shown in the huge sinuous line holding the Dreaming 'windows' in equipoise, was a rejection of white man's pretensions.

The selfhood expressed in the work is rendered in paint on canvas, a transitional medium already some way towards writing, in which narrative is harnessed to a surface and expressed through an arrangement of iconic and abstract marks. The serpentine line that wanders through the country of the painting is both the artist's journey and the self to whom the journey belongs. Bardon, who spoke to Tim Leura about this work, says 'the death figure in the painting is Tim's perception of himself in his own social context'. I take this to mean that the painter saw that his way of being in the world was dying. The painting is a magisterial expression of the genius generated by an oral tradition seeking to speak to a literate tradition. The painter records this struggle from within a consciousness of the self being torn loose from the unity of country, the senses, the essences of living things, the connectedness through time and place in the web of existence.

Most of us, looking at the work, would not come close to understanding its meaning without the interpretation that the painter entrusted to Bardon. No doubt much is lost in translation, but Bardon's attempt to communicate the depth and complexity of Tim Leura's intention is a window into a unique encounter between different ways of being.

Literacy allowed people to accumulate and store a much larger body of knowledge than was possible in oral cultures, but it also made it possible to become detached from the natural world, with its checks and balances and endlessly mutable wonders. Several years before painting *Spirit Dreaming through Napperby Country*, Tim Leura Tjapaltjarri painted *Sun, Moon and Morning Star Dreaming*. In this work, the dark, reddish ground can be seen through a mosaic of cloud. Men sit facing each other across campfires protected by windbreaks. The men are signified by red U-shapes, which represent the imprint made in sand by sitting cross-legged. The windbreaks are indicated by curved red lines, some of which are partly obscured by clouds. The men are waiting for the dawn, when they will rise from their fires and begin to dance. Above them, moving across the sky, the sun and moon make their own dance, which is about love. The symbol for the moon, which is female, is the same bent half-circle as for the men, but white. It moves about the white disc of the sun like a returning boomerang, now closer, now further away, but clearly caught in its orbit. The campfires of long-dead warriors are scattered across the sky, having turned into stars.

As you look at the painting, the fields of dots become points of light breaking over the land, and you sense the dancers rising and moving towards one another, feet stamping, voices rising, the sounds gathering like swarms of bees.

As I write this, conjuring a world that predates writing, I want to yell with astonishment that we inhabit a time and place where the perceptions that created this painting coexist with the internet and space travel and cookery books and market economics. They are perceptions that come from a place where words don't have edges, and they still have much to tell us about the country we live in.

2

Notebooks

Dusty, dog-eared, stained, my notebooks wear the evidence of hard use; of being shoved between car seats, rescued from the sticky fingers of children, written up by firelight under the bombardment of suicidal insects. They form a substantial pile, with brightly coloured A4 hard covers, easy to spot when mislaid, spiral bound for the convenience of folding them open and for notching a biro, which is tied on with string for additional security. Losing your only biro a hundred kilometres from the nearest source of a replacement is no joke.

Read consecutively, they reveal a trajectory, though towards what end is anybody's guess. The earliest notebooks are filled with the colours and textures of the country — drawings in ochres and charcoal, sketches of the landforms, grids of prevailing colours, notes on how the materials of the desert might be used for making drawings and sculpture. Plants are pressed between the pages, the brittle ghosts of some particular campsite or stretch of track. Words like *horizon* and *mirage* recur, hinting at the ideas that will come to preoccupy me. A sentence scrawled across a page of drawings reads: *horizon as faultline, fracture line in the consciousness*. It's one of those floating, half-understood thoughts that I will return to often, wondering what it was I actually meant.

Later, language predominates: a spooling narrative of events, places, people, observations, theories, ideas ... the writer as observer, maintaining a certain distance, conflicted, uncomfortable, alert to the disjunctions between white and Aboriginal lives:

> ... the importance of grasping the dynamic constant of family life, obligations, dramas.

> ... the whitefellas are always on stress leave, or are about to leave, or have done a runner ...

I still had the time to write daily journal entries, and the energy and the fresh eye to take nothing for granted, or to comment on what would later be too obvious to bother recording:

> ... hold onto the authentic voice, the awareness that you are considered rather stupid, and for most people are not much more than a convenience, a taxi service, a source of energy that generates interesting activities and, more importantly, money ...

And then something happens. Days are accounted for by lists: lists of chores; lists of names; lists of Aboriginal words; lists of food, tools, and equipment; lists of dates and meetings and payments. References to money business occur frequently. The writer's voice is reduced to marginalia, jotted down on the run:

> JK turned up for work with his mouth swollen from a fight. I told him to take the ice pack off so I could punch him in the mouth for being an idiot.

> J said if the community was run like a card game it would work better.

R said whitefellas don't trust Aboriginal people. I asked her if
Aboriginal people trusted whitefellas ...

The subtext of these later notebooks is the things that don't get
done. They are a record of loose ends and unfinished business, and of
my own lack of suitability for the multiple roles I find myself playing
simply because I am there. In their utilitarian prose, they tell the story
of a work in progress, where the cultures meet, abrade, enrich, and
undo each other.

This is the raw, uncensored stuff from which I've fashioned the
stories that have made it into print. This is the record of a place where
life happens to me — where I'm confronted with my limitations and
prejudices, challenged to the edges of my tolerance, embraced by
people whose lives I participate in without fully understanding them.
In bearing witness to my own life, I also bΔear witness to this world.
It's where I've been woken at four in the morning by a teenage boy
riffling through my belongings looking for tobacco, chased him off
in a fury, and discovered after he'd escaped over the fence with his
accomplices that he had lifted my wallet and car keys, been through the
car, stolen my head torch and binoculars, and would likely have stolen
the car if I hadn't mislaid the key to the gate padlock. I've had a Sunday
afternoon interrupted by kids setting fire to the visitors' quarters next
to the ranger base. The six-room visitors' demountable was reduced
to a twisted wreck, but we managed to save the hardwood verandah
and the protective roof, which were later incorporated into the ranger
compound. I've been enlisted to talk a young man down from a panic
attack caused by a potent variety of marijuana, and been hounded
by bullies of various creeds, races, and genders. There's always some
incipient drama simmering, generated by the activities of deranged
kardiya or the long-standing resentments between local families.

The notebooks confront me with a dilemma. To open them is to unleash the noise and vitality and contradictions of a world to which I have privileged access. I have a responsibility to the individuals who inhabit that world to protect their privacy, and a keen desire on my own behalf to protect the relationships I have developed with them. But I feel an equal responsibility as a writer to communicate the dynamic reality of ordinary lives, the robustness and resilience, the humour, intransigence, and adaptive opportunism that both counteract and contribute to the challenges of remote community life.

To attempt to write about these things is a risk. Not only do I lay myself open to attack from the cultural minders, but also to the risk of misinterpretation by the literate among those whose world I write about. To say to people, 'I have written about you to make you real to other members of the society in which you are marginalised and misunderstood' has little meaning to them, since they don't see themselves as marginalised or misunderstood.

I try to minimise the risk by creating locations that are similar but not identical to the ones revealed in the notebooks, inhabited by people who are similar but not identical to the people whose voices and characters live on the pages. Most of the characters are composites; occasionally, they are fictions. For example, all the incidents that follow happened, though not necessarily in the precise way in which they have been set down.

* * *

There's a photograph of him as a young man — lean, flash, arrogant, hair-raisingly handsome in his cowboy hat and tooled leather boots, the sleeves chopped out of his press-stud shirt to reveal rippling brown biceps. A man cultivating an image of himself to carry him through the world — white father, Aboriginal mother, time spent in one of the more notorious mission homes for half-caste boys; hints, never quite articulated, of sexual abuse, his beauty and the flaring violence in him giving credence to the rumour.

The last time I saw him, he'd begun to thicken and go soft. The fine edge of violence that had sent him to prison several times had been replaced by a vague, unfocussed sweetness. He seemed passive, compliant, only half in the world.

All the time smoking ganja, people murmured. *And grog, too much grog.*

You could still see the traces of beauty in her, too, in the grey-green unreliable eyes and the shapely discontented mouth. They must have made an astonishing couple, drawn together by their outsider status and good looks. She was smart, charming, manipulative, dangerous to know. She could lie barefaced, knowing you had witnessed the act she had just denied, knowing you wouldn't call her on it because of the tantrum it would trigger, the outpouring of abuse, self-pity, accusations of racism, and the possibility that she might hit you.

'We used to tease her all the time when we were kids,' one of her contemporaries tells me, chuckling. 'Make her really wild.'

'Wasn't that cruel?'

'Yeah, it was cruel. Kids still doing it today to the half-caste kids. They shouldn't do that.'

I've witnessed it myself, a bawling, furious child being tormented until she is incoherent with rage, pitching rocks the size of cricket balls into the grinning pack that knows to the finest calibration how to trigger the explosion. She's a child for whom I've had a particular affection since she was a laughing toddler hurling herself into the investigation of her world, knees skinned, head shaven for lice. Now this snot-smeared monster dissolves into a heartsore bundle of muscle and grief when I pick her up, and her tormentors cluster around us, innocent-faced and full of explanations.

'She started it. She bit Danika. She threw a rock at Junior and made him bleed.'

'Is that true, Ruby?' She nods, aims a kick at the nearest child, who bares his teeth at her. She's six now, dark-honey skin and curls, her fearlessness a provocation to those who would test her to see just how far her rage will take her. Her older brother is lost already, introverted and unresponsive, cruel to animals in a deliberate, premeditated way.

* * *

Betty Noir has a powerful, under-employed intelligence fuelled by a fermenting reservoir of grievances. In her presence I am always wrong-footed, clumsy, and inclined to dig myself into cultural holes. Betty will not brook any contradiction. To engage with her is to negotiate the eggshell-thin fragility of the wounded ego, to pacify, to acquiesce, to appease. To avoid her is to cause offence, to insult, to overlook. My friend Pam coined the name Betty Noir when I described this woman as my bête noir, because she brings out all my own anxieties and inconsistencies. She short-circuits the forms of communication I have evolved to manage daily life in a cross-cultural minefield. It's in this relationship, more than any other, that I feel the instability of the ground I occupy, where humour and goodwill are not enough.

We have worked together on several occasions, during which times she has told me her personal story. She was a clever, sensitive girl, keen to please, praised and encouraged by her teachers, hungry for the love and acknowledgement of her parents, who were absent and alcoholic when she was growing up.

While Betty has made many perceptive and critical observations to me about her family and culture, at the same time she asserts that everything is now fine, people are good and caring towards each other, the inter- and intra-familial jealousies have been resolved. I agree cravenly when she says these things, but we both know that they aren't true.

And so the relationship stumbles along, superficially amicable, undermined by uneasiness and distrust. I try to avoid having too much to do with Betty, but this is also a problem, because she has strong relationships with all the other influential members of the community, and to avoid her is not only obvious but downright dangerous.

What Betty wants is a moment of emotional reckoning of the kind I have always preferred to avoid, a stripping down and re-defining of the rules of engagement. Betty has the capacity to see her world in a large context — she has a grasp of the inequities of the position her people occupy that is more subtle than the facts of poverty and powerlessness. She has the capacity to jolt the agreed notions of normality out of kilter and to expose the faultlines on which that normality is constructed.

If I was braver, tougher, more honest, I would give her what she wants. I would put myself in a position of vulnerability and see what it reveals. But I know I don't have the emotional resilience to see it through. It's all I can manage to sustain the non-threatening relationships with the people who like me. So I leave Betty Noir to her religiously inflected grievances, while I hone my skills of evasion.

* * *

Marcia is renowned for speaking out of turn, batting the unsayable into the open. She has a mane of white hair and no teeth, and carries a butcher's knife in her handbag to cut up her food. When it suits her, she is a fine painter, and always generous with the knowledge she holds of language, flora and fauna, and the cultural practices of her desert childhood.

She grew up in the dormitory system of the old Mission days, a desert girl whose family walked in from the south to investigate rumours of food and men in frocks. She is literate, an attribute she keeps to herself. When she discovers that I remember the Mission days and the priests and brothers from those times, she says, 'That Brother Michael used to love Aboriginal womans. I said to him, "Hey, you brother, you supposed to love God."'

Since the death of her husband, a local man with unassailable connections to this part of the country, she has lost the status her marriage gave her.

'She talks wrong way,' people say when I challenge them on their treatment of her. 'She could get somebody killed.'

There's an intractable toughness at the core of desert culture. And an intractable toughness at the core of the old woman, who is always good-humoured, ready to forgive the slights and to forget the oversights. She holds no grudges towards me for the times she has been left behind, when the group consensus has dictated that she not be included. There is a subtle charity in her attitude towards white people, as if she grasps the uncertain ground we occupy.

Marcia doesn't gamble. She doesn't humbug for money, and she is scrupulous about paying back the small amounts she occasionally borrows from me. I invent reasons to take her out to look for bush tucker and bush medicine so I can pay her some of the money allocated for cultural activities.

Lena worries that Marcia will disappear into the bush and that we will have to sit around all day waiting for her to come back.

'She's too deaf, can't hear you calling out for her. And she's too quick when she's hunting, we can't keep up with her.'

When Marcia is hunting, another dimension enters her personality. When she sees fresh tracks, it's as if the creature that made the tracks flees through her mind's eye. There's a forcefield of inevitability between the old hunter and her prey. She can move faster than a respectable old woman has any right to move, and some of us suspect that when our backs are turned, she flies, leaving the smoke of small hunting fires to mark her flight path.

* * *

I think, contemplating these scuffed containers with their compromising contents, that I should have quit years ago, when I knew enough to make sense of what I observed. Now I know too much to make sense of anything. The sheer weight of the material is overwhelming. I look at the battered pile, and what I see, through them, past them, is a place — hard blue light, dusty wind, red ground — and the people whose lives belong to and are shaped by that place.

3

Blow-ins on the cold desert wind

Each year I drive from my home near Canberra to the Tanami Desert and spend several months in an Aboriginal community that has become my other home. The trip takes a week or two, allowing for the incremental adjustments that make my arrival one of recognition, pleasure, and ambivalence.

There was a year I did it differently, flying directly to Alice Springs and travelling the thousand kilometres of corrugated and sandy desert track squashed into the back of a troop carrier with nine or ten elderly Aboriginal artists. We arrived in the early hours of the morning, less than twenty-four hours after I had left Canberra. The vehicle headlights lit up a disorderly world of damaged houses, broken cars, lean, furtive dogs, and accumulated rubbish. This was a number of years ago, when I was still sorting out the uneasiness of my relationship with the place and people, and I felt the rise of old anxieties and discomfort. It seemed that having departed from the orderly, over-planned surrealism of the national capital, I had arrived at its sinister twin.

As I helped to drag tattered foam mattresses and assorted bundles from the back of the troop carrier, I thought of the plans and policies manufactured in the tidy hillfort of Parliament House, and imagined them on their trajectory across the nation encountering a zone of refraction somewhere in the upper atmosphere, arriving as a mess of shattered fragments on this windy plateau. This image has stayed with me, a visual metaphor for the sustained capacity of remote Aboriginal Australia to subvert the best intentions of successive state and federal governments.

One of the results of moving on a regular basis between predominantly white urban Australia and predominantly black remote Australia is an awareness of the gulf of perception between those people for whom Aboriginal Australia is a reality and those for whom it is an idea. An idea can encompass a number of abstractions. Reality, on the other hand, must encompass a number of contradictions. The way in which these contradictions are bridged by both white and black is largely through humour, irony, and a well-honed sense of the absurd — qualities generally missing from any public representation of white and Aboriginal interactions.

The whites who work at this interface talk about Aboriginal people all the time. Every conversation, no matter where it begins, ends up in the same place. These conversations are full of bafflement, hilarity, frustration, admiration, and conjecture. They are an essential means of processing the contradictions that one deals with every day.

The Aboriginal people talk about the whites, too, but I doubt that it is in the same sustained and obsessive way. I can't be sure of this, and it is something I will probably never know. What I do know is that the Western Desert word for white person, *kardiya*, runs like a subliminal refrain under the currents of ordinary conversation. No matter how much time one has spent, or how strong one's relationships with Aboriginal people are, the word follows you about like a bad smell. It is not intended as an insult; it is simply a verbal marker to underline the difference between *us* and *them*.

It becomes an insult, however, if one is Aboriginal. In the volatile world of family and community politics, it is the greatest insult that can be levelled at anyone who is suspected of harbouring kardiya aspirations and values. To take on any form of authority over your peers opens you to such an accusation, as does the refusal to share vehicles, money, and possessions. People of mixed descent are continually reminded of their compromised status, and children with a white parent are frequently referred to as kardiya.

To be white exempts you to some extent from the network of responsibilities and obligations. It is accepted that you belong to an inexplicably cold and selfish branch of the human family. Refusals to share what you have are accepted with equanimity. However, the boundaries become more difficult to maintain as relationships deepen, and negotiating one's place in all of this is a continuing process.

By the standards of white Australian society, the life I lead is extremely provisional. I don't have a regular job, I don't own a home, and my annual income is in the bracket that attracts a low-income rebate on my tax return. In the eyes of the Aboriginal people among whom I work, I own a reliable vehicle, I can buy fuel when I need it, I always have food in the house, and I am allowed to run up an account at the store. These are indicators of wealth. Sometimes, as I weave my evasive course through a web of subtle and overt demands, carrying only small change in my pockets, walking instead of driving, so my car is not commandeered as a taxi to ferry people home with their shopping, making continual small adjustments and compromises against my better judgement, I catch a glimpse of the truly provisional nature of people's lives. When I buy diesel at $3 a litre, when I pay $5 for a carton of milk that would cost me half that in a southern supermarket, I appreciate the mirage-like nature of money in this world. I understand why the fortnightly pension cheque is converted to cash and lost in a card game an hour later. Paul Virilio, in *The Aesthetics of Disappearance*, says, 'Number games, like lotto or the lottery, with their disproportionate winnings, connote disobedience to society's laws, exemption from taxes, immediate redressment of poverty'.

If I was of an academic turn of mind, I would be tempted to pursue a thesis on the role and meaning of money in remote Aboriginal communities. There is no apparent logic to its availability. Acquiring it is a serious preoccupation, with none of the social prohibitions that disguise the same pre-occupation in Anglo-Australian society. It is easy to become cynical at the manoeuvring to prove traditional links to mining land and thus to gain access to royalties. It is easy to be appalled by the ruthlessness with which elderly painters are milked by their extended family, or to be exhausted by the relentless pursuit of payment for the imparting of the smallest snippet of cultural knowledge.

These are the cross-cultural tensions nobody talks about, except in those kardiya enclaves within the communities, as one tries to find ways to dissipate the frustrations and misunderstandings. I found an explanation that took much of my own cultural distaste out of the equation when I made an analogy between hunting and gathering for food, and hunting and gathering for money. It may not persuade others, but it works for me. One has only to listen to accounts of traditional itineraries to notice the preoccupation with food. Desert society evolved in the boom-and-bust economy of one of the harshest environments on the planet, and survival was predicated on the efficiency with which its resources could be utilised. My theory, not entirely frivolous, is that the same energy once spent on getting food is now spent on getting money.

To be white is to be seen to have mysterious access to money. Sometimes I think we are perceived by the desert Aboriginal people as money guards, standing at the door to vaults full of wealth, and doling out pocket money to them while we take all we want for ourselves. The government supply-lines that support remote communities are poorly understood by the recipients. In the tightening political environment, there is a growing emphasis on accountability and effective governance, with a number of training programs and workshops designed to assist communities. A few years into my regular stints in the community, I was co-opted to assist in the trial of one such program.

'The Australian Governance Story' was designed by the federal government in response to a request from Aboriginal communities to explain how government works in Australia. Its purpose was to give the people an overview of where they fitted into the larger structures of government, of where the money that supports their existence comes from, and of their rights and responsibilities in managing these funds and services.

Over the years of my involvement with the community, I have avoided the Gordian knot of bureaucracy, working instead on cultural mapping projects to record the stories and knowledge that people still hold about their country. A fortuitous encounter with a committed and imaginative public servant called Kerrie, one of those people without whom really hard challenges would never be attempted, resulted in us throwing ideas around about how our different enterprises might assist one another. My subsequent brief assignment as a public servant was an experiment, to see if my work could be married to the daily business of people learning how to manage their communities effectively. My reasons for taking it on were self-interested. I try to spend several months of every year in this place, and it is a constant financial struggle to find ways of doing so. Hunting and gathering for money has become a way of life for me, too.

This is how I find myself with the task of explaining 'The Australian Governance Story' to the community members, and persuading people to attend a workshop — a proposition that more or less cancels itself out. I am up against the deeply embedded suspicion of and resistance to white government-driven agendas, even when those agendas are in response to requests and proposals from the communities themselves.

The workshop is planned for July, the time of year when the congestion of visitors is at its most intense. One of the major disadvantages of belonging to a disadvantaged minority, particularly one that is central to our sense of national identity, is the relentless stream of government officials whose job it is to assess and redress those disadvantages. On any given day between May and September (after the wet season and before it gets too hot, which happens to coincide with the southern winter), a number of spanking-white four-wheel drives, their doors decorated with logos, will be parked in the dusty quadrangle outside the office, while the government officials they have transported compete for the attention of the community residents. It's not uncommon to find a disconsolate government rep hanging about with a satchel of information and no one to deliver it to.

In any small community there are a limited number of people who take on the responsibility for its social and practical maintenance. This is especially true of a remote Aboriginal community. Whether the issue is governance, childcare, aged care, social security, substance abuse, sexual health, store committees, education and training, tourism development, environmental management, fire control, dogs, housing, or garbage management, it is the same seven or eight people who are in demand. Meeting fatigue is endemic. Burnout is a recognised syndrome among white staff on communities, but little notice is given to the same phenomenon among the Aboriginal people. Often, when the pressure gets too much, they simply disappear for extended periods.

A three-day workshop is a big ask for people on whom the daily functioning of the community rests. It is a fine line I have to negotiate between the requirements of the government agency (I will call it ACRO) and the potential workshop participants. There are bureaucratic formalities to be met — numbers, names, the demographics of age, gender, literacy, and language, and signed agreements from participants that they will attend and complete the workshop.

This last requirement presents particular difficulties. It is as likely to scare people away as it is to commit them to coming. Signed pieces of paper are whitefella business, implicit with danger. I know that I can count on the core group of older women with whom I usually work, unless family business intervenes. They will come because I ask them to, because over the years we have established a relationship of trust and exchange. But family business takes precedence, and signed papers will not alter that. The risk of getting the younger, overburdened community members to sign up lies in giving them too much time to plan their escape.

I re-read the list of selection criteria that applies to my temporary position as an Australian public servant. At 'no 4. — Innovates', I find what I am looking for: 'able to develop solutions that are outcomes focussed and informed by a strategic perspective'. I interpret this to mean getting bums on seats by whatever means necessary.

Since Rebecca has discovered that we have the same-sized feet, she has been humbugging me relentlessly for the slip-on shoes I wear, unimpressed by my refusal on the grounds that they are the only shoes I've brought with me.

'What am I supposed to do, go barefoot?'

She looks pointedly at her own bare, hard-soled feet, and says nothing.

'You're a blackfella, you go barefoot all the time. I have to wear shoes, my feet are too soft.'

She throws me a grin that is knowing, charming, and manipulative. 'I got some old ones you can have.'

'I don't want your old shoes. I'm quite happy with these.' I beg a cigarette from her. My resolve to not smoke is disintegrating, as it always does within a few weeks of returning to the community.

'Where's that thing you got for not smoking?' She's referring to the nicotine inhaler I've been sucking on since I arrived. I take it out of my pocket and show it to her.

'Doesn't work?'

'Not under pressure.'

'Buy me a packet of cigarettes.'

I agree to do this. That way, I can beg one from her whenever I need to.

Rebecca is smart and literate, one of the people in constant demand to interpret the two worlds to one another. She fits the profile of the target workshop participant perfectly.

'You can have my shoes if you promise to come to the workshop.'

'That's, what do you call it ... coercion.'

'Fuck off. Do you want the shoes or not?'

'Okay, I'll come. Can I have them now?'

'No way. After the workshop. And you have to come all three days.'

She gives me a deep, resentful frown, one of her stock array of expressions, all bordering on parody, which crack into broad grins of amusement at the absurdities we are obliged to play out. The self-satisfied crocodile grin appears. She has established that the shoes are negotiable. Whether she comes to the workshop or not, we both know which foot the shoe is going to end up on.

Enlisting men was always going to be difficult. So many of the arenas in which their identity as men are formulated have been undermined. The radar alert for coercion is set at a hair-trigger. In any case, there are very few young and middle-aged men in the community, a fair proportion of them being in jail for various misdemeanours and crimes, mostly alcohol-related.

My key target is PT, a man of standing in the community and a member of one of the strong families. He is a short, square, suspicious man with a flaring temper, and has just returned from a stint in prison for cutting someone with a tomahawk. A few days before, I had given him and his wife a lift back to the community from a broken-down car. Later that evening, I encountered him with his son and brother-in-law trying to get the same vehicle going, and loaned them my torch and tools. I have also loaned him jerrycans of fuel on several occasions.

'I need you to come to this workshop,' I say to him. 'It's to teach people about how the government works, to help you to look after the community properly.'

PT's expression is sceptical, mildly amused. Most of what is important in the encounter is unspoken. There is an understanding that the situation is improvised, because neither of us has more than a bare glimpse into the other's thinking processes.

'You're strong. People respect you. If you come, some of the other men will come, too.'

The appeal to his vanity works. I get him to sign the paper. We both know that this is no guarantee that he will attend the workshop. What it does mean is that he will put in an appearance, and that this will help to swing a few of the men and boys to at least consider attending.

Payment is a problem. People are used to being paid for attending meetings. For those on the work-for-the-dole scheme, the hours spent in the workshop can be claimed, but for the rest there is nothing I can offer except the suggestion that it's in their own interests to participate. This does not wash with Lulu, who has the profile and character of a Roman potentate.

'You kardiya,' she says, 'always coming and telling us what to do. You want us to come to meetings, and then you won't pay us.'

Attack is the best form of defence with Lulu, who is one of the community powerbrokers.

'Listen, if you were white you'd be expected to pay for a workshop like this, not be paid to come.'

She leans her bulk back in the chair and smirks, satisfied that she's made me say something she can hold against me later.

'Anyway, it's about how to manage things yourself, so you don't have to put up with kardiya telling you what to do.'

'You shouldn't get upset, Napuru. I'll come, just to help you out.'

And so it goes for the weeks leading up to the arrival of the training team. Kerrie wants a guarantee of twenty participants, preferably the younger, literate members of the community. I tell her I can't guarantee anything, but I'm doing my best. Rebecca checks every day that the deal with the shoes is still on.

I receive a list of questions from the trainers:

- Do people understand what it means to be a COAG site?
- Do DOTARS, DEWR, ICC and OIPC have regional reps?
- What is the current status of SRAs in the community?
- Do people have an understanding of how the CDEP changes will affect them?
- Will they come under an RAE?
- How will it impact on NAHS, HACC and FACS?
- Who is the local RSP?
- Is the IPA funded by DEH or DIA?
- What is the role of the KLC? Does KALACC come under the same umbrella?
- Has anyone in the community accessed the ISBF?

- Should one approach KLRC or KIC for interpretive services?

With the help of Rebecca and her sister Julianne, I decode most of this curious document.

I am mending a flat tyre when the training duo arrives. They are called Bob and Deborah, and have been refining and delivering workshops to Aboriginal organisations for many years. They are experienced, good-humoured, flexible, and tough. In the face of their professionalism, I feel awkward and incompetent.

Kerrie and her ACRO team arrive the next morning. Things look moderately promising. The weather isn't too cold, and most people have stayed in the community in spite of it being school holidays. This has also made it possible to hold the workshop in the school library, which is comfortable, well resourced, and away from the distractions of the community. It is also potentially intimidating for people who don't usually sit at desks, but there's no better alternative. I have a list of seventeen possible participants, about half of whom I can be confident will turn up.

The workshop is due to start at nine. At eight-thirty I begin my rounds. There's a recognised protocol to this, which is to drive your vehicle as close as possible to people's houses and keep your hand on the horn until someone appears. After a few circuits, I've roused most of the people who have signed up for the meeting, and extracted promises that they will come down to the school after they've been to the shop. No one shows any enthusiasm. At nine, I do another round, and see Lulu about to climb into the Indigenous Protected Area (IPA) troop carrier, which is taking a group of young rangers away to a training workshop. I work her over with shameless emotional manipulation, payback for the many times she's done it to me.

'How can you do this, after you promised me? I thought I could trust you. This makes me really upset.'

She casts a backward glance at the troopie, which is too crowded to fit her in, and pats me on the arm. 'Don't worry, Napuru. I was going to look after these kids, but you need me, so I'll come with you.'

By ten-thirty about twenty-five people have wandered down to the school to see what's going on. The trainers give their introduction, and we break for morning tea, after which the numbers drop off to sixteen. PT has put in his promised appearance, lurking just inside the door, and ducking outside after half an hour for a cigarette. I join him.

'What do you think?'

He shakes his head. 'That stuff make my head hurt.' He finishes his cigarette, gives me a nod, and leaves.

After lunch, the numbers are down to nine. By my reckoning, the dropout ratio is one-third per session, which doesn't bode well for tomorrow. But the afternoon session becomes animated. Bob and Deborah know their stuff. They get people to unpick the network of organisations that service the community. Rebecca and Julianne spearhead a group of women who reveal a sound grasp of the organisational network, which is astonishingly complicated. I am in sympathy with PT — it makes my head hurt, too.

The challenge on day two is to get people to the workshop before the Tanami bus comes through on its bi-weekly run into Halls Creek. I collect them in twos and threes, and drop them at the school. Half of them circle around behind the toilet block, and beat me through the gate. They wave as I drive past, and someone calls out, 'Taxi', at which they all hoot with laughter.

I drive to Lulu's house to see if she is coming today. The previous day there was an incident involving her daughter, who has been flown out on the doctor plane. This accounted for most of the absentees from the afternoon session. There's no response to my car horn, but I see the curtain flicker in the front room. In attempting to get out of the car, I discover that the door lock is jammed. Lulu appears in the doorway to watch me climbing out of the window.

'What you doing, Napuru?'

'I can't open the door.'

'You should get that fixed.' She gets into the car. 'What we doing today?'

On the way to the workshop, several of my previous passengers flag me down for a lift back to the school. They inform me that the Tanami bus has broken down and that there's no run to town this week.

I am impressed by the training team, who adjust seamlessly to the changing dynamics of the group and keep everyone fully engaged. The day is spent in outlining the structure of the federal government and the lines of communication from the community, through to the various departments that are responsible for delivering services. Most people are not aware that there is both a state and a federal government. The most pertinent piece of information they absorb is that the budget is passed by law, and that once a certain amount of money has been designated it can't be altered and must be delivered through the appropriate channels. At the community level, money is an arbitrary and unpredictable resource, so the notion that it is a finite and regulated commodity is a novel one. The trainers tell them that the money is provided by taxpayers. 'Your money,' they say. This bothers me, since I know that no one in the community, apart from the white staff, pays tax, although I appreciate the need for people to feel empowered. It is another of those irreconcilable contradictions.

At the end of the day, everyone agrees to come at nine the next morning. They say I don't need to drive around and pick them up, although they enjoy seeing me climb in and out of my car window.

'You should get that door fixed, Napurrula.'

That evening, on the downward haul, there's an air of hilarity among the workshop team. I remark that I feel like a hapless victim of fate, and we discuss the need for more hap to deal with events like this. This leads to reflections on being gormless and feckless. The next morning, the team sport nametags that say Hap, Feck, and Gorm.

At eight-thirty, the wailing begins, and my stomach drops. Someone has died, and I feel the fear we all live with that it will be someone we know and love. Life is so precarious here, death frequent and sudden. It is Wendy's sister, a woman whose life has been violent and troubled for many years, who has died in Derby. I join the group of people offering condolences, and sit with Wendy while the older women join her in the protocols of sorry business. So much for the nine o'clock start. It's out of my hands now; people will decide their own priorities.

Evelyn comes by to tell me she is going out with her family to kill a bullock. She says she will keep some rib bones for me, indicating that she feels I need to be compensated for her withdrawal from the workshop. She's learned as much as she wants to know about the 'guvment'. Her own concerns are closer to home, in the refined and complex politics of family and country. Rebecca has also dropped out, with the excuse that she has to get organised to travel to her father-in-law's funeral. She wants to know if she can still have my shoes. We negotiate a debrief on the workshop when she gets back.

By ten o'clock, there are ten people in the library. The training team's new name tags pass without comment. After all, people here go by names such as Rimikus, Spieler, and Blah Blah. There is an air of empowerment among the stayers. They carry out enthusiastic role-plays of how to present a request to their state or federal minister. They have a far better grasp than I do of the labyrinthine structures at the lower levels of bureaucracy, which, I have come to appreciate, bear some resemblance to their own convoluted family and political structures. At the end of the day, they are pleased and happy with what they have learned, and eager for follow-up sessions. The training team have a substantial list of suggestions to implement from the trial. Everyone but me seems to think that something has been achieved.

The next day, Bessie comes to the office and asks me to ring the treasurer to ask him about funding for her outstation. I find the number of the treasurer's office and tell her to ring him herself. Monica appears with a photocopied piece of paper that shows the line of funding support for the Indigenous Protected Area.

'You can help me?'

'What for?'

She shows me the paper. 'This for money, isn't it?'

'Only for the IPA.'

She throws the paper in the bin.

Julianne comes in and asks me when I'm going to pay her for her work as the interpreter for the workshop.

'That's ACRO's business. They haven't paid me either. Where's that list telling us who to ring up?'

Lulu comes in and parks herself portentously in the chair beside my desk.

'Napurrula, you know I'm always working to help people, old people and young people together, and kardiya, too. I should get paid for that.'

Evelyn comes to tell me she's got some rib bones for me in the freezer at her daughter's house.

During a lull, I lock the office and make my escape. The community is quiet; today there are no visitors from the other world. The cold desert wind that seems to rise in agitation at the influx of too many outsiders has dropped, and the day is clear and sunny. I climb through the car window into the driver's seat, avoiding the broken mirror-stem where the rear-vision mirror has been pulled off by a child doing chin-ups.

'You should fix that door, Napurrula,' someone calls out. 'It looks like a Aboriginal car.'

Lulu appears at the passenger door with her shopping.

'You can give me a lift home, Napuru?'

In the car, she says, 'That was a good meeting. We should have more like that.'

4

'Kardiya are like Toyotas': white workers on Australia's cultural frontier

'Kardiya are like Toyotas. When they break down,
we get another one.'

— remark by a Western Desert woman about whitefellas who
work in Indigenous communities.

This comment was relayed to me by my friend Jess Jeeves, whose experiences I used for one of the kardiya in the story. I had no notion when I wrote this essay that it would go viral, would be included in the induction material of many Indigenous organisations, and would continue to be circulated a decade after its publication. The essay's inclusion in this collection is an opportunity to acknowledge Jess's inspiration.

Unlike the broken Toyotas, which are abandoned where they fall, cannibalised, overturned, gutted, and torched, the broken kardiya go away — albeit often feeling they have been cannibalised, overturned, gutted, and torched. They leave behind them dying gardens and unfinished projects, misunderstandings, and misplaced good intentions. The best leave foundations on which their replacements can build provisional shelters while they scout the terrain, while the worst leave funds unaccounted for, relationships in ruins, and communities in chaos.

There are many reasons why kardiya break down. Some break themselves, bringing with them baggage lugged from other lives, investing in the people they've come to help with qualities that are projections of their own anxieties and ideals. Eager and needy, they are prime material for white slavery, rushing to meet demands that increase in direct proportion to their willingness to respond to them. They create a legacy of expectation and dependency, coupled with one of failure and disappointment.

A more common cause of breakdown is the impossibility of carrying out the work they are expected to do. Two factors in particular are not included in any job description. The first is that if the work involves interaction with Aboriginal people, which is usually the case, this interaction will be so constant and demanding that there will be no time left to carry out the required tasks. The second is that, by default, the kardiya's function is to be blamed for everything that goes wrong. Blaming the kardiya is the lubricant that smooths the volatile frictions of community life. For someone of robust temperament and sound self-esteem, this is irritating but manageable. If one has an overheated sense of responsibility, or a tendency towards self-blame, it's an opportunity to experience the high point of personal failure.

Awareness of remote Indigenous communities fades and flares in the national consciousness. Revelations about child sexual abuse provide a brief window during which it is possible to speak aloud truths that would previously have seen the speakers branded as racist and their voices neutralised. The Northern Territory intervention exposes the government's unerring capacity for wrong action under pressure, and its default response of coercive control. Urban Indigenous voices muffle the shouts and murmurs from the desert, until payback-induced violence and police shootings bring the remote Aboriginal world sharply back into focus.

There is, however, one story that doesn't get much mileage: remote Indigenous Australia has a significant white population that is disproportionately influential while being unequipped, unprepared, or unsuitable for the work it does. There are the good people, who are overworked and undervalued; and there are the sociopaths, the borderline criminals, the self-righteous bullies and the mentally unhinged, who gravitate to the positions that no one else wants, entrench themselves, and contribute in no small degree to the malaise that haunts Indigenous communities.

It is mandatory for anyone wishing to work in Antarctica to undergo a physical and psychological assessment to establish whether they will stand up to the stresses of isolation, the extreme environment, and the intense proximity to other people. All the same factors exist in remote Aboriginal communities, along with confronting cross-cultural conditions. Yet there don't appear to be any recognised training programs for people who aspire to work in a community, or any screening criteria to weed out the mad, bad, and incompetent who prowl the grey zone of Indigenous service delivery.

The remote community is a kind of parallel universe, where career paths, if they exist at all, travel laterally or downwards. The famous quip about mercenaries, missionaries, and misfits has a lot of truth to it, and each type covers a spectrum, from highly functional through incompetent to downright destructive. Under pressure, both strengths and weaknesses become exaggerated, and what in normal circumstances would be merely a character trait (stubborn, orderly, conscientious, volatile, flexible, timid) can become the quality that makes or breaks a person.

This desert culture, where the power of family and country encompasses and transcends all other preoccupations, is where the crossed purposes of Indigenous and non-Indigenous expectations are at their most extreme. It's probably the zone of greatest discomfort in Australia, a place where the white noise of the kardiya world and the babel of Aboriginal voices create a static through which we blunder, grinning and waving like mad people, signalling that we mean each other no harm, though harm frequently occurs.

The contradiction at the heart of the story is that for the quality of desert Aboriginal lives to improve in the terms demanded by humanitarian standards — in health, education, housing, and the like — the people themselves must become more like we kardiya, and to become more like us requires them to relinquish the identity from which their resilience and sense of self is drawn. Without their Aboriginal identity they are reduced to society's dross: the poorest, the least employable, the shortest lived, the least literate, the substance abusers and losers and wife-bashers. And one of the most powerful ways in which they keep hold of that identity is by defining it against white people.

Among the older people, holding onto traditional culture is the force in which they believe, but the young are like the young in every culture. They don't listen to us, the old people complain, while the young people move in flocks, plugged into iPods and clutching mobile phones, trying whatever drug is available, dreaming of becoming rock stars and film stars and sports stars, using sex as an antidote to boredom. The cultural structures are still there, in skin names, family relationships, identification with country. But they are loosening all the time, as the fine, tough threads of high knowledge are wearing out, leaving behind a shadow knowledge that carries the fear of punishment without the protocols and understanding with which to manage it.

Against all this uncertainty, this great, loose, mutating cosmology, the kardiya are conspicuous and ubiquitous: busy, bossy, cranky, frequently behaving badly. They are running the schools and the offices, the clinics, the stores, the art centres, the police stations. They are the service providers and project co-ordinators. They control the money and make the rules. They live in fenced compounds with their pay cheques and cars and the choice to stay or go. They exacerbate, simply by being there, the antithesis of themselves.

There is, for the time being, no alternative. Kinship pressures make it extremely difficult for a local Aboriginal person to sustain a management position, and the few who take on such a role are subject to constant demands, and abuse if they refuse to comply. The mobility of people means that skills training is intermittent, and commitment to work is provisional. Take the kardiya out of the picture, and the Big Men, the powerbrokers, will fill the gap. This is not unique to desert Aboriginal society. It has happened in every place where a colonial power has abdicated without leaving a self-sustaining system in place.

For the newly arrived kardiya, bright-eyed and full of enthusiasm, the initial welcome is gratifying. She is thrilled to be taken in hand by one or more Aboriginal people who are friendly and knowledgeable, and is moved almost to tears when she is awarded a skin name.

'You Nampitjin, sister for us,' the new kardiya is informed. She feels privileged to be invited into an ancient and arcane sisterhood, and listens eagerly to the complex explanation of how she is now related to everyone.

'Sister for me and Gracie and Sabina, mother for those young girls. This old lady your mother, and same for that one over there. This little boy here, he's your *jaja*, grandson.'

Everyone is delighted, and there is much laughter and good feeling.

It takes a little time for New Kardiya to notice that while her sisters and mothers and daughters and aunties are very much in evidence, there are many others who stay away. She doesn't understand that she is colonised territory. Invisible to her, power struggles of ancient lineage and epic proportions are being played out. *This is our kardiya — hands off.*

She becomes aware of mutterings and silences, and tries to find out what they mean, but the workload has escalated to such an extent that there is no time to pay attention. The previous kardiya has not acquitted several important grants, the deadlines for which are now long overdue. Continuing funding for the organisation is dependent on the satisfactory acquittal of these grants, but much of the necessary information doesn't seem to exist. The filing system is idiosyncratic, consisting of cardboard boxes with obscure acronyms scrawled on them in felt tip. The felt tips themselves, along with all biros, pencils, and other writing implements, have disappeared. Attempts to contact the previous kardiya are met with silence: emails bounce back; mobile numbers no longer function.

New Kardiya curses Previous Kardiya as incompetent, lazy, and irresponsible. According to her Aboriginal directors and helpers, Previous K also failed to pay them money they are owed. No records of these financial transactions exist.

'She took that money with her,' they announce. 'That was our money. She stole it from us.'

New K is horrified that someone would take advantage of people who live in such dire poverty. She adds 'criminal' and 'sociopath' to the list of adjectives pertaining to Previous K.

In the first days of wanting to appear willing, available, and caring, New K has allowed people to use the office phone for essential calls.

'Nampitjin, I need to ring up to find out about my uncle's funeral.'

'Nampitjin, I got no money from Centrelink this week. I got to ring up and find out what happened.'

'Nampitjin, I got to go to court next week. Can you ring up and charter a plane for me?'

This last request raises a flicker of alarm. Surely this is outside the jurisdiction of her job?

Her refusal is taken philosophically. *It was worth a try — you never know with kardiya what they are prepared to do.*

In her search for the missing information, New K discovers caches of energy bars and Minties stashed in drawers and cupboards and filing cabinets. This is further evidence of the peculiar, pathological nature of Previous K, who, it turns out, was also called Nampitjin.

News of the phone access has spread. People are queuing to use it for increasingly long conversations, some of which appear to be social rather than urgent. Important calls, for which New K has been waiting in order to deal with the acquittals, fail to get through because the line is constantly engaged. People waiting to use the phone enlist New K's help to decipher letters they have received from government agencies relating to welfare payments, court cases, and child custody.

'Don't you have someone whose job it is to deal with this stuff?' she asks.

'They always too busy,' she is informed. 'That kardiya in the office, he always growling, won't do nothing to help us.'

During the two-hour lunch break, New K locks the office and replies to all the calls she has missed. Since she has also missed lunch, she eats several of Previous K's energy bars.

With the job comes a troop carrier, a powerful LandCruiser designed to carry a dozen people and negotiate the rough desert roads. She has never driven such a vehicle, and the first time she manoeuvres it successfully through the sandy creek crossings and deep gutters of the back road she is filled with an immense sense of achievement.

Encouraged by a constant refrain of 'Keep going, keep going' from her passengers, she overcomes her reluctance to tackle some of the nastier patches of track, and is rewarded with their approval.

'You good driver, Nampitjin. Now you can take us hunting.'

Part of the job brief is 'to facilitate cultural activities', which, according to her Indigenous cultural advisers (so far, consisting entirely of members of the Sambo clan, whose name skids across her consciousness like a dark blip, impossible to process), means taking them hunting all day, every day. At first, this is a thrilling novelty — this is what she is here for, to experience the desert and its people, to learn to identify bush tucker and recognise animal tracks, to have pointed out to her the evidence of ancestral travellers who left their traces in the hills and creeks and waterholes. It is here, away from the tensions of the community, that things begin to make some kind of sense: patterns begin to emerge of kinship, stories, and country.

As a prelude to going hunting, there is a ritual that involves an hour or two of driving around, waiting, embarking and disembarking of passengers, loading and unloading of gear, shouting, waiting, retracing tracks, shopping, waiting, arguments, sulking, more embarking and disembarking, until New K is in a state of exhausted frustration. She's learned, however, that to drive off before everyone is ready is not worth the days of growling and recriminations that follow.

The office work mounts up. By working late and inventing figures, she's managed to acquit the grants, but there is a backlog of projects, cataloguing, sorting, and filing, and the new grant applications have to be written and submitted. She discovers that the funding process functions within a self-cancelling system in which each grant is dependent on funding being guaranteed by its state or federal counterpart. So far, she has been unable to find the centre of the logjam, the submission that will start the process rolling. She rings the umbrella organisations that have been set up to facilitate the process, and encounters instead several new layers of bureaucracy that must be negotiated. Helpful voices refer her backwards and forwards between agencies called FATSIC and KRAPP and WACKO. The voices all sound alike, and she begins to imagine a single office buried deep in some labyrinthine gulag, monitored by a shabby creature shackled to a bank of telephones each labelled with the appropriate acronym.

On the days when she manages to avoid taking people hunting, she starts work an hour earlier in order to get some essential chores done before the mob arrives, taking a circuitous route so that no one guesses she is on her way to her workplace. She walks, leaving the troop carrier locked in the compound where she lives, to avoid being flagged down and used as a taxi service. Experience has taught her that once she picks up passengers, she can spend the entire morning ferrying them between the shop, the clinic, the school, the art centre, and the various camps. She has learned not to turn on lights or fans, as this alerts people that there is someone in the building. It's too early to respond to the messages on the answering machine, which will have to wait until the lunch break. The supply of energy bars is running low. She will need to order some more.

She has begun to develop friendships among the other kardiya in the community. Vinnie, who runs the art centre, is eccentric, but warm and sympathetic. Her assistant, Simon, is a little intimidating, with an ironic sense of humour, but is also amiable and friendly. But it is to Ben, who works in men's health, that New K is especially drawn. She tells him about her difficulties with the phone, and he suggests a solution. 'Unplug it at the wall and tell them it's broken. Most of the community phones are broken anyway, so they won't check.'

She takes his advice, and although it means she can't use the phone herself during working hours, it makes a dramatic difference to the number of visitors to her office.

Ben has worked intermittently in the community for several years, and is well liked by the locals for his good nature and relaxed attitude to time, work, vehicles, and money — all the things that most kardiya are stitched-up and anxious about. That Ben's life resembles the lives of his Aboriginal friends escapes New K's notice. What she does notice is his helpfulness, his craggy good looks, his charm and humour. She doesn't yet know that he has been implicated in liaisons with most of the eligible kardiya women in the community.

On Ben's advice, she has declared a two-week moratorium on hunting expeditions, while she catches up on the paperwork.

'You have to set some boundaries,' he tells her. This is rich, coming from Ben, but New K doesn't know that. There are a lot of things she doesn't know about Ben.

On day five of the hunting ban, Nelly Sambo Nampitjin and her sisters descend on the office. 'You never take us hunting any more, Nampitjin.' They cluster around her, managing to appear downtrodden and intimidating at the same time. 'Those old ladies, they might die soon. Never get back to their country before they pass away.'

The old ladies in question look convincingly frail, sitting on the verandah like a pair of ancient stick insects. A passing camp dog lifts a leg, and is walloped ferociously with a walking stick by the less blind of the two. They are sisters born in the bush, their old minds reaching back to a time before kardiya, before missionaries and soup-soup and stock camps, before schools and clinics and art centres, when the world was a seamless fabric woven by the Law.

New K explains to the Sambo sisters that if she doesn't get the grants in, there will be no money to run the office or keep the troop carrier going, which will mean no more hunting, no more film projects and recording of stories. Everything will fall down. Her job is really hard because Previous K left a big mess, and she is trying to fix it up.

The mention of money and Previous K reminds everyone of the money they have been done out of, and Nelly suggests that New K might be able to make reparation. She agrees to do her best to sort something out once she can find some record of the payments. She also agrees to take everyone hunting on the weekend instead of spending the two precious solitary days catching up with her displaced self.

Despite starting an hour earlier and working through the lunchbreak, she does not seem able to make any inroads on the workload. The one person she had tracked down who had been helpful with the grant submissions has resigned, or been promoted, or committed suicide. She has noted that Vinnie and Simon are often still at work in the art centre at ten o'clock at night. Ben has warned her that Vinnie and Simon set a benchmark of superhuman standards, which makes her feel more inadequate, since she has been unable to produce even moderate results. How Ben manages to do his job and remain relaxed and sanguine is a mystery to her.

New K begins to stay late at the office, munching her way through the remaining Minties and energy bars, having ordered a new supply with the weekly bush order that Vinnie has delivered on the mail plane. By the time she gets home she's too exhausted to cook anything, so she has a tin of smoked mussels and a double gin and tonic, and falls asleep in front of the television. Her skin has broken out in sore, red pimples, and she has become alarmingly thin. Small cuts fester and go septic, and when she visits the clinic she is informed that she has a staph infection, and is put on a course of antibiotics. The nurse advises her to use an antiseptic soap, wash her hands frequently, eat properly, and take better care of herself.

Vinnie, who is aware that things aren't going well with New K, tells her it's time she took some time out, that the only way any of them manage to function effectively is to take regular breaks away from the community to rest and recuperate.

'I can't go away,' New K wails. 'I'm so far behind with the grants — I haven't even started the planning for the next round of projects. I don't know how anyone gets anything done.'

'You have to eat properly, and take regular breaks, and make time for yourself,' Vinnie tells her, although New K can't for the life of her see when Vinnie makes any time for herself.

'I go walking,' Vinnie says. 'Nobody's interested in walking unless they're hunting.' She doesn't mention that she takes her walks at five o'clock in the morning.

'Make time for yourself,' Simon says. 'Set boundaries. Remember, you're only human. Don't work too much overtime.'

'But you and Vinnie do,' New K points out.

'Vinnie and I are not good role models,' Simon says. 'I only do it because of Vinnie. We're setting up a structure that no one will be able to maintain. It's ridiculous.'

'Relax,' Ben says. 'Drop over to my place and have a joint. We can watch a movie — I've got Foxtel.'

She takes up Ben's suggestion. They get stoned and have sex. For a couple of weeks, New K is happy. Ben is charming and funny and good-looking and a thoughtful lover. The workload seems manageable, and the Sambo sisters make jokes that New K now has a *nyupa*. She wonders how they know, as she and Ben have been very discreet. In week three, she meets the new nurse from the clinic, leaving Ben's house at seven in the morning, and learns that Ben has no idea that she takes their sexual activity as something more than mutual entertainment. He is baffled and discomfited by her furious tears.

She feels assaulted by the landscape. Everything scratches, prickles, burns, abrades. It is all so appallingly physical. She feels the need to protect herself from it, and by implication from the people. When the Sambo sisters make jokes about her love life, she shouts at them and locks the office.

Because Ben is part of Simon and Vinnie's circle, New K no longer socialises with them. Anyway, she doesn't need to, because she has a new friend. Susie Nakamarra comes into the office one afternoon when New K is struggling to draft a management plan for the next year's projects, and makes suggestions that are insightful and helpful. She fills New K in on some of the local politics, both black and white, and invites herself for a cup of tea at New K's house.

The friendship blossoms. Susie regales New K with stories of her adventures growing up in and out of the community. The stories are violent and hilarious, and reveal a world that is both exotic and dangerous. New K fails to notice that most of them centre on the stupidity and bad behaviour of other people, and how Susie's wit and intelligence always proves superior. In return, New K confides her disappointment with Ben, and Susie tells her things about Ben that are shocking and possibly untrue.

When Susie asks to borrow the troop carrier, New K says she's not really allowed to lend it, but she doesn't refuse outright. It's obvious that Susie is a responsible person, and it seems ridiculous that kardiya rules should apply to her. She is, after all, half white, fathered by an itinerant stockman back in the cattle station days, and has been to boarding school and trained in a variety of skills.

Susie doesn't press the request, and New K offers her a gin and tonic with guilty relief. It's supposed to be a dry community, but as long as kardiya drink quietly inside their own homes, they are left alone. The two women get sentimental and maudlin, and tell each other the secrets they only tell their best friends. Susie's are dark and terrible, and New K is shocked at the horrors her friend has undergone. Her own troubles pale in comparison.

The second time Susie requests the use of the troopie, New K agrees. Nothing bad happens. The vehicle is returned on time, undamaged, although it is almost empty of fuel and the interior contains an astonishing amount of rubbish.

'It's the kids,' Susie says by way of explanation. 'I told them to clean it up, but they forgot.'

The next time Susie borrows the vehicle, two days pass, during which time New K becomes frantic. Three days later, she receives a visit from the local police, who tell her that the troop carrier has been impounded in the town of Garnet, three hundred kilometres away. Its driver (not Susie, who seems to have dropped from sight) has been charged with drink-driving, driving without a licence, supplying minors with alcohol, and assaulting a policeman, and New K will be required to give a statement about how the vehicle came to be in his possession.

For the next month, during which time Susie remains invisible, New K is embroiled in a mess of legal paperwork and bureaucratic reprimands, although the expected dismissal from the job doesn't arrive. She is unaware that she was the only applicant for the position, and that Previous K is suing the organisation for psychological damage incurred while at work.

One morning, New K encounters Susie outside the community store, and timidly suggests that Susie owes her an explanation. In retaliation, Susie calls New K a racist bitch and hits her with the bottle of tomato sauce she has just bought. The nurse who patches New K up at the clinic says that Susie is bad news, and that this is the second time she has assaulted a white woman she has befriended. At this point, all parties agree it is in New K's best interests that her appointment be terminated, and she flies out on the weekly mail plane.

The Sambo sisters and their extended family are disappointed to see her go.

'That Nampitjin said she was going to get our money back for us.'

'*Yuwayi*, she said that, but she never gave it to us.'

'Must be she kept it for himself.'

'That Nampitjin did a bad thing, keeping our money.'

The program is shut down for several months while the position is advertised and a replacement found. There is only one applicant, someone who is seduced by the prospect of working on the cutting edge of Indigenous culture, in a remote location imbued with the spiritual glamour of the desert. On her arrival, she is delighted to be awarded the skin name of Nampitjin, and a little baffled at the filing cabinets filled with Minties and energy bars ...

Sometimes the protagonist has better instincts than New K when faced with Susie or her equivalent — a natural skill at recognising which boundaries must be held and which can be more elastic. He or she may have a sense of humour that thrives on the absurdities and contradictions of daily life, and a sneaking admiration for the consistency with which Aboriginal people insist on being Aboriginal. Such a person has a chance of finding some sort of equilibrium, establishing sustaining relationships and focusing on small, achievable goals. What he or she doesn't anticipate is that insurmountable difficulties will be generated by other white people.

In a small, isolated community in an extreme environment, perspectives tilt, passions flare, and petty irritations assume the proportions of murderous hatreds. The Aboriginal inhabitants observe whitefella behaviour with close attention, witnessing feuds and coups, fisticuffs and power struggles, and a constant turnover of personnel.

A certain percentage of kardiya who work in communities don't like Aboriginal people. Some of these people are paid very large sums of money to do things that can't be achieved. As it's apparent sooner or later that the projected outcomes are not achievable, they have to conceal this for as long as possible. It's not the unachievable outcomes that are the issue — after all, there's a long and glorious tradition of non-achievement in the field — it's the pretence that all is well, the ticking-off of irrelevant performance indicators, the recycling of minor successes as major outcomes, and the snowstorm of paperwork couched in incomprehensible language.

Into this situation comes the enthusiastic assistant, handicapped by a sharp intelligence and a tendency towards independent thought.

For the incumbent manager, who has often established some functioning structures under difficult circumstances, the assistant's suggestions and implied criticisms are irritating. It is even more irritating if the assistant shows a natural affinity with Aboriginal people, and within a few weeks forms better relationships than the manager has done in a couple of years. A stand-off quickly results. The assistant is stonewalled, overridden, ignored, obstructed, and undermined. In retaliation, the assistant begins to alert his Aboriginal friends that things are not going as they should. This is a bad move. Regardless of the justice of his position, he can't expect support from the Aboriginal people. To them, it's whitefella business, best left to the kardiya to sort out, although it provides plenty of gossip and entertainment. The Aboriginal friends begin to fall away, foreseeing a power struggle in which they don't want to be implicated. After all, the manager has implemented a structure of payments and privileges, and better the devil you know ...

Neither the manager nor the assistant has an intimate friend onto whom they can offload their anxieties and frustrations. The manager is reclusive by temperament; it's not Aboriginal people in particular he dislikes, but people in general. The assistant is outgoing and makes friends easily, but the skewed environment and the persistent yet unacknowledged persecution has thrown him off balance. His confidence damaged, he becomes assertive and unreliable. Forced onto the defensive, he becomes obsessed with his situation, and is exhausting company to the people who sympathise with him. No one has the energy to listen to his repetitious, circular, self-defeating diatribes. They've seen it all before, and know how it will end.

The manager is a wily bird. He hasn't reached this level on the food chain by accident. He has an instinct for the power of injustice, its capacity to send crazy those who believe that justice is an entitlement. Unimpeded by empathy or compassion, he knows he can sit this one out while the assistant works himself into an untenable position and quits.

The manipulation of injustice as a means of maintaining power is not only employed by the unscrupulous, who know what they are doing, but by the self-righteous, who believe that they are acting for the greater good. Among the kardiya who end up on Aboriginal communities, the self-righteous flourish, feeding their sense of superiority on the conviction that they alone understand the needs of Aboriginal people — that, among the opportunism and incompetence of the resident whites, they alone are driven by motives free of self-interest. A particular sort of blinkered stupidity often accompanies self-righteousness, and in the smaller communities it can be toxic in the extreme.

The couple who came to be known as Super Kardiya and his Super Nyupa belonged in this category. He was a self-righteous bully and she was a self-righteous protector of the helpless Aborigines. For two years they managed a community in which I had been working on a regular basis, and they made it plain from the outset that part of their agenda was to drive out as many of the other kardiya as they could.

'I will protect these people as if they were my own children,' the Super Nyupa announced, glaring down at me from her considerable height, the inference being that they needed protection from the likes of me. I was in the community at the invitation of the traditional owners, my funding came from an independent source, and most of what I did involved the traditional lands beyond the community boundaries. So long as I kept out of the new management's way, the worst I had to endure was hostile glares, limited access to the office (and my only access to a telephone), and the ambient tension that prevails in such circumstances.

Not so fortunate was my friend the architect-builder, who had been coming to the community for years, during which time he had developed a team of local builders and had embarked on a project to build a community centre. He had spent several months each year overseeing and completing stages of the project, applying for and getting continuing funding, and building longstanding relationships based on trust and respect. It was a model of sustainable processes and achievable goals, and it was intolerable to the Super duo, who set about sabotaging it with the commitment of their high moral fervour. The money for the project had to be administered through the corporation, which allowed them to obstruct his access to the funds, refuse to sanction already-agreed projects, and send him slowly mad with helpless frustration. The lacklustre response of the local mob, among whom he tried to enlist support, left him nowhere to go but away, feeling done over and betrayed.

We both belonged to a group who had longstanding connections to the place, and had formed a network of people with a range of professional skills that could be brought into play to help the local people achieve their aspirations. Through a process of consultation, we had identified those aspirations and were discussing what might be achievable in the short term when we were halted by the hostile new management. Against their determined authoritarianism our carefully moderated consultative processes didn't stand a chance. And the reality was that the community could continue to function without the long-term strategies and plans we had identified, but it couldn't operate without a bookkeeper (her role) and a works manager (his role). We were routed, and several years of work came to a standstill.

Having driven out the architect-builder and kneecapped the support network, they set their sights on the shopkeepers and the co-ordinator of the Indigenous Protected Area. The shopkeepers were easy picking, since the shop was also under the jurisdiction of the community corporation. A campaign of micromanagement saw the incumbent store managers pack their bags and go, and over the next couple of years the numerous replacements were systematically bullied as soon as they showed signs of wanting to run things their own way.

The assault on the Indigenous Protected Area required more complex strategies, as the IPA was embedded in the aspirations of the founders of the community, and was the only organisation that offered long-term possibilities of meaningful employment, tourism development, land management, and cultural rehabilitation. The IPA's weak point, which the Super duo were quick to exploit, was that it was subject to the jealousy and suspicion that simmers around matters to do with country. Among the local people were those who felt their own power base threatened by the IPA and were readily manipulated into a plan to relocate the IPA staff and office to a community near the northern boundary of the designated area. The story of how this was achieved is too complicated to tell here, but the damage was considerable and the repercussions continuing.

At some point during their reign, which overlapped for a year with that of an unstable school headmistress who also belonged to the self-righteous category, I caught myself out in an interior rant about the destructive, self-interested jealousies of the Aboriginal mob I was working with. It went something like this:

Why can't they see how damaging it is to spend all their energy being suspicious and resentful of one another?

Why can't they put their personal and family vendettas aside and work together towards an outcome that would benefit everyone?

Why doesn't Jakamarra understand that his morose, manipulative sulking is the obstacle that stops him from achieving what he wants to do?

Why does Nungarrayi waste her considerable intelligence thinking up new ways to persecute and undermine the sister of whom she's insanely jealous?

In the midst of all this, a small voice said, *Hang on there, wait a minute — let's do a stocktake of the kardiya politics right now.* A headcount arrived at a resident white population of twelve. The configuration of hostilities among them was as follows:

- Super Kardiya and the storekeeper have recently threatened each other publicly during a community meeting.
- The storekeeper's wife has just assaulted the Super Nyupa, who is laying charges.
- The Super Nyupa and the headmistress only communicate by fax.
- Super Kardiya has threatened to spear the builder who replaced the architect-builder.
- The nurse, who is married to the builder, is not speaking to the Super duo.
- Super Kardiya has appropriated the IPA water trailer, and refuses to give it back.
- The headmistress has banned the IPA co-ordinator from the school, on the grounds that his relationship with one of the teachers, aged thirty, is immoral.
- The teacher in question is being subjected to merciless bullying by the headmistress.
- Three of the four remaining teachers have aligned themselves with the headmistress to protect themselves, and are therefore not speaking to anyone in the IPA.

- Because of my support for the IPA co-ordinator and his teacher girlfriend, I have recently been subjected to a drive-by shouting from the headmistress, who specialises in this method of attack.
- The Super duo have installed a screen door on the office building, and control the only key, so the rest of us can only gain access to our own offices when it suits them.

There have been times when the white population has consisted of mature, sensible, capable people who co-operate with and support each other, and the difference in the mood and function of the community is dramatic. And occasionally, when the planets are perfectly aligned and whatever unpredictable entity that rules the universe is in a benevolent mood, a group of exceptional people gathers, works together with skill and generosity, and achieves remarkable outcomes. Several times now, I have had the good fortune to be part of such a team, and it's the one thing, apart from the resilience and humour of the Aboriginal people, that allows me some optimism for the future.

The high-handed behaviour and interventions of Super Kardiya and Super Nyupa finally provoked the local mob out of their passivity. It's a mistake that kardiya often make, assuming that because Aboriginal people seem disengaged and uninterested, they are incapable of acting decisively in their own interests. Action, when it occurs, can be sudden and cataclysmic, and so it was with the routing of the Super duo, beheaded in a coup that drove them out of the community in a matter of days.

That they had been able to reign unchecked for a couple of years shows how poorly the systems and structures imposed by government on remote communities function, and how easily they are abused. No matter how good the strategies and programs developed at the policy level, the delivery on the ground is where it counts and where it consistently fails.

There are some excellent people working in remote Indigenous communities. If this wasn't the case, things would be much worse than they are. But, too often, they work in isolation, expected to meet criteria that have no bearing on the reality of the work they do, in circumstances of which their superiors have no grasp. For the petty powerbrokers, this is very satisfactory, allowing them to build their personal fiefdoms and fulfil their potential as unmitigated arseholes. For the committed, hard-working, responsible individual, it is demoralising and heart-breaking.

Why is it like this? Is it because Aboriginal Australia is still felt to be a retrograde country not fit for white people, a wounded, contaminated place to be avoided for fear of being contaminated oneself? Does it still occupy the dark corners of the collective white imagination?

In his introduction to the magnificent book on the Papunya art movement, *Papunya: a place made after the story*, Geoffrey Bardon describes his arrival in Papunya in 1971: 'I introduced myself to a group of drunken, foul-mouthed and violent men who, as I was to learn, were the settlement's administrators.'

During the 1960s and early 1970s, when my family lived in the Tanami, we would bypass the Aboriginal settlement (they weren't called 'communities' until the late 1970s) near the Tanami track as if avoiding a dirty secret, a festering rubbish tip into which the worst white trash had been thrown. I have no doubt that there were some good people working there even then, but the reputation of the place was self-fulfilling. Although things have improved since those days, the legacy lingers, not only in the lack of status associated with working in a remote community, but in the lack of interest among qualified and competent people to take on the jobs.

It's seen as contaminated ground, too hard to negotiate, which provides no career path. Instead, it's a bureaucratic nightmare and a cultural minefield, working with a recalcitrant and ungrateful Indigenous population who want what whitefellas have, but don't want to do what whitefellas do, who define their Aboriginality against the whitefella presence in their midst. In an environment that calls for the best and brightest, too often it's the sociopaths, the self-righteous, the bleeding hearts, and the morally ambiguous who apply for and get the jobs, and provide the example of white society against which the local people formulate their resistance.

During the era when Australia was responsible for the administration of New Guinea, the Kiaps who worked as patrol officers were trained at the Australian School of Pacific Administration. They studied law, anthropology, language, administration, health, research methodology, reporting, and people management. Today, anyone who works for an aid agency undergoes a thorough induction in the cultural and social environment they are about to enter, and is alerted to the challenges they can expect to encounter. But I've heard it said on a number of occasions by people who have worked in extreme environments overseas — Afghanistan, East Timor, and the like — that none of their experiences in those places compare to the difficulties they encounter in Indigenous Australia. And yet successive Australian governments don't see the necessity to train and prepare the people who work on our own cultural frontier.

This may be motivated in part by the assumption that Aboriginal people should be trained to fulfil these roles. Empowering Aboriginal people to run their own communities is one of those rhetorical platitudes that has been bandied around since the emergence of self-determination as a political ideology, and in theory it is the obvious goal towards which all energy should be directed. In practice, it often results in the most competent and functional people being set up for failure.

The mentoring and support for Aboriginal community workers in the process of taking responsibility is rarely available, and when it is available is never sustained for long enough. In all likelihood, the mentor will be one of those overworked and undervalued kardiya with their own manifold problems, and the competent Aboriginal person will already be in constant demand by every agency operating within the community, will be juggling complicated family politics, and will be subjected to hostility and jealousy for aspiring to be like the kardiya. Being fast-tracked beyond their level of competence achieves two negative results, neutralising their effectiveness in the roles they were already fulfilling, and setting them up to fail in the jobs to which they have been promoted.

Returning to the community shortly after the demise of the Super duo, I find it becalmed. It has gone into voluntary administration, and is waiting for the arrival of a temporary administrator. The shop is being managed by interim emergency storekeepers, and the most competent Aboriginal woman in the place is juggling roles as office manager and IPA co-ordinator. It is apparent that the most useful thing I can do in the circumstances is to take over the position of temporary IPA co-ordinator, as the work I usually do is contingent on that position being filled. This frees up my friend to do some of the things she is better equipped to do, and promotes me to my own level of incompetence.

A dramatic change for the better has taken place in the school. It has a new headmaster, who is keen to enlist whoever in the community has something of value to offer the kids, and a mature and experienced staff has replaced the batch of cowed first-year teachers. The regional council has initiated a program to mentor young adults, and has put in place a skilled German woman with a natural sensitivity in dealing with cultural and social complexities. The new resident nurse is a warm-hearted, intelligent man. In spite of the difficulties at the administrative level, the resident population of kardiya are decent, emotionally mature people whose first concern is to do as good a job as possible. With luck, the present situation will move beyond damage mitigation to some positive achievements. But it's a fragile balance. A single individual could tilt it back into the dysfunction and unpleasantness of recent times.

Meanwhile the local people carry on with their own preoccupations, taking the measure of this new batch of kardiya, who, for brief or extended periods, will control the resources of their world. Kardiya are unpredictable and unreliable. Even the best of them make promises they don't keep. It is necessary to extract the maximum value from them while you can, because tomorrow or next week or next year they will be gone, and there will be a whole lot of new ones to break in.

5

Country needs people: mapping and minding shared lands

They lit fires to burn out the animals for tucker mate, no other reason, and somehow or other the 'goodies' have explained that away as caring for the environment instead of permanently altering the environment. People, usually from the city or some exalted place, bemoan the state of the so called 'camps', and wring their hands but in actual fact that is how these people lived as hunter gatherers for they ate a section of the country out, befouled it, and moved on to continue the cycle for they knew no better and in fact had to do that to scratch an existence. Give a bush aboriginal the choice of a house or an open shed and he will pick the open shed every time.

As an opening quote for an essay about Indigenous ecological knowledge, the above passage was too good to pass up. The lapse into biblical cadences as the writer hits his stride, the seamless segues, the sweeping non sequitur about open sheds ... After all the advocacy documents and academic essays I've been reading, to encounter a comment so bracingly, unashamedly racist is a salutary reminder of the spectrum of attitudes I'm writing into. The scepticism about Indigenous people 'caring for the environment' is shared by many who would not put their views so robustly.

The quote comes from a thread of online comments, posted in response to an article in *The Australian* about a carbon-credit arrangement between the North Kimberley Fire Abatement Project and Qantas. Workers employed through the federal government's Indigenous Ranger programs carry out managed patch burns during the cool weather to pre-empt the fierce hot-season fires that burn vast tracts of country, destroy wildlife and habitat, and generate carbon emissions. The emissions created by the low-intensity fires are subtracted from the estimated emissions of uncontrolled wildfires, a baseline figure established over several fire cycles when no managed burns have occurred. The difference constitutes the carbon credits. High-emitting businesses can voluntarily purchase these credits to offset against their own emissions. The money feeds back into the Indigenous Ranger program that carries out the burning.

Most of the comments that followed the *Australian* article targeted the notion that corporations could purchase credits that allowed them to continue to pollute; several said that climate change was a furphy, so the whole thing was a waste of money; and one suggested that the young Indigenous ranger featured should get a real job. Others claimed that bushfires in the hot season were the norm, and that burning in cool weather was interfering with nature:

> Burning in winter is not the same as what used to happen naturally — hot large fires in summer. It is obvious why we prefer the manageable winter burns but that is not how nature used to do it. So already we are 'messing with nature' so at least admit it and stop fussing when we release CO2.

Whatever the origins and intentions of traditional burning practices, the ecosystems that early white settlers encountered were a result of many thousands of years of deliberate burning. And while nature no doubt played its part in generating fierce summer bushfires, fifty years of aerial imagery documenting fire activity near the community of Parnngurr, in Western Aiustralia's Western Desert region, illustrates the difference between 'natural' and man-made fire. The Martu people continued to live a traditional desert lifestyle until the 1960s, and returned to the desert in the early 1980s when the land rights movement established communities in their homelands. Aerial imagery suggests that the interim two decades, during which regular burning did not occur and fires were generated by lightning, was a period of fierce hot-season wildfire. While this is evidence of what happens when the region is left to 'nature', it also shows that the Martu's patch-burning strategy was a deliberate and effective way of avoiding such fires, and that humans had probably been interfering with nature since they invented tools and language.

Growing recognition that the Australian ecological landscape is a product of human-generated fire has provoked a shift in thinking, exemplified by Gareth Catt, the fire-management officer working with the Martu at the time this essay was first published. He is of the opinion that 'an appropriate human-driven fire regime is natural, and a wildfire regime should be viewed as feral'.

In late March 2012, I was based in Parnngurr while gathering material for an exhibition called *We Don't Need a Map* — a collaboration between Martu artists, the Martumili Artists East Pilbara Art Centre in Newman, and the Fremantle Arts Centre, and bankrolled by BHP. The object of the exhibition was to show the many dimensions of Martu culture, both contemporary and traditional. My job was to research the paintings included in the show, collecting as much information about their content as possible. Equipped with maps (the irony wasn't lost on me), a Martu wordlist, and photographs of the paintings and the artists who had painted them, I embarked on what would become an ecological treasure hunt.

This was my second trip into Martu country. Most of the artists involved with the exhibition lived in the remote communities of Parnngurr, Punmu, and Kunawarritji, and many of them belonged to the generation that had grown up in the desert. Their country, east of the Pilbara, overlaps the Great Sandy, Little Sandy, and Gibson deserts, and occupies a substantial section of the zone labelled 'useless' on a map drawn in 1926 to illustrate Australia's regions of habitability and opportunity.

Our trip from Parnngurr to Punmu, to talk to artists, had been cancelled because of rain. The Parnngurr Indigenous Ranger team was heading to the Canning Stock Route to do some controlled burning, so I decided to accompany them some of the way, along with the Martumili field officer, Carly, and three Martu women. The youngest, Thelma Bidu, acted as an interpreter for the two senior women, Kumpaya Girgirba and Jakayu Biljabu, who had been adults by the time they moved from the deep desert to Jigalong mission in 1963. Within twenty years, Kumpaya and Jakayu were back in their home country as a result of the homelands movement. Their knowledge and authority were peerless, and to go out on country with them was the kind of serendipitous opportunity you can't plan for.

We convoyed with the ranger team as far as Warntili, a magnificent red claypan near the Canning Stock Route, full of water after the recent rains. The rangers continued on, but the Martu ladies, Carly, and I camped at Warntili for several days. It had been a good wet season, and the country was a bountiful mosaic of old and new growth. Anywhere that the spinifex was mature enough to burn, the old ladies set fire to it, revealing the burrows of *parnajarrpa* (sand goannas), a food staple in the traditional days and still a significant addition to their diet. In a single afternoon, the three women caught and killed two dozen reptiles, some of which they ate the same evening. The rest they singed, eviscerated, and put into the car-fridge to take back for family. 'On the way home we'll show you a really good hunting place,' they told us. I wondered what sort of country could be better than where we were.

The really good hunting place, recently burned by the rangers, looked like the remnants of a scorched-earth policy — incinerated wattles, a few dusty bloodwoods throwing a thin shade, the red, sandy soil coated with fine, black ash in which the bright orange mounds of *parnajarrpa* burrows stood out like signposts. We had barely pulled over before the women were out of the vehicles and scurrying across the burned ground. Kumpaya and Jakayu, well into their seventies, were soon specks in the distance. A couple of hours later, they were back with half a dozen reptiles each. They showed us how to remove the intestines by squeezing them out through the anus. Carly acquitted herself well, but I was content to be an interested bystander.

Several of the paintings I researched for *We Don't Need a Map* referred directly to fire, depicting country patterned with fire mosaics. When I pursued this thread, a sophisticated understanding of burning practices emerged. The different stages of burning and growth had specific names: the newly burned ground so beloved of the old ladies was called *nyurnma*; the period when plants were fruiting and seeding was *nyukura*; *manguu* was when spinifex was ready to burn again; and *kunarka* was when the old-growth spinifex had taken over, eliminating diversity and setting up the conditions for destructive bushfires.

The Martu had worked for years with American anthropologists Doug Bird and Rebecca Bliege Bird, who had been researching the impact of anthropogenic burning, and it was apparent that the extended conversation about fire had found its way into the Martu repertoire of painting country. Not only did paintings show country 'cleaned' by fire, interspersed with new and established vegetation, but they also showed specific types of vegetation: solanums and acacias, eucalypts and grevilleas, and seed-bearing grasses. My main informant was Nola Taylor, one of those indispensable interpreters who thrives on the stimulation of working with white people. Having worked closely with the Birds, Nola was used to communicating the finer points of burning practices.

This experience of researching Martu paintings led me to a similar interrogation of *Yarrkalpa* (*Hunting Ground*), a painting purchased by the National Museum of Australia and a key work in its exhibition *Songlines: tracking the Seven Sisters*. (See chapter nine and colour section.) The five-by-three-metre painting was the centrepiece of a collaboration between eight Martu women, artist Lynette Wallworth, and singer Anohni, formerly known as Antony Hegarty. Wallworth used overhead time-lapse photography to film the making of the painting, and the immersive multi-screen result shows the painters materialising, disappearing, and reappearing as they create the landscape, dot by dot, on the canvas, to the haunting accompaniment of Anohni's unique voice.

The artists paint what they know and what they do: burning country, tracking reptiles, gathering plant food. The Seven Sisters, known as *Minyipuru,* flit across the western side of the painting, pursued by an ancestral stalker called Yurla, intent on capturing the sisters for sex. Their presence is just one strand in the fabric of Martu daily life. They are a seasonal constellation, their appearance an indication that the country is dry and that care must be taken with burning. The community of Parnngurr is represented by a tidy grid near the centre of the painting, with the sports oval to the north. Two rivers anchor the composition and orientate the landforms. The painting is a topographic replica of the landscape around Parnngurr: ranges and dunes and sand plains, creeks and rock holes and soakwaters. Each artist painted a section of the canvas from her own embodied knowledge, describing places, memories, ancestors, seasons, resources, burning, hunting, and living.

Yarrkalpa is an encyclopaedia of seasons, burning practices, and resources. It is also a crosscultural document influenced by many years of interaction between the Martu and ecologists, anthropologists, archaeologists, linguists, land-management experts, artists, art projects, Indigenous Ranger programs, and cultural-maintenance projects.

During my study of *Yarrkalpa,* Nola interpreted for Kumpaya, who had painted strips of alternating colour to indicate sand dunes and swales, and the plants that grow on them. Nola, an artist herself, specialises in painting fire scars, drawing on the satellite imagery she is familiar with through working with the American anthropologists. On *Yarrkalpa,* she painted the mosaic patterning of freshly burned country, old and new growth, and the variety of food plants that are dependent on fire. '*Nyurnma*,' she said, pointing to blackened patches of canvas. 'Good for *parnajarrpa*,' Kumpaya said. The other fire-painter, Ngamaru Bidu, was less forthcoming. 'Pretty flowers,' she said, when I pointed to a multicoloured section, pretty flowers being the generic term for plants that have no specific use. The area she painted writhes with energy, like flames rippling across the landscape. After several days of consultation, my reproduction of the painting was annotated with plant names: where they grow, how they are used, what birds and animals they attract, and whether they are eaten by camels or threatened by buffel grass.

Among the maps I took with me on my first visits to Martu country was a reproduction of what came to be called the Waterhole map, originally drawn on three doors in Punmu in 1987, when Sue Davenport was recording cultural material with the Martu. She facilitated an exercise in collective Martu memory, in which the names and locations of nearly 600 waterholes were recalled through songs, and marked on the hand-drawn map. When compared to the waterholes found during subsequent aerial and GPS surveys, the locations of the original waterholes proved remarkably accurate.

The paintings I was researching for *We Don't Need a Map* were full of named sites, so it was a natural step for me to locate them on the Waterhole map. Along with fire, the tracks and activities of the ancestors, the seasonal routes people travelled in the *pujiman* (bushman) days, and edible plants and animals, the paintings made references to underground streams that came to the surface after heavy rain, and places where fresh water sprang out of salt lakes. Another feature was the convergence of subterranean flows to a waterhole or soakage. Intrigued by the apparent knowledge that people had of underground streams, I applied a satellite elevational mapping program to the area covered by the Waterhole map. That an ancient river, which formed the extant Percival Lakes system, lined up with the subterranean drainage channels was no surprise, but so did all the mapped waterholes, including the wells of the Canning Stock Route, and the locations where people said underground flows came to the surface. The Martu know the waterways in their country, both above and below ground.

In 2014, a group of nine Martu elders, including two senior men and several of the women who painted *Yarrkalpa,* produced a painting called *Kulyu,* now housed at the Museum of Contemporary Art in

Sydney. Another five-by-three-metre canvas, *Kulyu* encompasses the entire Martu determination, an area of approximately 136,000 square kilometres. It was painted in response to fears that the tailings from uranium mining would pollute the underground water system, and shows the interrelationship between the subterranean waterways and the ecosystems that they support. To paint *Kulyu*, brothers Muuki and Waka Taylor first laid in the underground flows, which were then layered over with mud-coloured paint to represent the earth above the aqueducts. On top of this, the artists painted the topographic features of the country, showing how the underground streams feed the surface waters that support the ecosystems on which the Martu depend. (See colour section.)

Paintings like *Yarrkalpa* and *Kulyu* reflect the evolving conversation between the Martu and the organisations and individuals who have aspirations for, and designs on, their culture and country. As proof of knowledge is required, it is provided in ever more sophisticated ways, and it seems only fair that non-Indigenous Australians try to develop an equal sophistication in interpreting that proof.

The Martu have retained considerable agency in managing their affairs through two key organisations: Kanyirninpa Jukurrpa (KJ), which focuses on land, law, and culture; and Martumili, which focuses on art. Both organisations were established at the behest of senior Martu custodians, and both operate on a model in which the administration and management are predominantly non-Indigenous while the advisory board and on-ground expertise are Martu.

KJ first came across my radar during one of my stints as an interim co-ordinator of the Paruku Indigenous Protected Area, in the south-east Kimberley region. I found that the best material about desert-based Indigenous programs had KJ's fingerprints all over it. The more I learned about KJ, the more it seemed a model of an Indigenous organisation delivering what it had set out to do.

Although formally established in 2005, KJ had its origins during the resettlement of the Martu homelands in the mid-1980s. Relationships forged between the Martu people and particular whitefellas during that time persist to this day, and these have provided the foundation of mutual trust, respect, and communication that are the hallmarks of KJ's success. Although the designation of Martu country as 'useless' contributed to it being used for rocket-testing in the 1960s, this also meant that it has remained more or less pristine desert, apart from some mining activity. When the Martu returned to their homelands they had retained a strong sense of cultural identity and an extensive traditional knowledge of culture and country. But they knew that their future depended on forming partnerships that valued both whitefella and Martu skills and experience.

The serendipitous combination of people of intelligence, vision, trust, and skill produced an organisational model for KJ that is grounded in Martu culture, adaptive to new ideas and technologies, and committed to cross-cultural partnerships. The Martu directors and advisers are consistently engaged in developing programs and projects, and KJ continues to attract high-functioning non-Indigenous staff, rather than the missionary/mercenary/misfit variety. Effective, professional people stay with the organisation, corporate knowledge doesn't get lost, and long-term partnerships are maintained.

One of those partnerships, providing economic dividends to the Martu and social and cultural dividends to the company, is with BHP. The mining giant contributes significantly to Martu projects and to the maintenance of KJ, which means that the organisation is not as dependent on government funding as many Indigenous support organisations are. The Nature Conservancy, a USbased environmental organisation, is another major partner, and the other support bodies listed in KJ's newsletters indicate that it has developed effective advocacy and communication skills, and that keeping an Indigenous organisation functioning at optimum level is expensive and complex.

I'm aware that by writing at length about the Martu I risk reinforcing 'the non-Indigenous Imaginary', a concept attributed to Indigenous academic Larissa Behrendt, referring to the stereotype held by many white Australians that Indigenous people are close to 'nature'. But the Martu are proof that it's possible to live in and maintain country. They exemplify how it can be done, with partnerships and complementary knowledge systems. Variations on this theme are being played out all over Australia.

In Australia, most of the population — including most of the Indigenous population — lives in major cities and large regional town. This leaves the practical husbandry of the continent to the handful of people who occupy the rest of it. How farming and grazing lands are managed is outside the scope of this essay. The rest, whether desert ecosystems, marginal pastoral country, coastal, savannah, or riparian systems, Indigenous Protected Areas, Aboriginal determinations, NGO conservation holdings, unallocated Crown land, state forests or national parks, needs to be managed for water, fire, ferals, endangered species, and weeds. The Indigenous Ranger program has emerged to address that need.

The Indigenous Ranger program evolved in an ad hoc fashion. It began with community-based teams such Arnhem Land's Djelk Rangers, which were established in the early 1990s to deal with a growing feral pig problem. The Djelk Rangers (*djelk* is a Gurrgoni word that means 'land' or 'caring for land') soon became the on-ground workforce for all environmental-management issues in the surrounding Indigenous landholdings. The team's role expanded to include the management of invasive weeds, fire, and water buffalo. Funding came from various sources, and was underpinned by the federal government's Community Development Employment Projects (CDEP) program, one of many attempts to create a culture of paid employment to replace the dole. By the end of the 1990s, the Djelk Rangers were working with a variety of scientists, developing a suite of skills specific to tropical savannah management and the evolving environmental challenges.

As Indigenous Ranger projects gained traction, so did the establishment of Indigenous Protected Areas (IPAs), a Howard government program implemented in 1997 to extend the holdings of the National Reserve System and to help with and influence the management of Aboriginal land. Land rights, native title, and the homelands movement had resulted in large tracts of land coming under Indigenous jurisdiction. The types of tenure varied from pastoral leases, which already carried certain conditions, to Crown land and near-pristine desert, and the Indigenous custodians often had neither the resources nor the expertise to deal with the economic and environmental challenges that confronted them. In the advent of Howard's program for land to qualify as an IPA, traditional owners had to commit to managing their country according to standards stipulated by the International Union for Conservation of Nature. While some Indigenous groups were uneasy about adopting these externally enforced practices, in spite of the substantial funding that would come with them, others took them up.

Indigenous Rangers were a natural adjunct to the IPAs, and both programs snowballed. CDEP wages paid for the ranger teams until the Working on Country (WoC) program was established in 2007. (As you can gather, we are in the acronym zone.) WoC provided dedicated federal funding for the employment of rangers, and established the status of Indigenous ranger as a professional occupation, with training in literacy and numeracy, first aid, data collection, firearms, fencing, welding, fire management, chainsaws, and pumps. In 2017, when this essay was originally published, WoC supported 109 Indigenous Ranger programs across Australia, providing about 2,500 full-time, parttime, and casual positions each year.

The Martu and the Indigenous Ranger program were made for each other. KJ's integrated social, cultural, environmental, and economic objectives allowed for immediate adoption of the program when it was formalised. From a single team in 2009, KJ now runs seven — including three teams of women rangers — out of Parnngurr, Punmu, Kunawarritji, and Jigalong, employing approximately 300 people. The knowledge of elders informs every project, and the Junior Rangers program is an integral part of the school system.

Martu rangers, advised by their elders and assisted by professionals in various fields, survey and look after waterholes and other cultural sites, cull camels and bait cats, monitor the status of threatened species (such as bilbies, black-flanked rock wallabies, and great desert skinks), and manage habitat, predominately by reinstating 'right-way' fire across the entire Martu lands.

The ranger program, in partnership with land-management and conservation agencies, has mobilised an Indigenous workforce with the potential to develop a unique suite of skills that are specific to particular ecosystems and that target the threats to those ecosystems. Often, feral animals are not perceived as a threat, especially when they have been incorporated into the local diet (as is the case with cats, camels, and water buffaloes). Although people are sanguine about killing animals to eat, the wholesale culling of a food resource is often resisted. It is only through consultation and the presentation of evidence that the impacts of ferals are accepted as long-term threats to country and culture.

Fire management emerges as central to the maintenance of healthy ecosystems in large parts of Australia, whether to promote the growth of fire-dependent plants and to maintain diversity and habitat in the spinifex country, or to limit hot-season bushfires and to protect fire-sensitive species in the Top End. People no longer walk the country as they used to do, and the old burning methods tend to be restricted to areas within easy reach of communities or along roads. The fire strategies implemented by Indigenous rangers require an integrated approach that draws on satellite technology and fire-scar mapping, along with Indigenous knowledge and the use of four-wheel drives and helicopters to reach remoter areas.

Country Needs People, a not-for-profit advocacy alliance now comprising more than forty frontline Indigenous land- and sea-management groups, published a report in 2016 identifying key conservation work being carried out by Indigenous rangers that included fire-reduction strategies, removing buffel grass, protecting habitats for threatened species, and managing feral animals, weeds, toads, and other invasive species. It's not a seamless story of success, of course. Some years back, members of a ranger team were implicated in the sale of contraband dugong and turtle meat on the local black market — as traditional custodians, they could hunt the protected species. It was an example of entrepreneurial resourcefulness, but it was also illegal, given the endangered status of the dugong. And with each Indigenous Ranger project there are always personalities and politics to contend with: particular families may dominate the ranger teams and IPA positions, causing resentment and friction; powerful individuals stall progress by holding on to jobs they don't fulfil; the competing demands of family, football, and funerals can make it difficult to pin down the workforce. The rangers occupy a complicated position: flagged as the great Indigenous employment success story, they are still subject to the embedded responsibilities of family and culture as well as the pressure to meet Western expectations.

As anthropology professor Jon Altman says in his contribution to a collection of essays, *Unstable Relations: Indigenous people and environmentalism in contemporary Australia*, 'They [the rangers] need to constantly mediate these two perspectives while being suitably deferential to more senior landowners, their parents and immediate family.' Altman lays out the challenges and contradictions of managing the exploding population of water buffalo in the Djelk IPA. Comprising ten clan estates, the IPA covers approximately 1,000 square kilometres, extending from the coastal flood plains and tidal river margins to the Arnhem Land plateau. It is an area of great biodiversity and high conservation value. By agreeing to have their lands declared an IPA in 2009, the Kuninjku traditional owners had committed to managing their country for environmental outcomes. In 2014, however, an aerial survey of water buffalo in Arnhem Land estimated that there were four times the number of animals that had been counted in a 1998 survey. Twenty thousand buffalo occupied the Djelk IPA, wreaking extensive damage in the wetlands, and contravening the agreed conservation principles.

Altman's essay is a case study in the multilayered complexities of dealing with what might seem to be a straightforward environmental issue that could be solved by culling. The introduction of water buffalo from Timor to the Cobourg Peninsula, in western Arnhem Land, is recorded as happening in the 1820s. However, the Kuninjku are not convinced that water buffalo are such strangers: the powerful and charismatic animal provides a high-protein staple for the Kuninjku, and status for hunters; it has a name, *nganabbarru,* in local languages, and links to myths and ceremony. According to older people, *nganabbarru* has been incorporated into the kinship system, and is thus connected to family and country. This sets buffalo apart from other feral species. (Except possibly the horse: I was once shown a horseshoe-shaped imprint in a rock in the Tanami Desert, and told that it was made by a *yawarda* (horse) in the Dreamtime.)

Although the Kuninjku recognise the damage that water buffalo are causing to the ecosystem by breaking down the natural barriers between saltwater and freshwater systems, the fact that the animals have created an environment in which they thrive goes some way to compensating for the loss of other habitats. Goannas and monitor lizards, a major food source with totemic significance, were almost wiped out by cane toads, which arrived in Arnhem Land in 2002. As buffalo replace the species people used to hunt and eat, Kuninjku are increasingly dependent on them as a food source.

In spite of these complications, an agreement was reached to cull 5,000 animals in 2015. But the local Bawinanga Aboriginal Corporation scuttled this plan when the prospect of selling buffalo to the live export trade raised the possibility of making money. While the idea seems reasonable, it had the hallmarks of dozens of money-making schemes that are cooked up between Indigenous corporation managers (usually white) and powerful local family interests, usually in opposition to IPA conditions. The people who come up with the schemes rarely have the expertise to deliver what they promise, and internal politics tend to sabotage projects before they get off the ground. It is not difficult to read between the lines of Altman's cryptic account in *Unstable Relations* of the failure of the Bawinanga live buffalo trade being caused in part by the sacking of the corporation's white senior management because they didn't listen to the traditional owners.

There are manifest tensions between the Indigenous concept of 'caring for country' and Western principles of environmental preservation. Richard Martin and David Trigger document this tension in an essay also included in *Unstable Relations*. It tells the story of Pungalina, a remote pastoral lease in the Gulf Country and the traditional land of the Garawa people, which was purchased in 2009 by the Australian Wildlife Conservancy and is now managed as a wildlife sanctuary by non-Indigenous caretakers. The Garawa hold native title over Pungalina, allowing them access to hunt and fish, and on a trip with traditional owners in 2012, Martin and Trigger recorded the discomfort expressed by the caretakers that the Garawa hunting rights posed a threat to the wildlife. The Garawa, in turn, were concerned that the conservancy planned to reduce the numbers of cattle that still grazed on the pastoral lease.

'They belong here now ... same as buffalo, pig, horse ...'

In fulfilling their roles, Indigenous rangers find themselves occupying a place where traditional obligations intersect with job accountability. They have access to wellmaintained four-wheel drives, high-powered rifles, and wages. Having access to vehicles and money can trigger toxic jealousies, accompanied by relentless humbug, and for some rangers the pressure is too much. But the robustness of the Indigenous Ranger program, and its emergence out of a real and growing need to manage extensive tracts of country, has seen it develop and strengthen. This is the live ground where contradictions between conservation values, economic accountability, and Indigenous aspirations to make a viable living on their land remain visible, volatile, and constantly evolving. Rather than treating this volatility as a problem, it should be part of a committed, long-term conversation.

As Tony Birch suggests in the closing essay of *Unstable Relations*, 'difficulty, or even impossibility, is as good a place as any to begin a new conversation'. While we are still some distance from beginning a conversation on impossible ground, starting from a point of difficulty is well within reach.

In a field littered with failures, the IPA and Indigenous Ranger programs are standout success stories. There is nothing comparable for cross-generational engagement of Indigenous groups, from the deep desert to the urban fringes. While the focus tends to be on the desert regions, Arnhem Land, and north-west Kimberley, the ranger groups and IPAs are Australia wide. A rumour in 2016 that the Indigenous Ranger program was to be downgraded to be part of the work-for-the-dole system (a return to the status it had a decade ago) sent a seismic shudder through the agencies involved. Emphatic denials came from the minister for Indigenous affairs and the Department of the Prime Minister and Cabinet, and commitments were made for funding until the end of 2018, and then extended to 2020.

This grudging, unpredictable, and short-term approach was redressed in 2020 when the federal government committed to spending a total of $714 million ($102 million a year) on ranger programs between 2021 and 2028. The March 2022 budget allocated an additional $636 million to the same time frame, with the intention of bringing the total number of ranger groups to 208, and the number of rangers to approximately 4,000.

The Indigenous Ranger program should be embedded in education, and not just in Indigenous education, and celebrated for its flexibility and potential. The program is committed to continual adaptation and scrutiny, offering a forum in which hard questions can be asked about the conundrums that plague both black and white understandings of responsibility, accountability, conservation, custodianship, autonomy, and dependency. It provides an opportunity to tease out contradictions and to challenge some of the generic statements about caring for country, whether they take the form of a comment post ('they ate a section of the country out, befouled it, and moved on'), or the claim that Indigenous people have an innate understanding of their environments and should be allowed to manage them without interference from whitefellas. This claim, designed to invoke the 'non-Indigenous Imaginary', was made by an Indigenous delegate at a conference called Mapping the Inland. She was staying on message to a room full of whitefellas, and was confident that no one would challenge her, but I'm not sure she believed the claim herself.

Funding for IPAs, which was due to be axed in 2018, received a reprieve in 2017 when the federal budget committed $1.1 billion to support existing IPAs, and $15 million for competitive and discretionary grants to assist consultation and planning for new IPAs.

In 2020, IPAs made up more than 46 per cent of the National Reserve System. A glance at the map of established and pending IPAs and other Indigenous-owned lands, which can be found on the National Indigenous Australians Agency (NIAA) website, shows a broad corridor of IPA land stretching from the Nullarbor to the Coral Sea: large Lego-shaped chunks of the Western Desert, the Pilbara, the Kimberley, and Cape York. The south-east quadrant of Australia is notably free of large IPAs, although there are clusters of dots that indicate that the program can be applied to very small areas. Two new IPAs, declared in late 2020, brought the total to seventy-eight, with another seventeen currently under consultation.

Although new IPAs are being declared all the time, the money to support them is limited, hence the need for income streams to maintain the capacity for people to live on and manage their lands. Partnerships are fundamental to this, where both Indigenous and Western knowledge is respected, and where shared concern for the health of the land is acknowledged. It's also necessary to find a balance between environmental imperatives and economically viable ways to live on country. For many Indigenous people, mining royalties are central to their economic survival, and programs such as the carbon-credit scheme reported in *The Australian* provide environmental benefits and an income stream that is not dependent on government. Some of these partnerships have been in place for years, providing income stability for the ranger teams who carry out the burning, and proving the viability of continuing support before the federal government committed to long-term funding.

There are hardline conservationists who believe that to preserve wild places, people must be excluded. To the Martu, indeed to many Indigenous people, such an idea is incomprehensible. In her study of the Martu fire regimes, Rebecca Bliege Bird identifies the Martu as a 'keystone species' in the maintenance of the Western Desert ecosystem. Tim Flannery, in his *Quarterly Essay* 'After the Future', suggests that this keystone role is now the responsibility of all Australians, with an emphasis on science-based fieldwork exemplified by non-government organisations such as the Australian Wildlife Conservancy.

The Martu understand the need for a 'two-way' approach and they have provided a benchmark for how to negotiate the future we share. The specialist skills of whitefella professionals are a resource that the Martu recognise and value, while they bring to the partnership the desert-forged sensibility that tests and adopts whatever is useful, and discards whatever is not.

6

Hunting the wild potato

'Why don't they cultivate the plants near the community, so they can dig them up when they want them?' David J asks. We have spent the afternoon looking for yams, walking and searching and digging with the two Walmajarri women who are my willing collaborators, always happy to induct visitors into the mysteries of Aboriginal culture.

'Because that would take all the fun out of it,' I say. It's the first response that leaps to mind, but when I think about it later, it seems to underline a fundamental aspect of the desert Aboriginal world. I could have offered more logical reasons that would have satisfied my friend. I could have explained that the common wild potato, or yam, *Ipomoea costata*, grows in particular soil types, and that it would be difficult to replicate the conditions in the stony ground near the community. I could have said that anything grown close to the community is at risk of being pillaged early by kids, dug up by dogs, or eaten by the resident camel or horse, and that it would be an invitation to subvert the good intentions of whichever kardiya has had the brainwave to streamline a practice that is about much more than gathering food. I could have drawn on the examples of many failed agricultural enterprises, and the explanations for why they failed.

I tease out what I mean by fun. There's the social aspect, the gathering of whoever wants to spend the day out hunting. There's the teaching element — the kids learning about so much more than how to find the yams and dig them up. On any given day they might harvest some bush medicine, or some bush tomatoes on their prickly stems, or come across an opportunistic find of coolibah bark, which people burn and reduce to a fine white powder to mix with chewing tobacco. There's the chance of finding a blackhead python basking beneath the warm surface of its burrow. There's the escape from the pressures and tensions of community life into an elemental world underlaid by the traces of the ancestors making their ruthless way across the landscape. It's a way for people to be alone in company, wandering singly or in loose pairs, the threads of relationship stretching and holding them as they spread apart into the quietude of hearing all that the country has to say.

'That would take all the fun out of it' translates as: the efficiency achieved by cultivating the plants closer to the community would be countered by the loss of social and cultural sharing, the settling and clearing of the mind, the reinvigoration of the psyche that wandering with intent provides. And it wouldn't be more efficient anyway.

It is interesting to bring people from my other life to visit this one. The people in this group are all friends and colleagues of mine who are artists, mostly sculptors. The three men are all called David. Two of the women are called Wendy. The others are Sally, Cathy, and Rachel. Wendy T and Rachel have been here before, but for the rest it's a first. The plan is to see how, as artists, they interpret and are impacted by the desert and its people. My working title for the project is *Undertow*, flagging the fact that all of us who make artworks about the land must feel the undertow of its original custodians. How to incorporate or acknowledge this, or whether one even wants to go there, is a question

I want to put to the others. I have not foreseen how difficult it would be to stretch myself between the two worlds.

My usual pattern when I arrive is to spend the first couple of days in a state of ennui while my whitefella brain goes quiet, and my other self, the one that has grown and taken shape over the years, emerges from hibernation, stretches, inhales, and fills with the energy and pleasure of coming home. Instead, I have eight individuals who have invested great effort and a lot of money to get here, who are depending on me to manage and interpret the place and people for them.

The coolibahs that surround the campsite are beautiful, especially at first and last light, but offer no protection from the gusty wind that blows from sunrise to midday. From this eastern prospect, the desert lake the artists have come to see is a samphire-covered plain that dissolves at the horizon in a blue shimmer that might as well be a mirage. The lake basins can dry back to pools and soakwaters, and expand to the dimensions of an inland sea. In past years, the shoreline has been less than a hundred metres from the campsite. When I look at the lake, I see it through time, drying and filling, white as bone, blue as a kingfisher's wing, and everything in between. The people who have not been here before see only the absence of water.

The first visit to the community is daunting for my friends, who are viewing it through whitefella eyes — a first impression that is always about rubbish and dogs and disorder. I can't see it that way anymore. Instead, I see how the Boxer family have managed to extend the lawn they established last year until it has covered most of the ground between their houses and the dusty communal park. The Boxers are gardeners, not of food plants, but of flowers and trees and grass. They always ask me to bring flower seeds when I visit.

The Johns clan have continued to accumulate cars in various states of dismantlement, raised on blocks made of overturned hundred-litre drums. There's status attached to how many cars a family owns, no matter whether they go or not, and the Johns are way in front.

The Lulu clan at the block on the northern end of the community have planted bamboo and frangipani, and are managing to extend their patch of lawn, inch by incremental inch, to fill the space demarcated by a ring of tyres painted white and sunk upright into the ground. The car that Lulu purchased last year, the old 100 Series LandCruiser wagon that used to belong to the Indigenous Protected Area coordinator, is still functioning. She has bought many cars over the years, and they have usually only lasted a few months. But she seems to have established some ground rules for this one.

I know that it is used primarily to take the kids out bush and to the lake. In the early years, when Lulu used to say to me, 'That's why I need a car, Napuru, to take the kids to the lake', I took it for one of the many platitudes that she would offer up to kardiya, the things she thought we wanted to hear. But now I know it *is* what she wants a car for, that keeping alive the connection her grandchildren and great grandchildren have to the minutiae and seasons of their country is fundamental to her life's work.

But all this is invisible to my friends, who stand around in polite discomfort in the little art centre, a self-managed enterprise that has survived the aspirations of several white co-ordinators and community managers. I've marshalled a contingent of the women elders with whom I work every year; they sit, apparently ignoring the visitors, although I know they are hyper-alert to them. I suggest cups of tea, and direct Cathy and Sally to the kitchen, where the sink is cluttered with unwashed cups. Sally comes back with a plastic bottle of what at first glance looks like detergent, but is in fact dog wash. 'It'll probably do the job', I say, but we decide on paper cups as a safer option. 'The tea needs to be strong, but not hot. Half-fill the cups with cold water. Lots of milk. No sugar for Evelyn. One sugar each for the others.' I know it all by heart, having made countless cups of tea for them over the years. Sal, who is a tea fascist of the boiling-hot, strong, sugarless, dash-of-milk variety, looks aghast.

We look at the paintings, the subtext on the Aboriginal side being the expectation that these well-heeled kardiya will buy some. This is not in the minds of my friends, who tell me later that they found the women impenetrable.

The wind begins shortly after daylight, and blows until midday — a gusty, dusty gale that makes it uncomfortable to work or keep focus. The discomfort is emerging as faultlines in the kardiya group dynamics, a minor sniping about the organising of the camp and the managing of the food. Several people have remarked that they had expected to be camping on the edge of a body of water. Getting everyone to a part of the lake where they can experience the water is becoming imperative.

But before we do that we have another task. In recent years, the school has had a stable era with a long-term headmaster and his wife, and teachers who have stayed for at least two years. Because of my work with the Indigenous Protected Area and the rangers, we have developed a tradition that whenever I return to the community I facilitate sessions with the schoolkids, rangers, and elders. This time, because I've brought a contingent of sculptors with me, we will run a sculpture workshop for an afternoon. The kids will be on holidays the following week, so it must happen within the first few days of our arrival.

The lake edges are rich in a slick grey clay, which a couple of us collect in buckets to make an adobe mix. The most available binding medium for the clay is dried horse manure, provided by the brumbies that live around the lake. We spend a morning at the camp folding manure into the wet clay, kneading it into smelly grey clods that are then swathed in Glad Wrap to keep them moist. We construct armatures from branches, grass, and wire, the plan being to plaster the adobe mix onto the structures, shape it, and let it dry.

The school session is a great icebreaker for the visitors. The kids are engaged and unselfconscious, the teachers enthusiastic. When the adobe mixture turns out to be too dry, we improvise, wetting down the mixture to make it easier to use, which also makes it easier for the kids to spread it from head to toe. David J has been nominated to do the initial demonstration, and he proffers the armature he has constructed: an elegant horse with a neatly hedged mane of grass.

'What do you think this is?' he asks the kids.

'Goanna,' they shout. 'Kangaroo, bullocky.'

'It's a horse,' David J says, and one of the kids leans over and takes a sniff.

'Smells like a horse,' he says.

There's some consternation when the kids discover that the clay is mixed with horse manure, but this is quickly over-ridden by the sheer pleasure of making an unholy mess in the pursuit of art. There are nine artists deployed among thirty kids, and three teachers supervising and participating. The concrete verandah becomes a swamp of clay, grass, sticks, string, wire, and feathers. David J's horse falls over under its weight of clay. 'Someone been shootem,' remarks the kid who said it smelled like a horse. The most successful of the sculptures, overseen by Rachel, is an echidna made from a lump of adobe with sticks poked into it and stones for eyes.

It's a couple of days later that David J asks the question about cultivating wild potatoes. We have spent most of the day with Shirley and Evelyn, who are mainstays of any projects I facilitate. Evelyn is also Napurrula, which makes us skin sisters, a relationship that has shifted from tokenism into something solid and meaningful as the years have passed. Her brother, who has recently died, was one of the first contingent of stockmen who worked for my family in the sixties, and this adds glue to the bond between us. I've asked the women to show the visitors how to find and identify bush tucker and medicine, so they accompany us to the wild potato grounds, where there are signs of recent digging activity. The looping vines and heart-shaped dark-green leaves of the wild potato plants are easy to spot, and yams are a staple winter food in this part of the country. The tuber grows some distance from the central stem, and is located by the crack it causes on the surface. This part of the hunt isn't rocket science. The trick, which I've never mastered, is how to tell whether the yam is the size of a walnut or the size of a football. Evelyn keeps digging at a crack I've identified, and eventually unearths a yam the size of a small carrot. Shirley has commandeered my light crowbar, so David J brings his heavy bar to help dig. After he has made a few passes at the sandy red soil, Evelyn gestures him away. 'Too heavy, might breakem,' she says, concerned for the yams.

Away from the community, these two good-natured women are relaxed and open, joking, and teasing each other and us. They take us to a place they call the Lounge Chair, a huge termite mound shaped like a couch with a back and armrests. The women sit on it, and Evelyn points to a kerosene drum jammed onto a small anthill close by. 'That's the TV', she says. Rachel sits beside them and asks what they are watching.

'McCleod's Daughters,' Shirley says.

'This is priceless traditional knowledge you're being told,' I tell the others.

David S asks how spinifex resin is sourced and made. Evelyn interprets this as a professional request, and directs us to an area where there has been recent burning. To find the resin, *wajarn*, in its unprocessed state requires a combination of spinifex, termite mound, and fire. The raw material must be cleaned of grit and dirt, and 'cooked' in a metal dish until it melts. What we collect is not good enough to produce resin of a quality that satisfies Evelyn, and she tells me we will find better *wajarn* at a different place. 'Another day,' I say. Most of the visitors are showing signs of over-exposure. Camping, cooking meals on an open fire, and showering every few days is tough, and the wind is wearing people down.

The following day, I take my friends to a place where they can make sense of the lake. It's on a spit of sand that divides the largest lake basin, the one we can see from our campsite, from a deep lagoon that is fed by one of the main channels of Sturt Creek. This time we are accompanied by Evelyn, Shirley, and my painting partner, Lulu. I'm anticipating an expanse of clean, white sand where we can walk, make a campfire, and cook dinner. Instead, the water in the lagoon reaches almost to the foot of the long dune that divides the two basins. The narrow channel between the lagoon and the big lake must have silted up during the poor wet seasons of the last few years, blocking the usual flow from the northern basin into the southern lake, leaving the lagoon levels much higher than the main basin.

The group are ecstatic. The tensions that have been building drop away. We sit or stand around at the water's edge, and Lulu recounts the story of Jintipiriny, willie wagtail, who whips his cousins the snakes into carrying out revenge on his behalf. Evelyn, Shirley, and Lulu mud the visitors, a ritual that involves having lake mud smeared on legs and arms and faces so that the snake that lives in the lake can smell them and won't harm them. I ask the Walmajarri women if they want me to take them home before it gets dark, or whether they prefer to stay with us while we cook. They are unanimous. 'We'll stay. We all widows, we got nothing to go back for.'

There are methodologies emerging among the group. Cathy, a ceramic artist who uses native flora as the motif for her vessels, has a set of processes that allow her to enter the place along her own established pathways — to look at plants, identify, collect, press, and draw them — and to source and test local clay. More than once, I pull what I think is a discarded can out of the fire, only to find one of Cathy's experimental pinch pots being cooked in it. Rachel has previously visited the lake with me and our mutual friend Pam Lofts. Her current practice involves making line drawings in space, using various gauges of wire to depict tools and domestic objects. The lake is edged with the slender, tall spikes of drowned salt wattle, *Acacia maconochaeana*, themselves a form of line drawing created by time and weather and the attrition of nature. Rachel collects shards from the skeletal trees, and crafts them into domestic shapes — a standard lamp, a chair — that she installs among the stands of dead acacia.

The others are absorbing and observing. Sally works with animal bones, and I have promised to find her a horse skeleton from a recent brumby cull. David S has discovered the burning-chimney effect of hollow coolibah branches, and is indulging his inner pyromaniac while claiming to experiment with bush-kiln ideas. Wendy T, the head of the sculpture workshop at the ANU art school, makes notational drawings on her iPad, searching out a calligraphy that she translates into pokerwork drawings, using heated metal rods to scorch the marks onto heavy paper. David J, who makes complex and highly engineered sculptures, is struggling to find a point of entry. Evelyn has noted his practical skills, and puts in an order for firewood and a load of horse manure for her garden. The other Wendy and David have Wendy's grandson with them. The child has hit the wall, and the couple have decided to cut the trip short and return to Alice Springs.

I'm not attempting to do any work myself. Paying attention to the needs of the group, and anticipating how best to make sure they get to experience a cross-section of this place I've brought them to, is taking up most of the space in my mind. Although camp morale improves with the removal of the small unhappy boy, there's still an undertow of tension. No doubt it's the result of the physical and psychological discomfort my friends are feeling, but it's a reminder that this place can never mean to them what it means to me. It's a sojourn from their normal lives, a glimpse of somewhere remote and exotic and largely without context, whereas for me it's central, necessary, cross-wired into my neural circuits and the geography of my body.

Gourmet campfire cooking has turned out to be one of the manifestations of displacement behaviour, and Shirley and Evelyn are happy recipients of the cakes, puddings, and other goodies that emerge daily from the camp oven. I pick the women up most mornings and bring them back to the campsite. Wendy gives a demonstration of pokerwork, using wire shapes constructed by David J, who makes flower shapes for Evelyn to burn onto a small coolamon. She and Shirley offer to show us how they used to cut coolamons from the trunk of a river red gum, but it's tough going, and my tomahawk isn't up to the job. 'Too hard,' Shirley says. 'Leavem. You can see how we used to makem. We use a chainsaw now.'

We make trips to locations I think will interest the visitors. The old mission site where Shirley spent a lot of her childhood is one of these, a haunting and haunted ruin resonant with other kinds of displacement. The adobe walls, constructed of slurried termite mound, have mostly collapsed, but the stamped-mud floors are intact, and Shirley gives us a guided tour of the remains of dormitories, the dining room, and the kitchen, the schoolroom, and the church. Her voice fills with pride and nostalgia as she recreates for us the architecture of her early life.

On our last day we visit an outstation built for Evelyn's family when her husband was still alive, but unoccupied since his death. It's a big day out, with a full quota of elders, young people, and kids. My friends get to participate in a spontaneous firestick-farming event when a group of teenage boys set fire to a spinifex-covered hill nearby. This prompts the little kids to leave off hunting the bats roosting in the outstation buildings, and to light up the foliage near our dinner camp, which requires a quick relocation of the vehicles. David S and Rachel look longingly at the fires erupting all around us. 'You can burn, if you like,' Evelyn says, and they grab burning sticks from the campfire and dash after the boys, who are hallooing from the other side of the stony hill.

That night, the two remaining Davids erect a massive hollow log chimney and a makeshift mini-kiln, and we have a spectacular night-firing of clay test objects. Rain starts to fall in the early hours of the morning, and at daybreak we are confronted with the job of packing up sodden and muddy gear. The subsequent dash to Alice through storms and long stretches of greasy road, punctuated by a freezing night at Yuendumu camped in the cars, and a last wild, waterlogged stretch before we reach the bitumen, ahead of flooding and road closures, provides a dramatic finale to the adventure.

While we regroup in Alice, attending to vehicle repairs and drying out the camping equipment, I ask my friends to write down what the experience has meant to them. It's too soon to know how it will manifest in the work they produce, but everyone says that spending the time with Shirley and Evelyn has been the high point.

A fortnight later, I'm back in Mulan, where I keep a low profile for a couple of days, maintaining a window of solitude while I shed the remnants of my other self before letting the undertow take me where it chooses.

7

Trapped in the gap

A few years ago, a friend of mine worked as a nurse for a men's health organisation on a remote Aboriginal community. One of his responsibilities was to accompany the men when they travelled to other communities for ceremonial business, and to attend to any illness or injury that occurred. At one of these events, he was approached by a young Aboriginal man.

'Hey, bro,' the young man said, 'you got any cold water?'

'I've got water,' my friend said. 'It's not cold, but you're welcome to it.'

'You got any cup?' the young man said.

'No, mate, sorry, only paper cups, and they've all been used. There might be one in the bin you can rinse out.'

'You can get it for me?' the young man said. At which point, my friend told him what he could do with his drink of water.

'The thing is,' he said, recounting the incident to us back in the community, 'there are whitefellas who would have gone through the bin for him. "Look, here's one, will this do? Hang on, there's a better one further down. Just let me wash it out for you ..."'

We laughed. We all knew people like that — the white slaves, abject and ingratiating, whose desire to serve Aboriginal people undermines basic mutual respect. They are at the extreme end of the spectrum Emma Kowal defines as 'white stigma' in *Trapped in the Gap: doing good in Indigenous Australia*, her treatise about white professionals working in the contact zone of remote Indigenous health.

Kowal has made an anthropological study of a group of white health professionals working in a Darwin research institute where she herself worked for some time. Among them are people she defines as 'white anti-racists', a category she teases out as a self-conscious positioning by white, left-wing, middle-class professionals who work in Indigenous affairs. 'White anti-racist' doesn't roll off the tongue, nor does it work as an acronym, but Kowal's choice of the term is deliberate. Its requisites are an active stance against racism, a belief that the problems afflicting Indigenous Australians are the direct result of colonisation and that the Australian government and society should foot the bill to redress this situation, and that Aboriginal people should control their own destiny, assisted by white professionals who will remain inconspicuous and aspire to make themselves redundant. A basic driver within this group is the desire to be recognised as a good white person, set apart from the racist norm.

Trapped in the Gap is an academic work that makes no concessions to the lay reader, and for this reason is unlikely to be read by any but the most committed, which is a pity, because the points it raises are central to the dilemma that white Australia tries and fails to negotiate again and again in its encounters with remote Aboriginal Australia. The zone that Kowal's protagonists enter, and to which I am referring when I use the term 'remote', is a place where cultural beliefs include the primacy of sorcery and the imperatives of payback, where the landscape is seething with presences that are mischievous at best and malevolent at worst, and where the pressures and expectations of whitefella society are flotsam in the deep currents of family and country.

One of the arguments Kowal posits is that the white anti-racist, in order to maintain a stance against victim-blaming, will identify structural rather than cultural issues as the cause of poor health (or poor education, unemployment, high crime rates, and domestic violence) in remote Aboriginal communities. This position assumes that when the structural obstacles are removed, the outcome will be a steady movement within those communities towards healthy choices — such as clean houses, healthy diets, regular work, and a commitment to education. In other words, they will then behave more like the majority of white people. Along with this argument goes the notion of 'remediable difference', whereby the differences between Aboriginal people in remote communities and the rest of the predominantly white Australian population is only skin deep, and that a level playing field will put things right.

That this is not what happens in remote communities suggests that the structural argument doesn't quite cut it. And this is where the white anti-racist begins to flounder. That Aboriginal people might not want the things that will make them healthier throws into question the purpose of the work the white professional is doing. It also raises the spectre of differences that run much deeper and are cultural rather than structural in their origins. And if the difference is cultural, and achieving better health outcomes means changing cultural attitudes, the white health professionals must participate in social engineering, which is the antithesis of what they believe in.

Kowal's protagonists are confronted with the irreconcilable contradiction that, in order for the frequently cited 'gap' to be closed, Aboriginal people must surrender or dilute their aboriginality, thus relinquishing or diminishing their power and their identity. This is their crippling moral dilemma: in their attempt to do good, they may in fact be doing harm. In a situation desperate for resources and support, the most highly skilled and scrupulous people are paralysed by the effects of this contradiction.

I put this conundrum to an Aboriginal friend who has worked for some years in the health arena, both in regional towns and in her own remote community. What did she think about the concerns of white professionals who feared that, by trying to improve Aboriginal health, they might be joining the long tradition of white values being imposed on Indigenous people? From her response, it was clear that she didn't lose sleep over the moral scruples of whitefellas. She had encountered those scruples as a zone of ambient anxiety, but they were background noise against the potency of racist slights she experienced as an Aboriginal health worker.

I took my question to one of the white nurses based in Mulan, the Western Australian Aboriginal community to which I have a long-standing connection. A man in his sixties, he had worked in remote-area health for years. Many of his views tallied with the white anti-racist position: the desire to facilitate Aboriginal people to take over the role he currently filled; and the belief that, with structural change, health outcomes would improve, and that Aboriginal people had the capacity to make their own choices. But when I pressed him on whether he thought it was necessary to change people's behaviour, he said yes. To encourage people to practise better hygiene and cut down on fat and sugar was part of his job, not an ethical issue.

'I'm not in the job to do good,' he said. He had fallen into remote nursing by chance, and found it suited him. He liked the work and the people, and was satisfied to observe incremental changes brought about by individuals. This set him apart from the white anti-racists, although, according to Kowal, some who continue to work in the field arrive at the same position, albeit after a period of soul-searching.

In the chapter titled 'Mutual Recognition', Kowal examines the constantly changing boundaries of both Aboriginality and anti-racism, and the sometimes farcical situations that arise from the sensitivities of both parties. In one example, signed consent forms are required for people to take part in a project. Some people want to participate, but don't want to sign the forms. The white project co-ordinator thinks that this is due to a legitimate cultural distrust of forms, while the Indigenous adviser believes it makes her mob appear primitive and stupid, and insists that she will convince them to sign the forms.

While the white anti-racists are hyper-vigilant in monitoring their own boundaries, they are also kept in a state of anxiety by the scrutiny of the Indigenous professional class. Kowal does not state this explicitly, but it is implicit in the nervousness with which members of her study group attempt to unpick the term 'Tribal Council'. Is it a relic of outdated anthropological terminology, or has it been reinstated by Aboriginal people from 'down south' (as 'blackfella' has been reinstated)?

In the contact zone, it is the white person who is on high alert, uncertain of how to interpret the ever-changing rules of engagement, while the Aboriginal people who live there have had long experience in extracting what suits them from the plethora of conflicting possibilities.

The most interesting chapter in the book deals with white stigma, unpacking the effects of an excessive attachment to the ideology of anti-racism. According to Kowal, the concept of white stigma is to perceive 'whiteness' as an inescapable contamination for which one must continually make reparation. One manifestation of this is to underplay the contribution of the white professional and to overstate the competence of the Aboriginal worker, often to devastating effect. I watched this play out in the south-east Kimberley, where an Aboriginal cattle manager was praised and assured by his white advisers that he was doing a great job, while the cattle station collapsed around him, along with his pride, his confidence, his identity, and his trust in white people. No one was prepared to tell him that the job was beyond his capabilities, or to help him to come to grips with contemporary cattle management and marketing. Any doubts he expressed about his abilities were buried under excuses and reassurances. In this particular case, I doubt there was anyone among the so-called advisers who had the requisite knowledge themselves.

The conjoined twin of white stigma is the black victim, resulting in a crippled partnership between the stigmatised and the victimised that has many refinements and variations, none of them pretty to watch. The committed anti-racist, blinkered by colonial guilt, cannot admit to the suspicion that when an Aboriginal person chooses to go fishing rather than to attend the meeting that has taken weeks and great expense to organise, the behaviour may not be cultural at all, but an expression of casual disrespect. When ideology excuses bad behaviour on cultural grounds, something abject enters the relationship.

The rigorous academic language that Kowal applies to her research may be necessary to counter the attacks that her ideas will elicit, but it does make the work less useful to the public conversation. After a hard day in the contact zone, I found it something of a challenge to spend my evenings unpicking the meaning from sentences such as: 'To escape essentialised Indigeneity, both Indigenous and non-Indigenous people "must de-couple Indigeneity from disadvantage and marginality from cultural and physical alterity and from callow moral dichotomies".'

Translated, Kowal's argument suggests that the way forward requires the victimised to let go of the advantages of victimhood, and for the stigmatised to relinquish the excoriating pleasures of the hairshirt. It's hard to imagine such ideas gaining traction in the current climate of racial politics but, as she points out, the existing model is gridlocked in its own contradictions.

From the solitude of my makeshift accommodation in Mulan, I can hear the night sounds of the community charged with the energy that ebbs and surges between people. In the years of returning to work in this small settlement on the edge of the Great Sandy Desert, I have learned to interpret those sounds. Everyone is connected through blood or marriage, an intricate network of relationships that coerce and protect, hurt and heal, entrance and terrify, without which life is unimaginable and identity extinguished. And just beyond is the violent, enchanted landscape, the domain of sorcerers and spirits and ancestral ghosts.

I wonder if part of the failure to persuade many of the people out here to choose safer, healthier, *whiter* lives is because what we offer, compared to what they have, is just too boring.

8

The seething landscape

In 2017, the blockbuster exhibition *Songlines: tracking the Seven Sisters* opened at the National Museum of Australia. Many years in the making, *Songlines* was a collaboration between the Australian National University, the National Museum, and the Indigenous people of the Martu, Ngaanyatjarra, and Anangu Pitjantjatjara Yankunytjatjara lands. Harnessing Indigenous storytelling, song, dance, painting, sculpture, and immersive visual and interactive technologies, the exhibition endeavoured to tell an ancestral Indigenous story.

In Australia, the activities of the Seven Sisters crisscross the continent. The names they are known by vary, as do the nuances of the story, depending on language group and country. Throughout the Central and Western Deserts, it's a tale of flight and pursuit, as the sisters flee the unwanted attentions of a sorcerer who pursues them relentlessly, spying on them, lying in wait for them, sometimes capturing one or several of them. The violence of his obsession thwarts his attempts to approach the women 'proper way', and manifests as a landscape that seethes and ripples with sexual desire, rendered unstable by a force that is both a primal sex organ and a relative of the ancestral snake that lives in waterholes and creeks — dangerous, unpredictable, everywhere.

The Jukurrpa, or Dreaming, is an active, continuous time, an animating presence in the land, reactivated whenever country is traversed by its keepers, or song and ceremony is performed. The Jukurrpa stories are the connective threads that weave the landscape into a tapestry of places and events, committing knowledge to memory by embedding each component of the story in a particular place, and recording it in song. The natural features of the landscape are the raw material of narrative. Around what already exists, the drama of creation, sex, violence, retaliation, flight, and survival is woven. The more intense the emotion attached to an event, the more indelible the memory of the place where it happened.

Among the Martu, the Seven Sisters are called the Minyipuru, and their pursuer is Yurla. The songline begins at Roebourne, on the north-west coast of Western Australia, and travels eastwards around 600 kilometres to Pangkal, a rock hole some forty kilometres north-east of the Telfer mine. In the beginning, there are many more than seven women, and the number is diminished by the arduous business of bringing landforms into being. Several paintings in the *Songlines* exhibition depict events at Pangkal, where the Minyipuru camp and perform ceremonies, transforming into rocks as they become weary, while others are born out of the landscape to take their place. It is here that the women taunt Yurla by flying above him and revealing their genitals, and his penis makes an independent appearance, bursting through the rock hole as if penetrating the earth itself.

The women flee south to a site east of Parnngurr Rockhole, where Yurla spies on them. It is somewhere around here that his penis tracks them along a creek bed and bursts out of the ground beneath their feet. The Minyipuru take refuge on a hill to the north, where they can be seen sitting down as a line of rocks along the ridge. Yurla hunkers nearby, his penis/snake coiled in waiting beneath the hill.

Connected by an almost umbilical link to the sisters, Yurla seems a manifestation of the landscape, a force of nature in the guise of a man. Although the Minyipuru torment and outwit him, they are unable to shake him off or harm him. In contrast, when the women encounter a group of men at Kalypa, near Well 23 on the Canning Stock Route, they fight them off with digging sticks.

'We never came for you', the sisters cry, 'We are our own selves', in what may be the earliest known statement of female autonomy. They beat the men unconscious and fly away.

The encounter at Kalypa is described as the first meeting between men and women. Unlike Yurla, the men are considered to be the ancestors of living men, and the Minyipuru ceremony for Kalypa is performed by men and women together.

The Minyipuru separate, regroup, gather food, dance, and perform rituals in a landscape rendered threatening and unpredictable by Yurla's relentless pursuit. At Pangkapini, Yurla captures one of the sisters, and the others offer to stay with him if he will gather firewood for them. While he is collecting the firewood, the Minyipuru rescue their sister, and when Yurla returns he hears them giggling, and looks up to see them flying above him, taunting him. He builds a ladder in an attempt to reach them, and they push it over, leaving him crawling after them in desperation. At this point in the telling, he is described as 'poor fella'.

Although the story as told here is predominantly a women's story, there are elements that belong to men, in which they identify with Yurla and acknowledge that he transgresses in his stalking of the Minyipuru.

Yurla embodies the desire for the forbidden, for which he suffers humiliation and disappointment, although he also inflicts fear and harm. One could put various interpretations on this story — that sexual obsession makes fools of men, that pursuing your desires above all else is a futile enterprise, that female solidarity prevails. While all these elements are present, to interpret the story only as a morality tale is to undermine its psychological power. It cleaves to the emotional truth of human experience in all its arbitrariness, a reflection of desert life and survival.

The trajectory of the sisters across the country is a means of naming and remembering sites, their resources, and their significance. As the Minyipuru dance, run, and fly across the Martu landscape, zigzagging from waterhole to rock hole, fleeing Yurla, sometimes outwitting him, sometimes falling victim to him, they map the waterholes and mark the country, creating landmarks and enacting ceremonies, weaving a picaresque tale that is menacing and hilarious, cheeky, violent, transcendent — and, above all, memorable. Soaring together across the night sky, chased relentlessly by the priapic old man, the Minyipuru leave their traces everywhere.

While the paintings depict sites where the Minyipuru rested, performed ceremonies, and encountered Yurla, they also record the artists' home country and personal recollections, and the routes and activities of other ancestral beings.

Of the many permanent waterholes, lakes, and ephemeral soaks visited by the Minyipuru, several are also visited by the Wati Kutjarra, the Two Men whose wanderings crisscross the Western Desert. The Minyipuru Dreaming track intersects in many places with other songlines — some of them major, like the Wati Kutjarra, and some of them local, like KurrKurr the night owl, whose eye popped out when he was speared, creating the underground pool called Mujingarra.

The Martu are famous for being among the last Aboriginal people to live a traditional way of life in the desert. Many Martu elders, people in their seventies and eighties today, grew to adulthood with little knowledge of the world beyond the desert. Some of them had encountered the droving mobs along the Canning Stock Route, so were aware of white people, horses, camels, and cattle, but had never seen motor vehicles, and believed the aeroplanes that passed over their country to be flying demons. For many of the artists involved in the *Songlines* exhibition, their first encounters with white people occurred in the 1950s and 1960s. This was the period when they 'came in' to the settlements and missions, most of them to Jigalong mission, where relatives had already settled.

In 1964, shortly before the first proposed testing of a rocket from the Woomera rocket range, a group of Martu were spotted in the Percival Lakes area, in the direct firing line of the rocket. The story of the attempt to find the group, composed entirely of women and children, and to shepherd them to safety, is told in the book *Cleared Out* by Sue Davenport, Peter Johnson, and Yuwali (2005), and in the 2009 film *Contact*, written, directed, and produced by Bentley Dean and Martin Butler. The book and the film focus on Yuwali, a teenage girl at the time of the episode. It is an astonishing tale of pursuit and evasion, a contemporary version of the Minyipuru. Coincidentally, there were seven adult women in the group, although their pursuer, unlike Yurla, was a gentle and gentlemanly character called Walter MacDougall, a patrol officer employed by the Woomera-based Weapons Research Establishment to clear the projected firing line of people.

Yuwali's account of fleeing from the patrol — of the women separating and regrouping, signalling their whereabouts with fire, running through the night to reach a spring or rock hole, stopping to find *warmula* (bush tomatoes) or *minyarra* (wild onions) — is an archetypal desert story of terror, resourcefulness, and physical endurance. Like the Minyipuru, the women stay just out of reach of the patrol, terrified but curious, leading their pursuer in a dance. It is not until a second patrol is organised that contact is made, when two Martu men accompany MacDougall and are able to communicate with the women and persuade them to stop running. In a twist of the Minyipuru story, the two Aboriginal men immediately claim the two youngest women as wives, although this is later overturned by Martu kinship laws.

The land rights movement of the 1970s saw the development of homelands and outstations. By the 1980s, many of the Martu who had come into the missions in the 1960s had returned to one or other of the communities — Parnngurr, Punmu, and Kunawarritji — established in the heart of their traditional lands. While the communities provided a school, a store, and a clinic, people were able to maintain their traditional practices, including law business and hunting.

The Martu are among the foremost practitioners of anthropogenic fire — fire lit by people — for the maintenance of plant and animal diversity in the desert. Fire, in the hands of people who know how to use it, is a sophisticated tool. Regular and sustained mosaic burning by Indigenous people brought a degree of predictability to the desert's resources. This finely integrated relationship continues today among the Martu, after a hiatus during the years when people moved into the missions and stations. The return to the desert communities reactivated the burning practices, although they were limited to within easy travelling distance, creating ideal conditions for comparison between the anthropogenic fire patterns close to the communities and regular campsites, and the lightning-generated fire patterns in the regions that people no longer visited. The maintenance of these practices led to a long collaboration between the Martu and the American scientists Doug Bird and Rebecca Bliege Bird, which resulted in a sophisticated understanding of Martu burning practices by the scientists, and a sophisticated articulation of those practices by the Martu.

In 2005, with the assistance of Peter Johnson and Sue Davenport, the Martu established Kanyirninpa Jukurrpa (KJ), an organisation dedicated to the maintenance of cultural knowledge. KJ supports the Indigenous ranger program, which provides on-country employment for many Martu, and to which the elders make a unique contribution with their experience of growing up in the *pujiman* (bushman) days. Today, the rangers use helicopters to carry out burning of less accessible regions.

Around the same time that Kanyirninpa Jukurrpa was established, the painting collective 'Martumili', based in Newman and designed to service art sheds in the various communities, brought Martu art into the public domain. When the Martu women began painting, the story of the Minyipuru and their ancestral stalker was their first subject. As the Martumili painting enterprise expanded, the Martu also began to represent country in large collaborative paintings with an ecological detail that reflected their knowledge.

In *Yarrkalpa* (*Hunting Ground*), the creation of which is the subject of Lynette Wallworth's immersive film installation in the *Songlines* exhibition, the rich and complex patterning of the Martu landscape represents the stages of growth and regeneration wrought by burning. (See colour section.) Depicting a world intimately known to the women, *Yarrkalpa* shows the country around Parnngurr, the community where many of the artists live today.

The Minyipuru traverse the western side of the painting, from east of the Parnngurr rock hole to the hill in the north, stalked by Yurla and his restless penis. They are a part of the quotidian landscape, a manifestation of the omnipresent Jukurrpa, enmeshed with the activities of daily life. The south-east quadrant of the painting shows a vibrant patchwork of fire scars, the result of regular local burning that regulates and stimulates the growth of food plants. If you were to sit down with the painters and ask them to explain the burning practices, they would tell you that there are several distinct stages of burning and renewal. *Nyurnma* is freshly burned country, which reveals the tracks and burrows of reptiles, especially when it is still covered with ash. *Nyurnma* includes the first growth of green shoots, followed by *nyukura*, when plants mature and produce edible fruits and seeds.

Manguu means the spinifex is ready to burn again, and *kunarka* is old-growth spinifex that will burn fiercely and cause hot-season bushfires if struck by lightning.

The content of *Yarrkalpa* is encyclopaedic. Apart from the collaborative process that created it, and the visual and sound elements of the installation that make it an immersive sensory experience, each artist has brought their own knowledge and experience to the sections they worked on. Embedded in the painting are individual stories and accounts of the *pujiman* days, the dance of ancestors across the landscape, the nuanced knowledge of plants and animals, of seasons and fire, of permanent water, of ephemeral soaks and underground seepage. The depiction of a small patch of *tinjil* (white coolibah trees) in the upper-right section of the painting indicates many things: the ground is low-lying and waterlogged in the wet season, it has grasslands favoured by bush turkeys, it is a good place to dig for wild onions, and in winter the witchetty grubs will fatten in the trunks and branches. Every part of the painting is dense with information, either literal or implied. The south-west corner of the painting is Kumpaya Girgirba's rendition of *nyurnma* (freshly burned country) for hunting *parnajarpa*, the goanna that is a staple bush food, caught in astonishing numbers when the conditions are right.

Because of its appearance in the night sky at particular times of the year, the Pleiades cluster is associated with seasonal change, and has likely served this function since early humans tried to establish some predictability in their world. Perhaps the first migrations out of Africa brought the cosmological narrative with them, welcoming the seasonal reappearances of the Seven Sisters as familiar celestial companions in a strange new world.

Today, the songlines of the antipodean Seven Sisters contribute in significant and essential ways to the maintenance of our Indigenous cultural knowledge.

9

The man in the log

On one of my regular visits to Alice Springs, I was told the following story. At the Ngaanyatjarra Pitjantjatjara Yankunytjatjara (NPY) Women's Council, a secondee from inner-city Sydney was sharing an office with Linda Rive, an interpreter who had spent a good deal of time living in remote communities in the Western Desert. Linda mentioned that when she first worked out on the lands there was no accommodation for visiting whitefellas, and she had lived for months at a time in a *wiltja*. The secondee heard the word, which means a traditional shelter, as 'wheelchair'. Constrained by good manners from asking what disability Linda had, and having been told by the co-ordinator of the placement organisation not to ask too many questions, but to listen and learn, she absorbed this information.

'It was pretty cramped,' Linda said. 'Especially when other people moved in with me.'

The secondee wondered how this might be managed, and towards the end of her placement she commented to her colleagues that Linda was a remarkable person who had lived for months in the desert in a wheelchair, sometimes even sharing it. By the time the story made its way back to Linda, it had become local legend.

I love this story for several reasons. The image it conjures up, of

Linda trundling over the dunes in her wheelchair, people clinging all over it, is much more beguiling than the reality of living in a shelter made of branches and spinifex. But, more importantly, it reveals how easily wires can get crossed; how readily we accept the improbable or outlandish when we are in unfamiliar territory; how acquiescence and good manners can allow the preposterous to go unquestioned. It's a perfect introduction to an essay about communication at the edge of the incomprehensible.

The Aboriginal world is the radioactive core of Alice Springs, impacting on everyone who lives there, even those who aren't involved with the organisations that service, support, and incarcerate Aboriginal people. Whenever I return, it's like entering an energy field in which the cultures ripple through one another, obscuring, illuminating, interrogating, undoing. The deficit aspects of Aboriginal life are in full view, and the counterpoint to that deficit is a dynamic, enmeshed, inspiring enterprise playing out in multiple ways.

I was in Alice Springs to research a project called Uti Kulintjaku, which translates from Pitjantjatjara as 'to listen, think and understand clearly'. In Pitjantjatjara, to listen properly and to understand are synonymous. You can't listen if you don't understand the language of the other people in the conversation. This isn't a difficult concept, but it often seems to elude the grasp, or at least the capacity, of governments, educators, police, and health professionals.

Since the publication and viral circulation of an essay I wrote several years ago, 'Kardiya are like Toyotas', about the dysfunctional world of whitefellas working in remote communities, I've been on the lookout for examples that run counter to that trope. These examples stand out because they share a suite of characteristics that are rare or absent from most of the organisations that service Aboriginal people.

The organisations and projects that meet my criteria are anchored in long-trusted cross-cultural relationships, have evolved as a response to the wishes of Aboriginal people, feature engaged Aboriginal participation, involve high-functioning white people who are in it for the long haul, share an equal respect for different ways of knowing and being, build on what is already there, and are process-based and responsive to change.

The Uti Kulintjaku project has all these elements, but what I find especially compelling is the way it provides a framework for a conversation about the underlying psychological forces that drive human behaviour. This conversation is carried out across languages and between cultures with profoundly different belief systems, but which are attributed equal value. The project employs skilled interpreters so that people can think in their own language and share complex ideas, teasing out words and their meanings with precision and subtlety. Everyone involved with Uti Kulintjaku speaks about it with a kind of wonder. It's the first time I've heard desert Aboriginal people express such enthusiasm for a project that isn't embedded in country.

Over several weeks, I sat in on evaluation interviews and spoke to people involved with the project. There was something unique and important going on, something more than good practice and productive outcomes, though that was unusual enough.

Uti Kulintjaku evolved from the Ngangkari (traditional healers') project, which was also developed by the NPY Women's Council, beginning in 1999. The Ngangkari project brought traditional healing practices to the health system in Central Australia, to help deal with the crisis in mental health among Aboriginal people. Conventional treatments were failing, and when Anangu (Western Desert people) were asked why, they suggested that their own healers were being ignored and should be brought into the process.

To begin with, there was resistance from doctors, who were

afraid that the Ngangkari would discourage Aboriginal patients from accepting Western medical treatment, but the Anangu healers insisted that their role would be complementary. After all, most of them were on various forms of Western medication. The presence of Ngangkari at Alice Springs Hospital became commonplace, producing a marked improvement in the mental health of Aboriginal patients. The Ngangkari were astonished to learn that Western doctors couldn't see or feel the spirits that are essential to human balance and health. How could they treat sick people if they couldn't see if their spirits were out of alignment? Ngangkari believe the spirit is intrinsic in the breath, and must be in its proper place for a person to remain healthy. According to senior Ngangkari Toby Minyintiri Baker, 'Spirits are not particularly difficult to work with. If you can see them, you can get them! They are not overly clever or trying to get away or escape you. They are just confidently themselves, and just need to be where they should be!'

The success of the Ngangkari project exposed the need to apply what had been learnt back on the lands, where mental-health resources were scarce and youth suicide was on the rise. As the conversation between Western psychiatric professionals and Anangu traditional healers evolved, it became apparent that there was little common language with which to talk about mental-health issues. Interpreters had been employed all along; but as the questions became more specific, the interpreters struggled to find the words to frame them, or the answers when they came. Consequently, in 2012, a small grant was sourced to run a project that focused on defining and translating words for various states of mind, and Uti Kulintjaku was born.

Many of the Aboriginal members of the Uti Kulintjaku team belong to Tjanpi Desert Weavers, the collective of artists who produced the transgressive female tree spirits first shown in the 2013 *String Theory* exhibition at the Museum of Contemporary Art in Sydney.

They also collaborated with Fiona Hall on the exhibition *Wrong Way Time* for the 2015 Venice Biennale. They were the instigators of and key participants in the 2017 exhibition *Songlines: tracking the Seven Sisters* at the National Museum of Australia. Some members also sing with the Central Australian Aboriginal Women's Choir, which toured Germany to great acclaim in 2015. They are involved in every major creative enterprise in the Western Desert. Many, though not all of them, are Ngangkari. They are directors of the NPY Women's Council, highly proficient speakers of language, and comprise an encyclopaedia of Western Desert knowledge. They bring a broad-spectrum approach to a problem that is generally constrained by Western medical science.

I meet four of these women at the home of Angela Lynch, program manager of the Ngangkari and Uti Kulintjaku projects, and her partner, Patrick Hookey, who speaks Pitjantjatjara and has agreed to interpret the conversation. In the course of the discussion, I ask the women what message they would most like to pass on to the politicians in Canberra.

'We need to think about that,' they say. The women talk quietly to each other over dinner. When the meal is over, we regroup, and Rene Kulitja, a powerhouse for whom Uti Kulintjaku has been transformative, speaks for everyone.

'*Nganana palyani nganampa katjaku munu untalpaku. Tjana-nku walytjangku kulira, atunymankunytjaku munu kunpuringkunytjaku.*'

Patrick translates: 'We want to do this project for our daughters and our sons, to look after them so they can be strong, to help them think for themselves.'

It's the cry of parents everywhere, but there's great poignancy in this carefully articulated statement. The challenges faced by these parents are gargantuan. The gap is great between the oldest people, who grew up in the bush, and the youngest, who inhabit a world of mobile phones, internet banking, and consumer goods. The young people are safer, and their chances better, if they stay on the lands, where family support remains strong. In town, instead of them reaping the benefits of the resources it offers — education, jobs, stimulation, creative opportunities — their more likely outcomes are substance abuse, crime, violence, incarceration, and, all too often, death.

'The government needs to keep helping us,' Rene says, 'because for us there are two roads, one to a good life and one to death.'

That these women are driving the push to address mental-health problems is not surprising. Suicide, drugs, alcohol, and violence in many forms have affected their own children and grandchildren. But that's not all that brings them to the meetings. In the Uti Kulintjaku evaluation interviews, the women consistently talk about how excited and challenged they are by the conversations with the Western mental-health doctors, and how they love gaining knowledge that expands and develops their ideas, digging into their languages to find words to describe the complex psychiatric and emotional problems afflicting their families. Coming together to share experiences, support each other, and workshop ideas makes them strong. It enables them to go back to their communities and practise what they have learnt.

In a meeting-fatigued culture, people make the effort to travel vast distances to attend Uti Kulintjaku workshops. This is almost unheard of for anything other than funerals, football, family business, and gatherings to celebrate country. There is a sense of meaning, but also of progress.

The workshops begin with the Anangu interpretation of the previous workshop and what has happened in the interim. Their experiences are the baseline from which to broaden the conversation into physiological and psychiatric explanations of cause and effect. Fundamental to the process is the inclusion of skilled interpreters. Their presence enables the Anangu to think in their own languages, to reflect on and share what they know, and to recognise that they have a considerable body of knowledge to bring to the cross-cultural

Kulyu, 2014, Ngamaru Bidu, Jakayu Biljabu, Bowja Patricia Butt, Kumpaya Girgirba, Noelene Girgirba, Karnu Nancy Taylor, Muuki Taylor, Ngalangka Nola Taylor, and Waka Taylor, synthetic polymer paint on linen, Museum of Contemporary Art, purchased with funds by an anonymous donor, 2014. Image courtesy of the artists, Museum of Contemporary Arts Australia, and Martumili Artists. Copyright © the artists. *Photograh by Jessica Maurer*

Spirit Dreaming through Napperby Country, 1980, Tim Leura Tjapaltjarri and Clifford Possum Tjapaltjarri. Copyright © estate of the artist. Licensed by Aboriginal Artists Agency Ltd

Yarrkalpa – Hunting Ground, Parnngurr Area, 2013, Kumpaya Girgirba, Yikartu Bumba, Ngamaru Bidu, Nancy Taylor Karnu, Janice Nixon Yuwali, Reena Rogers, Thelma Judson, and Nola Taylor, 300 x 500 cm, acrylic on linen. Image courtesy of the artists, Martumili Artists, and the National Museum of Australia. Copyright © the artists. *Photograph by Jason McCarthy*

Text overlay of *Yarrkalpa* by Kim Mahood. *Photograph by Jason McCarthy*

The Man in the Log, 2018. Copyright © Rene Kulitja. *Photograph by Angela Lynch*

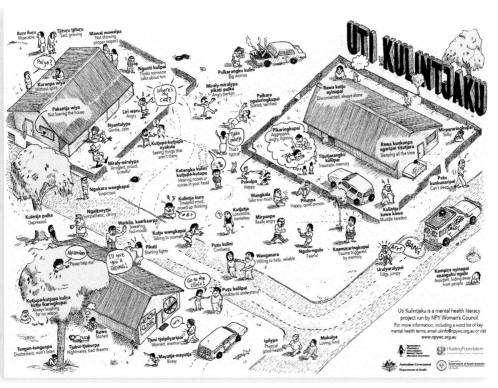

Uti Kulintjaku poster, 2014. Copyright © Joshua Santospirito and NPY Womens Council

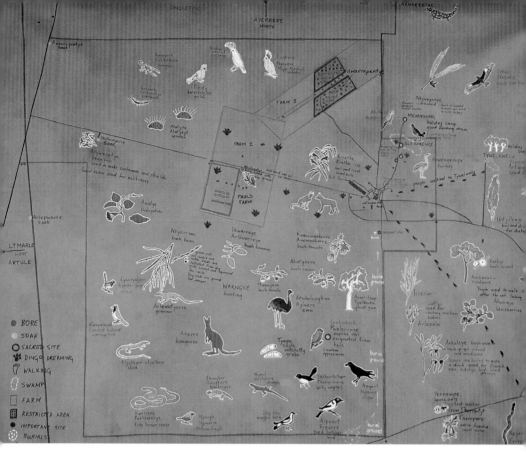

Painted map showing Indigenous knowledge of country in and around the Alekarenge land trust, 2019. Copyright © Kim Mahood, the artists, and Centrefarm. *Photograph by Kim Mahood*

Painting the Alekarenge map, 2019. L–R: Nancy Long, Nita Dickenson Holmes, Judy Kong, Kim Mahood, Rosieanne Holmes, and Rene Long. *Photograph by Kerrie Nelson*

Kim Mahood working on the University of WA map, 2019. *Photograph by Jason Thomas*

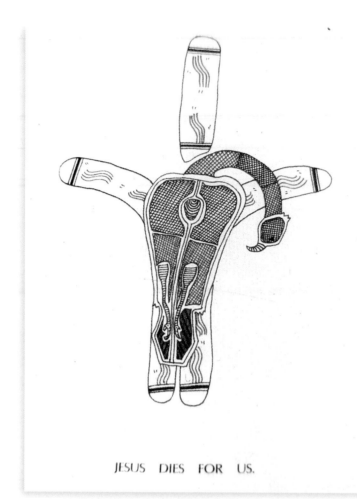

JESUS DIES FOR US.

'Jesus dies for us', 1983–84, Matthew Gill, pen and ink drawing on paper, from the suite of drawings *Stations of the Cross*. Copyright © Warlayirti Artists

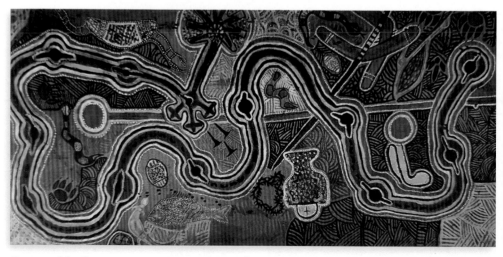

Stations of the Cross, 1982, painting, Matthew Gill, Greg Mosquito, Ronnie Tax, John Lee, and Gary Njamme. Copyright © Warlayirti Artists

dialogue. The drilling down into language has given them the words to articulate the developmental stages of Anangu child-rearing practices, and how these have been affected by cultural change. Old words are being revitalised to describe new conditions. As Rene says, 'We are looking for a new way of using the old way in the new world.'

It was clear to me from listening to the evaluation interviews that it was a transformative moment for all the Anangu women when they were shown a scan of the human brain. This occurred after they had questioned one of the doctors about why Western treatments are administered, and how they work. The doctor used the scan to demonstrate the functional impact of trauma on the brain, and how that carried through into behaviour and treatment. Apart from recognising trauma-related behaviour in their communities, the women understood that they had all suffered trauma — the loss of a husband or child (often both); family members going to court and prison; chronic illness; exposure to violence, alcoholism, and drug abuse; and poverty — which compromised their capacity to look after others.

With this realisation, stress-management techniques — painting and meditation — were introduced to the workshops. Mindfulness exercises were taken up with enthusiasm. Psychiatrist Dr Marcus Tabart, the clinical director of the Central Australian Mental Health Services, and a member of the Uti Kulintjaku team, says, 'It was very amusing when mindfulness was introduced to the ladies and they said, "Well, why didn't you do this sooner?"' The women challenged the practitioners' assumptions that some Western approaches would not be applicable, and vice versa.

During an extended evaluation interview, one of the women, speaking through an interpreter, says how important she finds the self-reflective exercises for self-management and 'stress clearing'. After talking about especially difficult problems, such as abnormal sexualised behaviour among children, she puts her distress and sadness into the painting exercises, and observes herself as she paints. She says she can feel the painting working as a continuous clearing process. 'When I begin I feel heavy, and then when I put my stress into the painting I can feel myself getting light.' As the interview proceeds, the shy, quietly spoken woman becomes animated, articulate, and confident. The conversation is seamless, everyone slipping between languages in a familiar and well-tried process.

Since its inception in 2012, Uti Kulintjaku has produced books, a language compendium, an iPhone app, videos, posters, and methodologies to manage the catastrophe of intercultural damage. One of the most popular resources is a bilingual poster illustrating and providing words for various mental and emotional states, including the behaviours and feelings associated with depression and psychosis. (See colour section.) The drawings convey humour, bringing a light touch to a heavy subject. Schools and clinics use the poster to open up the conversation about mental health. People put it on their walls at home, and children treat the poster and associated flash cards like a board game, identifying themselves and people they know by their moods and behaviours.

A beautifully illustrated book published by the NPY Women's Council in 2017, *Tjulpu and Walypa* tells the story of two girls: Tjulpu, who has a good life supported by family and culture; and Walpa, who is lost in the world of alcohol, family violence, and her unsupported pregnancy. Although published originally in English, the book crossed the literacy barrier by speaking to the girls whose lives follow Walpa's trajectory, documenting their experience and offering a way through, and reinforced the values that provide Tjulpu with the love and support of kin. According to a woman who worked intensively on the book, it also serves as a warning to girls at risk. 'You want to end up like Walpa?' she asked her granddaughter when she deliberately missed the plane from her community back to boarding school. The question was effective: 'It cost us money for another plane, but she got on it!'

The Pitjantjatjara and English version, *Tjulpunya munu Walpanya*, is now available.

Yankunytjatjara woman Margaret Smith loves being part of Uti Kulintjaku. The bilingual dialogue has alerted her to the sophistication of her own languages, Yankunytjatjara and Pitjantjatjara. She illustrates her point by mentioning words for the many refined aspects of listening and thinking. While she speaks about her pleasure in working with the other women, it's the conversation with the doctors that really stirs her enthusiasm, especially when the concept of *tjukurpa* enters the discussion.

Tjukurpa refers to the Dreaming, or creation period, when ancestral beings made the Law that underpins Aboriginal culture. It also means history, and story, and how culture functions in present-day life. The meaning is dependent on context, and the difficulty of pinning down a precise interpretation conveys the challenges faced when eliciting cross-cultural understanding is the purpose of a project.

Margaret uses tjukurpa to describe the Greek myths introduced into a workshop about addiction.

'Working with the doctors — they have their tjukurpas, too ... The one with the grapes, they made them into wine. And the one where she goes underground.'

Craig San Roque, a local community psychologist and psychoanalyst with many years' experience working with Aboriginal people in Central Australia, told the story of Dionysus to the Uti Kulintjaku team. Using props to illustrate how Dionysus encouraged excessive drinking and dangerous behaviour, and how the effects of alcohol and addictive behaviour permeate the present day, San Roque showed that European culture had ancient instructional stories. The women were enthralled to learn that white people had a form of tjukurpa, including a story about grog. They discussed the impacts of addictions on their own families and communities, and a visiting doctor suggested they might explore a relevant tjukurpa story during the painting session the following day.

What happened next is now Uti Kulintjaku folklore. Overnight, five women — Pantjiti McKenzie, Rene Kulitja, Nyunmiti Burton, Maringka Burton, and Ilawanti Ken — identified one of their own stories as the tjukurpa for addiction, made telephone calls to seek permission to tell it, and gathered the materials with which to make a miniature version of the trapped man and his grieving wives. (See colour section.) This was produced with a flourish after the painting session, accompanied by the telling of the story and a discussion of how it applied to contemporary life:

> A good man, a husband and provider, goes hunting one day and chases an animal into a hollow log, where he becomes hopelessly stuck. While wailing and singing, he manages to hobble back to his two wives, who are baffled by the sound coming from the advancing log. When they realise their husband is inside, they fling themselves about in grief and try to free him. Failing this, they squeeze water-soaked grass through a small opening so he can drink, and then lead and carry him in search of a Ngangkari powerful enough to set him free. After much difficulty and the efforts of several Ngangkari, the log is cracked to reveal the shrunken, emaciated, excrement-fouled body of the husband. With the care of his wives and the advice of the healers, he is slowly restored.

Whatever the ancient meaning of this tjukurpa story, the metaphor of entrapment has resonated with modern Anangu. It has been variously interpreted to mean that men are trapped in their shells, unable to communicate their problems; that they don't know what their role is anymore; and that they are trapped in cycles of alcohol and violence. The women lament that 'when that man is trapped, he hasn't got his full potential'. The metaphor is extended to young people trapped by substance abuse, and to all Anangu trapped by cultural breakdown. The wives who refuse to abandon their trapped husband symbolise the women in the Uti Kulintjaku project who refuse to give up in spite of the scale of the challenges they face. To escape can't be accomplished alone. It's a heroic task, requiring the combined resources of doctors and culture and family.

Embedded in cultural memory, 'The man in the log' story provides a psychological traction that's missing from Western approaches to Aboriginal mental health. That the women immediately made the connection between the European myth and an equivalent tjukurpa suggests that there are vast metaphoric resources in their culture, waiting to be tapped.

Digging into their tradition-rich past to discover what has made them strong and resilient, the women also identify the *aalpiri*, the name of the instructional wake-up call that began the day of the desert-dwelling Anangu. Aalpiri — jokingly called the morning rooster — gave a dawn bulletin of how things were travelling in the Anangu world, reinforced right behaviour, resolved disputes, and outlined the activities for the day before people got up.

A performance of the aalpiri has been filmed out on the lands, along with a recitation of 'The man in the log'. The plan is to broadcast them on Indigenous Community Television, the channel watched throughout the Western Desert, with the aalpiri heralding the start of daily programming.

I saw the film as a work in progress. The intended setting of sensational desert scenery is washed out by a flash flood, and Ilawanti

Ken declaims the tale of 'The man in the log' against a backdrop of crumbling demountables. She is enthroned on her mobile walker, and accompanied by Pantjiti McKenzie singing the eerie song of the trapped man trying to attract the attention of his wives.

With the development of 'The man in the log', the Uti Kulintjaku team decided it was time to invite Aboriginal men into the project. The women chose the men: effective leaders and individuals of status in their various communities, ranging in age from twenty-five to seventy-plus. The facilitator of the men's group, Martin Toraille, says that having been chosen by the women, the men feel pressure to act. Faced with a challenge so vast, and seeing men as a significant part of the problem, they want to get out and start fixing it — to stop the violence in their communities, and keep people safe — but don't know where to begin. It's early days, and the concepts and processes are very new. It's the first time a men's group has been established within the NPY Women's Council, and the first opportunity these men have had to talk together in such a facilitated and focused way.

The brain imagery showing the effects of trauma also had a huge impact on the men. Jamie Nyaningu, the only Anangu man whose interview I observe, speaks passionately of the need to manage traumatised kids properly. According to the team psychiatrist, the men are already doing the right thing — calming people down, providing care and support — but need to enhance and develop these skills. Jamie talks of a trauma toolbox, and of finding the tools to put in it. The interview is held in English, which Jamie speaks well enough, but he flags, struggling to articulate his thoughts. When asked if he has anything more to add, he says, 'I might be worn out, eh! I'm tired.' I'm tired, too, just from listening. Trying to communicate complex ideas in the absence of an interpreter is hard work.

Stephan Rainow, from the Nganampa Health Council, first worked with Anangu in the 1970s, helping to build the communities during the homeland movement. Invited by the men to be part of their team for the Uti Kulintjaku project, he says this model should be adopted by every organisation, as the level of discussion is something people want and need. 'People should be talking about this stuff, what's driving the cultural engine.' Instead, the fatigue caused by relentless, endless meetings about housing and budgets and the like is contributing to the mental-health problems that Uti Kulintjaku is trying to address.

Behind the revelatory experiences of the Uti Kulintjaku workshops is the hard slog of writing reports and grant applications, the constant pursuit of funds to keep the multiple strands of the project going, and the logistical challenges of getting people from remote desert communities to town for the workshops and supporting them while in town, and mobilising crews for bush trips.

Angela Lynch says it's difficult to put a tangible value on the most significant outcomes of the project, which are incremental rather than quantifiable. For example, information and strategies teased out in the workshops in Pitjantjatjara and Ngaanyatjarra trickle out into the communities via word of mouth. The same information, limited to English, doesn't travel. It's a critical point, but a fine one, and hard to position on the performance indicators around suicide prevention.

Ngapartji-ngapartji (working together) is fundamental, and the mutual respect and affection is palpable. People's lives have interwoven over time — in some cases, thirty or forty years — as they have committed to work towards whatever is possible. The white members of the Uti Kulintjaku team are as challenged and enthusiastic as the Anangu, their minds stretched, and their sense of awe amplified by this engagement with a parallel reality. The excitement, humour, and shared aspirations are implicit in every conversation and interview.

'This is one of the most exciting and encouraging and hopeful developments that I've seen in Central Australia for the twenty-one years that I've been here,' says Marcus Tabart.

Without the Uti Kulintjaku process of listening, thinking, and understanding clearly, 'The man in the log' may never have struggled into the Anangu repertoire of ways to approach the fractious terrain of contemporary life. Maybe, back in the days when we were all more connected to the mythic world, these stories didn't need to be made conscious for them to work their healing power. It would be strangely appropriate if an Aboriginal metaphor about a man trapped in a log shows all of us a way forward.

The people and the project are inspiring and humbling, and make my own work seem self-absorbed and irresponsible. *I can do self-absorbed and irresponsible*, I tell myself, as I pack up my notebook and voice-recorder. *I'll pay my dues with an essay to get the story out there.* If people could learn to listen properly they would understand that Uti Kulintjaku offers a glimpse of this unique cultural potential, where ngapartji-ngapartji, based on generosity and trust, enriches both sides of the encounter.

The revolutionary work of Uti Kulintjaku doesn't translate easily into conventional funding parameters, and crossing the borders of South Australia, Western Australia, and the Northern Territory complicates things further. The Northern Territory Primary Health Network withdrew support for Uti Kulintjaku in its 2018 July funding round. Small grants allowed some threads of the project to continue, but the structural core of the program — the cross-cultural workshop discussions between Anangu and health professionals, supported by interpreters and reinforced by developmental evaluation — remained without funding until mid-2022.

By contrast, the Uti Kulintjaku Watiku (men's) group, with its focus on addressing destructive behaviour and its causes, and providing role models for young men, ticks all the right boxes, and has attracted continuing funding for its various projects. Among these is *Tjanimaku Tjukurpa, how one young man came good*, an illustrated book written in Pitjantjatjara, Ngaanyatjarra, and English. Like *Tjulpunya munu Walpanya*, the story of two girls with different backgrounds, *Tjanimaku Tjukurpa* is a redemptive parable in which family and culture nurture a lost young person back into self-respect and a fulfilling life. The book reflects the lived experience of Aboriginal boys and men, and addresses both the real-life challenges of the story it tells and the literacy gap that is part of the problem.

Meanwhile the Uti Kulintjaku women have taken up meditation with gusto, partnering with the organisation *Smiling Mind* to produce audio and video meditation apps, initially for their own use, and later targeting children and young people. I suspect it's the first time *Smiling Mind* has been faced with the conundrum of including the sound of a gunshot in a hunting meditation designed to calm down agitated young men.

With the promise of reinstated funding for Uti Kulintjaku's workshop model, it will be interesting to see what new and creative insights emerge from the complex process of listening, thinking, and understanding each other clearly.

10

Lost and found in translation

The vast continent is really void of speech ... this speechless, aimless solitariness was in the air. It was natural to the country.

— D.H. Lawrence, *Kangaroo*

Unlike many city-dwelling Australians, the desert holds no terrors for me. Instead, like D.H. Lawrence, I find the cathedral forests of the coastal regions oppressive and disquieting. Lawrence brought to his descriptions of the Australian bush the same overwrought sensitivity that created the claustrophobic emotional landscape of *Sons and Lovers* and the appalling, majestic insularity of the Italian mountain village in *The Lost Girl*. He was the writer who made explicit an intimation of some non-human presence in the Antipodean landscape, and while I have a different interpretation of the 'speechless, aimless solitariness' he attributed to the country 100 years ago, his instincts were good.

In his depictions of Australia in the 1923 novel *Kangaroo*, Lawrence expresses the ambivalence of many visiting Europeans and settler Australians. For Somers, who stands in for Lawrence as the novel's central protagonist, the Australian bush is host to a watchful, menacing presence:

> But the horrid thing in the bush! ... It must be the spirit of the place. Something fully evoked to-night, perhaps provoked, by that unnatural West-Australian moon ... He felt it was watching, and waiting ... It was biding its time with a terrible ageless watchfulness, waiting for a far-off end, watching the myriad intruding white men.

By the end of the novel, Somers has fallen in love with the landscape. It is no longer silent or watchful, but mysterious and enchanted, and he can hear its muted, incomprehensible call:

> Meanwhile he wandered round in the Australian spring. Already he loved it. He loved the country he had railed at so loudly a few months ago ... it had a deep mystery for him, and a dusky, far-off call that he knew would go on calling for long ages before it got any adequate response, in human beings.

By the time Lawrence visited Australia in 1922, the remnants of the coastal tribes in the southern part of Australia had been incarcerated in missions or driven inland, and their languages mostly silenced. What Somers/Lawrence heard, I think, was the fading murmur of those languages.

Because English is not the first language of the Australian continent, many early writers about the landscape heard only an echo of their own anxieties. These anxieties arose from their perception that the land was empty, inimical to people, or inhabited by ghosts and savages.

This cognitive unease about the land and our relation to it, the suggestion of the uncanny so powerfully articulated by Lawrence, continues to haunt much Australian writing. Much of *Kangaroo* is set on the south-east coast, the part of Australia now largely tamed by habitation, although traces of the uncanny still linger among the scarred sandstone cliffs and light-fractured forests of the Hawkesbury and the South Coast. But the genre of the hostile and haunted landscape reached its zenith in *Voss*, Patrick White's re-imagining of the explorer narratives. Based loosely on the experiences of Ludwig Leichhardt, *Voss* relocated the uncanny to the inland, and conflated the European trope of seeking enlightenment in the desert with the Australian mythos of death by landscape in a novel that reads like a protracted hallucination.

White's genius is in his invention of a desert that exists only in the imagination, drawn from his experience of the Middle East and on the desert paintings of Sidney Nolan (which are also largely imaginary, although Nolan did fly over and visit some Australian deserts). The country of *Voss* is a vehicle for the aspirations and passions of men. It does not exist apart from Voss and his party; it is felt rather than seen, a force, sometimes benevolent, sometimes malevolent, an emanation that precedes and envelops those who travel through it. It has less physical substance than the rooms and gardens of the Sydney society that constrains Voss's female counterpart, Laura Trevelyan.

Voss was published when White was forty-five. A year later, the third novel of a twenty-three-year-old literary prodigy called Randolph Stow won the Miles Franklin award. *To the Islands* is the story of a Catholic priest, Stephen Heriot, who flees a remote mission believing he has killed an Aboriginal man, learns humility, discovers meaning, and dies among the Kimberley rocks.

Stow was the writer, when I was in my teens, who described the kind of world I came from, in which the landscape was paramount. *To the Islands* might have been set on the south-east Kimberley mission that shared a boundary with the cattle station where I lived. *Tourmaline* could have been the town on the edge of the Simpson

Desert where I spent the drought-stricken years of my early childhood. I discovered, long after the event, that Stow lived for a time with his mother in the Perth suburb of Peppermint Grove when I was a wild and reluctant inmate of the boarding school just down the road, writing an impassioned critique of why I preferred his *Midnite* to *Animal Farm* as an example of satire. Stow spoke to me as no other Australian writer has done before or since. *The Merry-go-round in the Sea* invoked the sensory immersion in place that I knew from my own childhood (and described the competent women and charismatic, damaged men who inhabited it). Years later, when I read *Visitants*, I recognised the encounter between different kinds of consciousness that needled my own psyche.

But the landscapes in *To the Islands* and *Tourmaline* are also imagined. They are settings for the search for meaning out in the metaphysical void, Stow's version of the explorer narratives, the apotheosis in the desert that he makes explicit in his poem 'The Singing Bones':

No pilgrims leave, no holy-days are kept
for these who died of landscape. Who can find,
even, the camp-sites where the saints last slept?
Out there their place is, where the charts are gapped,
unreachable, unmapped, and mainly in the mind.
[...]
Time, time and time again, when the inland wind
beats over myall from the dunes, I hear
the singing bones, their glum Victorian strain.
A ritual manliness, embracing pain
to know; to taste terrain their heirs need not draw near.

'A ritual manliness'. D.H. Lawrence, Patrick White, Randolph Stow, and the current exemplar of the genre, Nicolas Rothwell, are male, white, the inheritors of a philosophical and spiritual tradition embedded in European scholarship and a European imagination.

Ironically, the writer who most perfectly embodies this sensibility, and one who made the sojourn into the wilderness before writing about it, was female. *Tracks* by Robyn Davidson is the account of her solo camel trek in 1977 across the Gibson Desert from Uluru to the West Australian coast. Davidson's quest spoke directly to the great Australian hunger for insights into whatever secrets the desert might hold. That the seeker was a wilful and beautiful young woman sent the pulse rate of the nation into overdrive, and that she survived the journey, rather than succumbing to the obligatory death by landscape, created a myth that still overshadows the life of its progenitor.

After the gendered detour of *Tracks*, the literary expedition was cajoled back on course by another articulate Englishman, Bruce Chatwin, with his half-fictionalised account of his own Australian desert sojourn. Interpolated with notations about nomadism, walking, dreaming, companion predators, and Moleskine notebooks, Chatwin's *The Songlines* was the first popular account of the ancestral routes that mapped the activities of Indigenous creation beings. A captivating confabulation of ideas, *Songlines* was an invigorating and, to some, infuriating contribution to Australian desert literature.

The explorer narrative continues in the writings of Nicolas Rothwell, stories haunted by nostalgia and a sense of loss, populated by white men searching for meaning, as in *The Red Highway*, 'chasing after some kind of pattern, some redemption they think might be lurking, on the line of the horizon, out in the faint, receding perspectives of the bush'.

What is consistent in all these books is the presence of Aboriginal people in various configurations. Apart from the young Aboriginal guide, Jacky, who accompanies Voss's expedition, the Aboriginal figures in White's novel are spectral, capricious, and unknowable. They lurk on the periphery of the explorers' vision, coming into focus only when an apotheosis is required — to spear the saintly Palfreyman, whose character is later confused with that of Voss, or to encourage the boy Jacky to murder his master. They reflect the existential menace and the alien, impenetrable nature of the country.

Stow's Aboriginal characters in *To the Islands* are individual, troubled by the incomprehensible behaviour of the whites, struggling to identify right action in a conflicted world. Part of the priest Heriot's spiritual journey is the recognition that his own birthright as an Australian is founded on the murder of the people he has been trying to convert and control. Stow himself, unable to tolerate the contradictions he perceived in a settler landscape that had usurped the Indigenous world, left Australia in his twenties to find a more comfortable psychic fit in the landscape of East Anglia.

In *Tracks*, Davidson meets and is accompanied for a while by Mr Eddie, a Pitjantjatjara man who shows her the practical details of desert life, and allows us a glimpse of the desert as *ngurra*, home, domesticated and friendly, before Chatwin recolonises it with his bravura insights. Rothwell, who has immersed himself in desert landscapes and cultures for many years, seeks in his recent writing, especially *Belomor*, to invest the traditional Aboriginal world with a cultural density and intellectual complexity comparable to that of Europe.

In spite of — or possibly because of — what we are beginning to understand about the webs of kinship and song that connect every part of the country, a deep ambivalence continues to permeate the stories we tell. It has taken a long time for literary forms of writing to pay attention to the sounds that hum along the arteries of the country. The prohibitions against non-Indigenous writers entering this terrain are intensifying, and the ground is pretty complicated for Indigenous writers, too, who have to prove their credentials in an increasingly complex territorial domain.

Had there been a single Indigenous language, a single Indigenous identity, things might have been different. But there were likely around 500 languages spoken on this continent when the First Fleet arrived, some 200 of which are still spoken today. And their imaginative power belongs to the spoken form. As far as I know, there is not yet a literary tradition in an Australian Indigenous language. Indigenous languages are being written down in order to preserve them. Stories are recorded and transcribed as the languages that articulate them fall out of use. Languages are being reconstituted from fragments embedded in place names and historical documents and memory. What kind of languages these will be, and what purpose they will serve, is yet to be imagined. If they contain enough of the original sounds and meanings, maybe they'll reawaken the ancestors, and there'll be a new conversation between people and country.

In a recent essay, 'Can my country hear English? Reflections on the relationship of language to country' by scholar and academic John Bradley, who has worked for several decades with the Yanyuwa people of the Gulf Country, an elderly woman asks the question, 'Can my country hear English?' She concludes that the answer is no. In the same essay, a young man says, 'I want to learn my language so I can speak to country properly.' The importance of speaking to country in the language it can hear is fundamental to the continuing existence of country in its Aboriginal manifestation, and to counteract the invading literary tropes of emptiness and menace.

Bradley's essay goes on to describe how every performance of a song is unique, nuanced, and individual, and to show that an oral tradition does not mean an unchanging and unchangeable tradition. What it does mean is a tradition in which the naming and describing of everything that exists in a place is essential to keeping that place alive in the consciousness. To sing the country approximates bringing it into being in all its richness and complexity, and the loss of language — in particular, the loss of song — causes a formerly known, beloved, and meaningful place to revert to featureless, primordial space. Language and country can't be separated. The song brings the country into being.

There's a sea change occurring in the literature of place. Indigenous writers are entering the mainstream, and writing about the inland is being infiltrated by women's stories, both black and white. Less oppressed by the existential void, less impressed by the explorer narratives, they have an exuberance and vitality that is bringing into the language a very different sensibility, and one whose time has come.

In 2017, the National Museum of Australia hosted an exhibition, *Songlines: tracking the Seven Sisters*, that brought to the Australian public an immersive experience of one of the great Dreaming epics, the account of the Pleiades and their pursuer as they created the landforms, waterholes, and vegetation of the Western Desert. I worked on the exhibition as a writer and researcher, which drew me into the ancestral story of the Seven Sisters (called the Minyipuru by the Martu, and the Kungkarrangkalpa by the Anangu) as they fled across the desert, pursued by a lustful sorcerer named Yurla or Wati Nyiru. During this time, fragments of ideas and conversations, snippets of knowledge, and flickers of intuition began to coalesce. For a long time, I had been wondering whether there might be a collective consciousness, shared by the custodians of a particular country, in which the landforms of their country reflected their own psychological terrain, whether to walk around country was tantamount to walking around inside their own minds. These ideas had been lodged in me from years of messing about in the desert with Aboriginal people, lending myself to whatever task came to hand, talking to whitefellas as enmeshed as I was with this parallel reality. I had absorbed whatever came my way, often not grasping what I had learned until much later.

I was writing the wall texts that would give the viewing public enough information to interpret the exhibition, but not too much. This required me first to absorb myself in the exhibition content, and then to distil from it the essential elements of the narrative and translate them into succinct, accessible texts. I was familiar with the story and many of the locations, but this attention to detail brought into focus the sheer vitality of the songline, along with the nuances and differences that existed across the language groups.

We were working with sexually explicit material that had to be turned into a family-friendly show that communicated something meaningful and accessible to an audience with no prior knowledge of Indigenous culture. There were aspects of the story that could not be made explicit because of cultural prohibitions. The raw material was violent, gendered, hilarious, shocking, politically incorrect. I couldn't use words like 'penis', or 'rape', or 'blood'. It was an act of double-censoring, respecting Indigenous sensitivities and complying with museum requisites. While I grappled with the challenge of retaining the vitality of the story for a general audience, the suppressed content bubbled away under the surface.

Many of the ancestral stories don't translate easily across cultures, but the story of the Seven Sisters is universal. It is about the mismatch between male and female desire — the relentless pursuit of the sisters by Wati Nyiru, the hyper-vigilance of the women, the humiliation they mete out to the sorcerer when they get the chance, the sexual violence he inflicts on whichever of the women he can get his hands on, the rare moments of fear and shame when he wonders what is driving him, the mutual support the sisters offer each other.

The familiar tale of the lustful, powerful man making unwanted advances towards the reluctant woman (or women) makes it an ideal vehicle through which to explore the less communicable aspects of the songline. The old man sorcerer and the sisters are everywhere embodied in the features of the landscape. In Ngaanyatjarra country, the black caves of Wati Nyiru's eyes glare from under the brow-ridges of an escarpment, fixed on the boulders that are the oldest and youngest of the sisters. A cluster of rocks perched on the profile of a flat-topped hill are the Martu Minyipuru keeping out of reach of Yurla, who hunkers in a waterhole below. In the Anangu Pitjantjatjara Yankunytjatjara lands, Wati Nyiru turns himself into a quandong tree to seduce the Kungkarangkalpa with fruit and shade; they fall ill when they mistake his wandering penis for a carpet snake, and cook and eat it. At any moment the sorcerer's errant member can detach itself from its owner, burst out of a vulva-shaped rock-hole, penetrate a cave, and infiltrate the crevices of an escarpment. The country is alive, sexualised, and dangerous; safety is provisional and temporary; to survive requires vigilance and quick-wittedness.

There was much discussion, in the early stages of exhibition planning, of the meaning of songlines — what they were, what they did, whether the word 'songline' was a legitimate description of these mythic itineraries that animated the ancestral landscape. Philip Jones, author of *Ochre and Rust*, describes songlines as 'a kind of scripture, a framework for relating people to land, and to show that their relationship is inalienable ...' He also notes that 'regional songlines are connected to longer continental narratives'.

The major songlines, such as the Seven Sisters, are like arteries that carry the life force of the culture through the body of the country. The re-enactment of ancestral events draws on that arterial energy, and feeds back into it, in a cycle that makes deep time continuous with the present. The performance of ceremony and song at the creation sites, where ancient dramas are inscribed in the landforms, reinvigorates the Dreaming, ensuring that the country remains alert and alive.

The songlines are fixed in the landscape, but the performance is mobile. To perform the ceremony in the place where the story has its genesis is to carry out its most essential manifestation, but it can be performed elsewhere in order to communicate and educate. With permission, country can be danced and sung on other people's country. The performance, the *inma*, is the narrative expression of the physical body of the country.

As I burrowed into the meanings of the paintings, watched the videos, listened to the voices and the songs, and felt the country come alive within the context of what I knew of other places and other songlines, I began to understand something. This raunchy stalker-narrative about rape and revenge and humiliation, this tale of fear and hilarity and grief and resilience, about sex and manipulation and trickery, about a landscape volatile with the forces that surge through the human world, was a conduit of psychological energy, a way for people to perform the stark and violent dramas of their own lives and to draw sustenance from participating in a story that draws on a deep, shared past and a shared continuous present.

Beyond what I knew about the reanimation of place and the reaffirmation of tradition and identity was an embodied narrative that provided something necessary and regenerative for its performers. There was a visceral processing of lived experience going on, a re-enacting of sex and violence and empathy and grief and revenge and remorse and obsession that suggested that the performance of the story was a way of processing the traumatic events that people encountered in daily life — a performative pressure valve that acted out the injury, the agency, and the resilience of its players.

The Martu women Kumpaya Girgirba and Jakayu Biljabu tell with relish the story behind an often-performed ceremony at Kalypa, the site of Well 23 on the Canning Stock Route:

Yurla was watching all the ladies fly away in fear ... to Kalypa, where the women fought off a group of men who desired them ... All the men at Kalypa were from my people ... grandfather and all those men wanted wives. They begged the women: 'Stay with me only, stay with me.' Well, the women said, 'We never came for you, we are our own selves!' The women hit them and hit them ... until they all fell down.

Bryony Nicholson, in her contribution to the *Songlines* catalogue, describes the performance of a harrowing part of the story by women who identify as the current manifestations of the Kungkarangkalpa: 'In the performance ... was another telling of the story — one steeped in the shared experience of the sisters and suffused with feelings for family.'

Tjayanka Woods, a senior holder of the story, dances the role of the eldest sister, Kampukurta, who is attacked by Wati Nyiru while she is gathering quandong. In performing the grief and pain of this ancient event, the dancing provides an opportunity to express more recent grief and pain. The dying sister, Kampukurta, embodies the death of the woman who last danced the role, and all who have danced it before her. The sisterhood's empathy that accompanied the dancing reinforces the sense of being 'held' by their people and their country. To be 'held' is fundamental to the Anangu sense of wellbeing, and performing the *inma* is a way of sharing contemporary sorrow and its aftermath via the ancient but ever-present stories woven into the landscape.

More than a generous and entertaining insight into Indigenous culture, the public exhibition of the Seven Sisters songline is a powerful expression of an integrated world view, in which the land is as conscious as the people who live in it, and the relationship between kin and country is indissoluble. The desire to share this living story with the wider Australian population is an attempt by its custodians to make an active and viable space for different cultures to interact with and recognise each other.

It's what is happening at this interface that excites me. Through long-established partnerships, collaborations grounded in trust and friendship and respect, plus technologies that allow for different kinds of storytelling, voices in their multitudes are making themselves heard, framing new stories along with the old.

Back in 2000, I saw a remarkable exhibition at the contemporary art space 24HR Art in Darwin. *Two Laws ... One Big Spirit* was a painterly dialogue between Rusty Peters, a Gija artist from the Kimberley, and the New Zealand-born pakeha painter Peter Adsett. Over a period of several weeks, the artists each produced a painting on alternate days in response to the other, beginning with *The Waterbrain*, Rusty Peters' painting of his conception site.

The exhibition should be on permanent display as the focus of a continuing cross-cultural discourse. It's a fabulous-looking show, in which European modernism converses with Indigenous symbolism, the literal engages with the metaphoric, and the narrative meshes with with the conceptual. There is reciprocal acknowledgement between traditions that remain obscure to each other. In the painting *Two Laws ... One Big Spirit*, from which the exhibition took its title, Rusty Peters attempts to reconcile the Aboriginal and the whitefella belief systems at a conceptual level, suggesting that while the different laws may be incomprehensible to each other, they come from the same spiritual source. Adsett uses the material properties of paint to create a liminal edge between apparent opposites, making the equivalent point through abstraction. It's a dialogue that could only take place between painters. Adsett said that the sustained activity of making the work, side by side, day after day, finding in the process a means of communication without comprehension, became the most significant aspect of the project. To quote from the review I wrote at the time, 'In this encounter an Aboriginal man painting inside the boundaries of his country, paints his way into a conceptual language which makes the space for another kind of law, a different kind of country. And a white man paints his way into the liminal space where there is neither black nor white ...'

But for the purposes of this essay, I want to talk about *The Waterbrain*, the painting that started the dialogue. According to the artist, the waterbrain is a prerequisite for individual human existence. It floats in bodies of water, waiting for the pending human identity it will occupy and animate. This consciousness enters the human foetus and is reborn into the world, where it grows and learns, becomes adult, ages, and forgets before returning to the water to be recycled.

Rusty Peters' articulation of this concept, unique in contemporary Aboriginal painting, seems to have evolved as a result of conversations with the art impresario Tony Oliver, and manifested first in the painting dialogue with Adsett. Peters revisited this theme in the magisterial twelve-metre *Waterbrain* purchased by the Art Gallery of New South Wales in 2002, which charts the various stages of development of a human being. The final *Waterbrain* painting, produced in 2012, shows its disintegration as the ageing brain loses its memory.

Among the Yanyuwa of the Gulf Country, song converts the raw matter of space into a storied and inhabited place. To the Gija, the waterbrain is a sentient waterborne element that animates human existence. The Minyipuru and Kungkarrangkalpa songlines carry the lifeblood of song through people and country. This is a worldview in which country, the languages in which country is addressed and performed, and the people who perform the ceremonies comprise a sentient being that needs all its components to function — an autochthonous place-based consciousness articulated through song, embodied in dance, embedded in landforms, which flows between people and country through the conduit of the songlines.

And these songlines are not immutable. They embrace change, and evolve to incorporate strangers.

In 2006, while I was working at the small Aboriginal community of Mulan in the south-east Kimberley, my dog Slippers was run over and killed. I buried her at the foot of a sand dune near Parnkupirti Creek, which I knew was the route of the ancestral dingoes known as Kunyarrjarra, the Two Dogs, who created the Paruku lake system in the Dreamtime. I didn't know, when I buried Slippers, that her grave was close to a sacred stone 'put down' by the dingoes, but my inadvertent choice of a site in the heart of dog dreaming country was interpreted in my favour. Eleven years later, another dog died: Jiwawa, a chihuahua bitch (small dogs are popular in the desert) belonging to Hanson Pye, a senior custodian of that particular stretch of the dreaming track. The dog was having seizures, and Hanson brought her to me to see if I knew what was wrong. She had recently produced a litter of ten pups, and it was likely she was overwhelmed and undernourished — whatever the reason, she died while we were discussing what might be wrong with her. Hanson decided she should be buried next to Slippers so they would have company out there in the dog dreaming country. Later that day, we drove to the gravesite with the Ranger co-ordinator Jamie Brown, and Jamie and Hanson buried Jiwawa while I cleared the spinifex from Slippers' grave.

The following morning, Hanson came to see me, excited and troubled. He had had a dream, he said, in which Jiwawa and Slippers were running about and playing together on the sandhill, and Hanson, Jamie, and I were walking around together — the Two Dogs and the son, the mother, and the grandson, he said, referring to the kinship relationships between us.

He was agitated. The dream signified something, and he wanted it recognised. I suggested he write it down in Walmajarri, and together we would translate it into English and see how the story came out. This is what we produced:

Parnkupirti Kunyarrjarra Mapirrijati Marnpa
Two Dogs Together Again

Kunyarrjarra lo pila nganimpa wanjani
The two dogs left us
Ngajukura lu nyuntukura lu, Japangati lu Napurrula lu
My dog and your dog — Hanson's dog and Kim's dog
Kanga palipa Parnkupirtila kunyarr
We took my dog to Parnkupirti
Palipa yutukani kanyn Parnkupirtila
We three buried her in the dog dreaming place
Palipa yutukani manpa Napurrula kunyarrta
We buried her beside Kim's dog
Palipa yutukani Parnkupirtila jiljinga kanyn
We buried her at Parnkupirti sandhill
Kani palipa ngurranga kunyarr wanjani
We left her there in home ground.
Juju lu parnki manila kunyarrlu
It woke up the song of the Two Dogs
Winkirr mani mana ngajungu pukanja
In my dream last night
Ngaji, ngamaji, jaja — Japangarti, Napurrula, Japalji
Me, my mother, and the grandson — Hanson, Kim, and Jamie
Palipa waman kitpinga ruwa
We three were walking around together
Kunyarrjarra pilangan waman wanga
The two dogs were chasing around together
Kunyarrjarra pilangan palipinga

The two dogs found each other
Juju pilu pankimani
They woke up the Dreaming.

Although I don't believe in the Dreaming as a literal reality, I can't help but be glad that my dog has contributed to the living tradition of Paruku, and that her canine spirit has found a friend to play with out there in the dog dreaming place.

In his 1968 Boyer lectures, the anthropologist W.E.H. Stanner said, 'There is stuff in Aboriginal life, culture and society that will stretch the sinews of any mind which tries to understand it.' For those of us whose psychology has its origins in a different cultural tradition, to spend a long time in proximity to this potent psychological realm can tilt the self into a strange borderland, a hybrid form of consciousness that does not belong in either culture.

'What haunts are not the dead, but the gaps left in us by the secrets of others.' This quote is from 'Encryption', an essay by Nicolas Abraham and Maria Torok. They posit the theory that something can become entombed in the psyche, where it continues to live, a potentially malignant entity that fuels our preoccupations and seeps into our dreams — the absence, perhaps, of those lost languages that Lawrence mistook for silence? Or the country where charts are gapped — where places are unreachable, unmapped?

When that secret is the inaccessible heart of another culture, located in a place to which your own heart is beholden, something complicated happens.

This splinter of an idea embeds itself in my mind and festers. What happens if the live thing that has become encrypted in the psyche is another form of consciousness, one implicit in the landscape from which we draw our own sense of identity? What happens if that different consciousness infiltrates the one we have inherited? I think it's responsible for the edgy discomfort of the times we are in — the reluctance of white Australians to engage with Indigenous people for fear of transgressing some invisible boundary; the suspicion and scepticism among the diverse groups who identify as Aboriginal, or Indigenous, or First Nations People.

Since the first Europeans entered the consciousness of the country, speaking a language it couldn't understand, the country has been whispering back, its voices pitched to reach the psyche's inner ear. Lawrence heard the voices, faintly, and didn't know what he was hearing. Stow heard them, and couldn't bear to stay and listen. I've been hearing them all my life. I sometimes think that this extra sense has produced in me a kind of moral inertia, which manifests as an acceptance of the way things are, rather than as a desire to fix or change them. Up to a point, this is a good thing, but it can leach away the energy to feel strongly about things that warrant strong feelings.

I should, for instance, be troubled by the return of the cattle to Lake Gregory Station, the pastoral lease that occupies the same country as the Indigenous Protected Area of Paruku. The prospect is greeted with excitement by the local Walmajarri people. In the years since the pastoral enterprise collapsed, its custodians have never relinquished their identity as cattle people, their pride in being stockmen and camp cooks and drovers. The Indigenous Protected Area, declared in 2001, has not delivered outcomes comparable to those that the re-establishment of the cattle station is expected to provide. The reasons for this are complicated and frustrating, a case study in the multiple ways in which good intentions, poor communication, political correctness, and contradictory expectations can sabotage good policies.

The local people are entitled, as owners of the country, to use it as they choose, and there is growing pressure for Indigenous people to produce a viable income from the land they hold. Leasehold agreements are an emerging solution. That the cattle may have a significant environmental impact on this unique arid-zone lake system is an argument that has lost traction in recent years.

My feelings are mixed. The environmental threat from the cattle is significant, but under efficient management the enterprise may deliver some good outcomes for the local people, although I'm sceptical that the neighbouring community will be able to resist the temptation of free beef on their doorstep. And if certain families receive more benefits than others, it will activate the resentments that simmer beneath the patina of kinship amity.

It's a long time since any serious ceremony has been performed for the country. The eastern Walmajarri language particular to Paruku is spoken now by only the most senior traditional owner, who laments that when she's gone there'll be no one to talk to the lake in its own language. The cattle station taps into more recent dreams, of a way of life that people remember as meaningful and structured, when working the cattle was synonymous with time spent on country, and compatible with ceremony and kinship obligations. While this view is distorted by nostalgia, it's possible that the return of the cattle will provide a different kind of energy, a new way to perform and participate in dreaming the country.

It's an overcast morning in late May, and my youngest brother and I are bush-bashing across dense spinifex and wattle scrub, on a trackless stretch of the station where we lived as children. Our father named this place Skeleton Valley decades ago, to mark a labyrinth of eroded limestone several kilometres to the north, scoured by an anomalous watercourse to resemble the skeletons of imaginary monsters. The watercourse is the result of a system of lakes and swamps that only overflow in extreme flood conditions, decanting and back-filling between the dunes until the water builds enough pressure to cut through and find its way down to the extensive salt lake systems to the south. According to geological records, this occurs every thousand years or so, when the palaeo-channels of the ancient Tanami topography are activated, although some time in the deep past it must have been a lot more frequent.

We cross the southernmost of the sand hills through which the watercourse cuts its route, and drive down into the sandy creek bed at the centre of the channel. The creek is choked with ti-tree, and it's apparent that we can't drive the vehicles along it. The limestone formation is only three kilometres away, so we take water, cameras, my brother's drone, and my dog Pirate, and set out to walk the remaining distance.

The last time I walked this way was soon after one of those fabled extreme rainfall events. There was water everywhere, and the southern section of the creek was still flowing sluggishly. There was a crescent-shaped pool where a sandhill terminated, and a dingo watched me from the lee of the dune. Ti-tree seedlings were already sprouting across the channel with the boom-and-bust opportunism of the desert. I was looking for the limestone labyrinth on that occasion, too, but there were other people to consider, and the prospect of a slow drive home through dense whipstick wattle. If we were to get back to the homestead before dark, I had limited time, and it wasn't enough.

I must have come close, nevertheless, because in less than an hour of walking, my brother and I overshoot the site, which is obscured by the now well-established ti-tree. We check the GPS reading and angle back to the south-west, emerging from the tree-cover to an expanse of red earth from which weather-smoothed domes of limestone protrude. Beyond the domes is the vast bony excrescence, honeycombed by wind and water, that my father came upon more than fifty years ago, tracking strayed cattle as they chased storms into the desert. I try to imagine it as it would have been without the vegetation that has colonised the channel in the past decade. It might have been centuries since the watercourse last flowed when my father followed it south, riding a narrow-wheeled motorbike that must have been difficult to manoeuvre through the sand.

The precise GPS reading we're using is for the location of a small wooden box containing our parents' ashes, brought here on a family pilgrimage some years ago. That was the third attempt my brother and I made to find this place, having made a second foray the year after the floods, driving across country from the north, turning back when we ran out of time and tyres. It was not until the third trip, with a convoy of vehicles and more time to explore, that we were able to come in from the east, driving along the swales and working our way south-west around the sand ridges.

Stories accrete in the landscape, along with the meanings we attribute to them. I imagined this place, long before I saw it, and made it part of the itinerary of a fictional alter ego called the mapmaker. Her task was to draw ephemeral daily mud maps, predicting the events and hazards that lay ahead. She's as much a part of my connection to the country as the human ashes now absorbed into the growing coolibah, or the footprints we've made walking here today, some of which may last for years.

When I saw this place for the first time, it was stranger than I expected. It seemed then, and still seems now, like an intrusion from another reality, the trace of something ancient and incommunicable that was never meant to be revealed. The opposite of encryption, perhaps, where a greater mystery lies in what has been exposed.

From space, satellite technology shows a kink in the waterway, a geomorphic glitch that splits and redirects the flow. Some time in the ancient past, water seeped into some pre-existing form and replaced it with limestone. Was it before or after the cold, dry, windy centuries that laid down the sand ridges and choked the palaeo-channels? Certainly, it was before an invigorated monsoon triggered an era of high rainfall and turbulent water that churned down through the dunes and carved out this time-warped intersection.

Only a few rotting splinters remain of the box of ashes that we placed in a bony socket of limestone seven years ago. A young, white-barked coolibah has taken root in the cavity, which acts as a reservoir for water and nutrients. Across the honeycomb formation, other small, twisted saplings have sprung from their elaborately wrought containers. I imagine coming back years hence to find a garden of bonsai gums rooted in stone.

I would like some of my own ashes brought here, when the time comes, although I hope to visit again before that happens. When this place last heard its own language spoken is anyone's guess. I should have thought to bring the recording I made ten years ago of Dora Mungkina Napaltjarri, Ngardi speaker and traditional owner of this patch of the desert. I'll remember next time.

I am beset by a sense of time passing and time lost and things changing and nothing changing.

This brings with it a loneliness that intensifies as the years pass. The desire to share what I have experienced becomes more insistent, and the impossibility of sharing it becomes more acute. To write it down is the best I can do.

11

Flowers for Evelyn

It takes me longer than I expect to choose the flowers for Evelyn's funeral. The store is cluttered with cheap hardware, craft materials, cosmetics, picture frames, flowerpots, party costumes. Artificial flowers for Aboriginal funerals are a staple product, and there's so much choice that I find myself looking for blooms that remind me of Evelyn — tall, dark-red dahlias, purple delphiniums, and maroon and ochre roses, their cloth petals as full-blown as the real things. When did it become the practice at Aboriginal funerals to cover the grave mound with artificial flowers? In the deep desert they left the corpses to desiccate in the spinifex. Evelyn's people built platforms out of branches, and suspended the bodies above flat stones, reading into the spatter of dissolving body fat the story of who was responsible for the death.

While I'm pondering my choices, a swarm of Aboriginal children enters the shop, splitting into ones and twos, and moving with practised efficiency down the aisles. A girl of twelve or thirteen saunters past, sizes me up, and palms a small bottle of perfumed oil. She knows I won't give her away. A matronly shop assistant swoops on the girl, grips her wrist, and peels the bottle from her hand, gesturing with her jaw towards the door. 'Out!' The child swans away, followed by her cohort, shrieking and giggling as they make off down the street. It's a seamless piece of choreography, everyone playing the part they've been cast to play, the moves as familiar and practised as a long-running piece of theatre. When I pay for my flowers, the shop assistant shakes her head. 'Little ratbags,' she says, without anger.

The funeral is a day's drive from Alice Springs, in Western Australia. When my car breaks down 600 kilometres up the Tanami Road, 300 kilometres short of my destination, it feels like a replay of the trip I made fifteen years earlier with my friend Pam Lofts to attend the funeral of another Aboriginal woman, Patricia Napangarti Lee. That time, we made it with the help of the local station people and the staff of the Granites gold mine, and I know that the same network will get me there this time. In the years between now and then, Pam has died, too, of motor neurone disease.

I'd been aiming to camp at the turnoff to my old home, the cattle station my family established in the nineteen sixties, and it's when I stop near the abandoned roadhouse of Rabbit Flat that I realise I have a problem. Hanging onto the bull-bar of my twin-cab utility while I squat to pee, it takes me a moment to realise that the detached idler arm is the reason for the peculiar angle my steering wheel has adopted in the last half hour, and that I'm in trouble. It's not far off sundown, and I'm not far from where I had intended to camp, so I drive in the lowering light to the station turnoff, choose a clear space near a stand of mulga trees that will provide morning shade, let Pirate the dog out, collect some firewood, and think about what to do. The mulga branches make their familiar tracery against the fading red horizon, and my body makes its cellular adjustments of recognition that we are back on home ground.

My mobile phone shows a single bar of reception. This amuses me, given that I am in one of the remotest locations in Australia, and until six months ago it was rare to get one bar of reception where I live, thirty kilometres from Canberra, the national capital. When I climb onto my roof-rack, the phone shows three bars. I get down and light the fire, feed Pirate, make myself a gin and tonic from the emergency supplies in the esky, climb back onto the roof-rack, and consider who to contact. On a whim, I text my youngest brother in Brisbane, not because he can do anything to help, but because we have made several trips out here together, and he will know exactly where I am and how it feels — the night falling, the mulga wood fire flaring, the particular Tanami stillness that we internalised as children and which bonds us across political and other differences.

Within a few minutes, he rings back.

'If anyone else was broken down on the Tanami, I'd be worried,' he says.

I have a flash of regret that I'm someone no one worries about, followed by the knowledge that being worried about has always irritated me, and that it's been part of my life's project to become someone people don't worry about. We chat for a while, and I flag my options — to contact the station and see if I can borrow a vehicle to drive to the funeral, or to backtrack to the mines and hope to get my car repaired in time to make it under my own steam.

My brother rings off and I call the station, leaving a message when no one picks up. I also text my colleagues in Alice Springs, the team I'm taking leave from to attend the funeral, to let them know that I've broken down and will keep them in the loop. During the night, the fire burns down to a bed of coals, and I wake early to the intrusive presence of the small, persistent, moisture-deprived flies that appear every decade or so in response to some inscrutable climatic rhythm. While I'm boiling the billy for my morning cup of tea, the phone rings — it's the station manager, Mark, who has just picked up my message. I explain my situation, and he says he will come out and see what he can do to get me on the road. It's a fifty-kilometre drive, and it will take him a while to organise the tools he needs, so I brew another billy of tea, move the car so that the front end will be in the shade all morning, and settle down to wait.

The current station manager is the youngest son of the only other white family who settled in the Tanami in the nineteen sixties. As part of a move to rationalise the viability of Aboriginal-owned cattle stations, the lease was recently put up for tender and taken over by Mark and an older brother. My family left and his family stayed, but we share the knowledge of what it means to live here. Mark understands my imperative to get to the funeral. Evelyn's brother worked as a stockman for my family in the sixties, and Evelyn took to heart the fact that as a baby I was given the skin name of Napurrula, making me her sister in the Aboriginal kinship system. Apart from the relationship we had and the personal grief I feel, I am family, and this is something I have to do.

The other urgent reason to get to the funeral is because, at the request of Evelyn's daughter Megan, I'm bringing food for the wake. There's a crate of potatoes, onions, and sweet potatoes on the tray, and the back seat is loaded with boxes of lettuces, tomatoes, and avocados. Covered with wet towels, the salad vegetables are travelling well so far, but there's a time limit to their viability.

A LandCruiser pulls up beside me, with a toolbox and a welder tied down on the back.

'G'day,' Mark says. 'Let's have a look at the problem.'

He squats by the front wheel of my car and assesses the damage. It's a year since we last spoke, apart from the telephone conversation this morning.

'Don't you have a partner who can come on these trips with you and keep you out of trouble?'

'No,' I say. 'It's one of the things I forgot to do.'

He laughs, crawls under the vehicle, and sets about welding up the broken part. It's a serviceable job, and will get me back to the Granites, but probably won't stand up to 300 kilometres of corrugated road.

'Thanks, Mark. I owe you one,' I say.

I make my way back to the Granites turnoff and call the number for visitor enquiries. Time passes. Eventually, a woman emerges from the demountable building beside the entry boom gate, and invites me and Pirate into the air-conditioned interior to wait for the return of the senior mechanic, who is out in the field on a job. She's pleasant and friendly, and we chat for a while before she gives me the wi-fi password so I can use my laptop, and we both get on with some work while Pirate sleeps on the lino floor. More time passes, and the mechanic arrives, checks my car, unbolts the idler arm, and takes it back to the workshop to be repaired by a professional welder. Half an hour later he returns, re-attaches the part, and tells me I'm good to go.

Most of the day has been consumed by this process, and it's late afternoon by the time I get back on the road, with 350 kilometres to travel and a load of food to deliver. The lettuces and tomatoes are still in good order under the wet towels, although the waxed cardboard boxes they are packed in are getting soggy.

Because there's a time-zone difference of an hour and a half across the border, it's only seven-thirty when I arrive in the community, although it's been dark for several hours. The Sorry camp is at Daisy Kungah's house, where fires are burning and people are hunkered in groups that disperse into familiar individuals as they recognise my car and stand up to greet me.

'We was worrying for you. We thought you was coming this morning.'

'At least somebody worries about me. I broke down — took all day to get the car fixed.'

Given the unreliable vehicles everyone drives, breakdowns are too common to provoke comment. I made it, and that is all that matters. I find Megan, and embrace her while she keens, the ritual wail of shared grief I can never bring myself to make. Then I make my way around the assembled friends and relatives, embracing, shaking hands, beginning at last to feel my own sadness through this collective sorrow. Once the sorry business has been attended to, I unload the crates and cartons of food, hand out packets of tobacco, negotiate with Daisy that I will come back early in the morning to have a shower, and drive back to the river crossing, where I find a place to camp away from the road, collect firewood, light a fire, throw down my swag, and exhale.

Evelyn's death has been sitting in my mind like a parcel waiting to be unwrapped. It has not been possible, in my other life, to feel the loss properly. I could only hold open the space of grief until I re-entered her world and the visceral knowledge of who she was. She stalks across my memory in a dress the colour of the dahlia flowers I've brought to grace her grave.

* * *

She shows you a place on the river where the people used to camp in the old days, and tells you about a fight she remembers when she was young.

'Everyone fighting, spears, everything, fighting for days. It was like a war.'

Months or years later, someone else mentions the same fight.

'Yeah, that fight was over Evelyn. She was really young, maybe eleven, twelve, but all the men going wild, too much trouble over that girl. They bin marry her to that old man straight away to stop the trouble.'

At sixty, the wild girl is still visible in the wicked gap-toothed smile, the statuesque confidence of her body, her fearlessness. Because she is your skin sister, you have been taken by her and the other Napurrulas to bathe at a private spot on the river. They make a fire and heat water in a galvanised bucket, strip down, and soap themselves all over. You are the only one who dives into the chilly green water and swims; your thin, white body is as insubstantial as the ideas and theories that trouble your mind.

On the bank, the mass and substance of the women's bodies arrange themselves into gestures you recognise from Degas — here one is kneeling, arms upraised, shampooing her hair. Another bends forward to wash an outstretched foot. But there is none of the claustrophobia of Degas, the voyeur peering through windows and keyholes. Evelyn stands, opulent and regal, on a riverbank under a sky that goes on forever. You think of boulders and tree trunks and gleaming, dark fish. All that shining skin washed and polished. She has used hair conditioner as a skin lotion for lack of the real thing. When you get out of the water, she rubs some on your shoulders and back.

'This my country,' she says. 'I was born up there,' gesturing to the north-east. 'Watersnake dreaming.'

You know she's talking about the Rainbow Snake. Snake dreaming, river dreaming, this is where her power comes from. This is at the heart of her story.

She dries her hair with the skirt she took off, and pulls on a dark-red dress in which her body takes on the contours of a muscular animal. Later that day, a battered Toyota drives into the camp. Evelyn has been stalking up and down the road in the red dress. You know the driver of the vehicle, a genial powerbroker whose charm and transparent venality are irresistible. You know, because it has been told to you in dropped voices by different women, that he is Evelyn's great love, and that they have been kept apart by the Law since they were teenagers. What you now understand is that the day's arrangements, over which you thought you had some control, have been directed by Evelyn towards this seemingly chance encounter, that the leisurely morning, the bath, the red dress have all been part of a larger scheme to which you have been an unwitting accessory.

The tight-mouthed woman beside the driver is his wife. When Evelyn leans voluptuously against the car door and the man's heavy, sensual face turns towards her, the tension, sexual and otherwise, is palpable. You think of the wife, all the years of knowing that everyone knows, of knowing the Law is losing its authority, that with the death of Evelyn's elderly husband she still has the power to steal away other women's men. It was decreed years ago by the old men that Evelyn be banned from singing the songs and using the krin-krin plant from which love magic is made. Evelyn herself has shown you the plant, grinning her wicked grin at the folly of old men. With the advent of a new man in your life, she and the other women suggest they make some women's business for you, to which you agree. It works, but when you leave the place where it was made, it loses its power.

* * *

The river is its own country, an ancestral track and trade route from the savannah grasslands in the north to the dune fields of the Great Sandy Desert. Evelyn was a river woman, and now it has claimed her back. The flies wake me early, and I make tea and eat a bowl of muesli to ensure that I've had enough carbohydrates to get me through what will be a gruelling day. Pirate doesn't stray far. He knows we are about to enter territory that is dangerous for dogs, and that he will be spending most of the day in the car.

Daisy's house is quiet when I arrive, and I have a shower and put on black pants and a dark shirt to serve as funeral clothes. To enter Daisy's home is to enter an intermediate zone in which I am both family and a whitefella, where kinship trumps skin colour while allowing us to occupy our separate identities. On the basis of this relationship, Daisy suggests I buy her an outfit to wear to the funeral, and leads me through backyard shortcuts to the store, where she chooses a black skirt and white blouse, and a hot pie for breakfast. I pay for the clothes and the pie, and buy myself some energy bars and a carton of iced coffee.

Although the funeral notice says the ceremony will take place at 9.00 am, no one takes this seriously. Things can't go ahead until the prisoner plane delivers a grandson and a nephew who are currently in jail, and there's a car coming out from town with three great-grandchildren who have been taken into care. While Evelyn was alive, the kids were kept out of the welfare system; now she's gone, the structure she held together has disintegrated. It was put under pressure when Megan had to leave home and move to a town where she could have regular dialysis, and crumbled further when Evelyn's other daughter was killed while crossing the highway at night somewhere east of Broome. That loss broke Evelyn, and unleashed the grief and anger that had simmered since her husband's death. While he was alive, her status in his community was not challenged, but once widowed she was on shifting ground, a river woman living on someone else's country. This might not have mattered had she been less forceful and volatile, but she had a big personality and a short fuse. She buried her daughter in the graveyard of the community where she had lived the greater part of her life, and then left it for good. That's why she is being buried here instead of in the country where our friendship fledged and grew.

The great-grandchildren arrive, the boys wearing white shirts and ties, the little girl dressed in a pink dress, shoes, and socks. She must be four or five by now, and I'm glad to see that the pink dress and shoes have not tamed her. Within minutes of their arrival, the kids are swinging on the fence, the girl swinging higher and faster than the boys, with a sinewy grace and fearlessness that she has exhibited since she could crawl. There has always been something about her that draws attention, a creature energy that captivates and mesmerises. This is how Evelyn must have been as a child, the girl all the men were fighting over before she reached her teens.

As the morning wears on, the outliers and outlaws arrive, but there is no sign of the minister who is supposed to conduct the ceremony. It emerges, after questions are asked, that no one has remembered to invite him. The family regroup to discuss their options. There are two pastors in the community, members of opposing factions split by territorial and clan alliances that have caused frequent outbreaks of fighting in recent months.

One of the pastors is Evelyn's cousin, but the family decides that to also invite the pastor from the other faction will be a gesture towards reconciliation. It's an honourable choice, though not one I'm sure would have been endorsed by Evelyn, who relished her grudges. The other pastor accepts the invitation, and there's movement towards the basketball courts, where the ceremony is to be held. A folding table is set up, and someone asks me if I have anything to cover it with before the coffin is brought out. I go to my car, check on Pirate, and collect the sheet I use to protect my suitcase from dog hair.

By the time I get back, an alternative covering has been found, the coffin is in place, and Megan is beginning to melt down. She's had four days of dialysis in order to attend the funeral, and the heat and stress are beginning to take a toll. One of the aunts gets an arm under Megan's shoulder, gestures that I should take the other side, and together we try to support her as she collapses, hauling me and the aunt down with her. Although she's lost a lot of weight since she began her dialysis treatment, Megan is still a big woman, and she thrashes and howls while we grapple her heaving torso off the filthy concrete floor. Evelyn's body is in the coffin a few metres away, and to hold the howling, heaving body of her daughter channels my grief in a way that feels elemental and true. Megan tries to stand, staggers, indicates she needs to be near her mother, and we half drag, half carry her to the plastic chair that someone has put beside the coffin. She stretches her arms out and beats her fists on the pale wood chosen to match the colour of the milky water that represents her mother's country. Two camp dogs have staked out their territory and gone to sleep under the table.

The pastor who belongs to Evelyn's clan invites me to speak first. Somewhere in the flailing and wailing of the last fifteen minutes, I've lost the notes for what I'd planned to say, so I stammer my way through what Evelyn meant to me: how she helped me to navigate the Aboriginal world, how she was wise and brave and funny. I say that I have been privileged to know her and work with her for so many years, and that she has gone back into her country, and I hope it will take her in and hold her, at which point I break down and her son, Leonard, who has been standing behind me with his hand on my shoulder, leads me back to my spot on the concrete floor opposite the sleeping dogs.

Several more people speak, and then the officiating pastor takes over. He thanks the family for offering this possibility of reconciliation, pulls a shabby bible from his briefcase, and delivers a rant in which he does not mention Evelyn, but exhorts us all to take Jesus into our hearts and be saved. With references to biblical chapter and verse, he reiterates this theme many times, through a screeching sound system that escalates in pitch until it wakes the dogs, which get up and skulk away. Megan shudders and sobs and takes gulps of water, which she swills and spits into a growing puddle at her feet. The pastor persists until the restiveness of the crowd forces him to stop, and we make a break for our cars and drive to the cemetery for the final interment.

While the coffin is being lowered, the pastor has another attempt at enlisting us to the cause of Jesus, but he's lost his momentum. The crowd eddies around the grave, throwing handfuls of red earth onto the blond-wood coffin until it is almost covered. I hold onto my bundle of flowers until the great-granddaughter in the pink dress come to me and says, 'Kupiyu, give me the flowers.' *Kupiyu*, great-grandmother, is the name she called Evelyn and that Evelyn taught her to call me when we went out to collect firewood and go hunting.

'Okay, kupiyu,' I say, because *kupiyu* also means great-grandchild, and she takes the flowers and runs to join the other kids, who are watching the grave being filled in by the community grader. Although the machine is manoeuvred with great dexterity by its driver, it's too clumsy a tool for the final shaping of the grave mound, and one of the nephews borrows my long-handled shovel. When the job is done, he hands it back to me with a grin.

'Here, Auntie. You always growling us to bring back your shovel.'

The kids plant the mound of earth with the mass of artificial flowers, the heads of the dark red dahlias standing tall above the rest.

Goodbye Napurrula, goodbye my friend.

That she has gone back into the country feels like a reality rather than a sentimental conceit. The great-granddaughter stands at the head of her *kupiyu*'s grave, and I see the spirit of Evelyn, fierce and proud, and the web of kin and country holding the past in the present. What form it will take in this changing world is impossible to predict, but I have to believe that it will survive.

I stay long enough to share in the wake and to say my goodbyes to the family, who are clustered at the clinic where Megan is being monitored, having collapsed properly now that her mother is buried. It's long after dark by the time I leave, but I'm feeling wired from the roller-coaster emotions of the day, and drive until it's time to refuel. There's a spot where I often camp, in a range of low hills near an old mine site, but in the time it takes to siphon a jerrycan of diesel into the fuel tank, four pairs of eyes are glowing and circling within fifty metres of the vehicle. While I'm not usually troubled by dingoes, there's something unnerving about so many assembling so quickly. They probably won't bother me, but they are a real threat to Pirate, so I drive another sixty kilometres to the station turnoff where we camped two nights ago.

In the morning, the flies get me up at daylight. We are on the road by seven, and in Alice by mid-afternoon. I call in to the office to let my colleagues know that I'm back.

'We weren't worried when we heard you'd broken down,' they say. 'We knew you'd get through okay.'

12

From position doubtful to ground truthing

I imagine a series of maps shimmering across the roads and suburbs, the parks and farmlands and urban sprawl, recording the traces of Indigenous knowledge, inscribed with fragments of all those lost languages surviving in the names of places, whispering to the country in the language it can understand. I see it as something in which all Australians would participate, a shared enterprise in which each contributes what they do best. Discovering things together makes concrete what otherwise remains uneasy and unresolved. It's acknowledgement that does the real work of reconciliation.

When I wrote these words in 2008, for an essay in *Griffith Review* titled 'Listening is harder than you think', I had been making large canvas painted maps with the Walmajarri and Jaru custodians of Paruku, a terminal lake system at the northern end of the Great Sandy Desert, for four years. By then we had mapped family jurisdictions, dreaming tracks and sacred sites, frontier encounters, station days, and stock route stories, and had moved on to mapping the patterns of fire, water, and seasons as part of the Indigenous Protected Area (IPA) land-management program. Over the next decade, we would make a variety of maps to serve a variety of purposes. Map-making became the methodology through which we shared and recorded different kinds of knowledge, interpreting the world for each other on a template that embedded the Aboriginal story as the ground on which all other knowledge was located.

The early years of making maps with the Walmajarri and Jaru brought about a remapping of my own life, a recalibration of the co-ordinates by which I navigated the world. Until then, I had depended on part-time art teaching to support myself, and my visits to the desert were predominately artist field trips. As one mapping project led to another, and I committed to returning every year to Paruku, the teaching job ceased to make sense. It anchored me to a timetable that limited my time in the desert, and it didn't pay enough to cover my bush trips. I threw in the job and took a chance on getting enough work with the Paruku IPA to survive. Although I continued to make art, and to exhibit whenever I could, I abandoned the professional artist's trajectory that demanded regular self-promotion and constant attention to career opportunities.

The country provided a steady infusion of sensory information, and the mapping process revealed the knowledge and priorities of its Aboriginal custodians. I absorbed these things incrementally, often unconsciously. The effect of that destabilisation led to a different way of being and seeing, what I now think of as ground truthing.

Ground truthing is formally defined as the process of verifying through direct observation what has been inferred by other means — to walk the ground and see for oneself what is there. A place can carry many truths, and it takes time and attention to discover even a few of them. My version of ground truthing begins with the physical attributes of a place, and moves onto what has happened there. It puts people into place, which brings into play science, stories, husbandry, history, metaphor, and myth. This form of mapping has been called various things — co-mapping, cross-cultural mapping, counter-mapping, radical cartography. The wordsmith in me likes the flamboyant suggestiveness of radical cartography, but my bullshit detector finds it pretentious. There's nothing radical about what I do. The only surprising thing about it is that it hasn't been done before.

The underlying rationale of the map-making is that it is open-ended, responsive to the priorities of the people involved, and only provisionally driven by outcomes. One must find a point of entry for the participants, and then follow the trail where it leads. Whatever the overall purpose of the project, it begins with the Aboriginal people identifying what is important to them. This dictates what happens next, and next again, until the map develops its own logic. This is when the conversation can begin.

Part jigsaw puzzle, part treasure hunt, the act of making the maps requires you to search for the jigsaw pieces without knowing what the picture will look like until you have assembled it. And the maps are unique artefacts. The texture of the canvas, the scale, the handmade mark, the work-in-progress quality — they hover between a work of art and a utilitarian document that can be amended and elaborated. Because they are topographically accurate, the painted maps can be calibrated and digitised to provide base maps for use-and-occupancy mapping, language preservation, environmental management, and land-use planning. But their real power is in their capacity to tell stories, to open a space in which knowledge seduces rather than coerces, leaving room for the imagination to make its own interpretations.

In the introductory chapter to his book *Changescapes*, Ross Gibson distinguishes between structures and systems. A structure, he says, 'is founded on the permanence and solidity of its constituent parts and joints, whereas a system is a set of contingent relationships evolving, shifting while also persisting through time'. He goes on to describe a structure as something built to resist change, 'whereas a system is fluid, in slippery balance with mutability'. The maps I made with the Paruku people harnessed the structures of western cartography and adapted them to the slippery mutability of a system. Working together, we developed a methodology that connected image and text, place and metaphor, and spoke directly to the cognitive mutability that slips between visual, oral, and literate ways of understanding the world. On the one hand, it carried the topographically accurate authority of the conventional map. At the same time, it employed Aboriginal ways of embedding knowledge in place. The maps captivated and enthralled people. The Paruku mob felt vindicated and acknowledged. White people who participated in the mapping, and those who later saw the maps, felt that something of an inscrutable world had been made comprehensible.

I was invited in 2017 to participate in a research project interpreting the deep history of the Willandra region in western New South Wales. The invitation came from Professor Ann McGrath, director of the Research Centre for Deep History at the Australian National University, who was leading a project exploring Indigenous landscapes of national and international significance. My role would be to map the diaspora of the Indigenous families connected to Lake Mungo and its revelations of ancient Indigenous occupation. I was familiar with the prehistoric story of Lake Mungo through my association with the geomorphologist Jim Bowler, and knew something of the politics around the repatriation of the skeletal remains, but I had no connections with the contemporary Aboriginal people of the region. I accompanied Ann and her team to meet the main players in the Mungo story and to sound out whether they were interested in the mapping project. They were enthusiastic, and I accepted Ann's invitation.

It was the first time I had worked outside the desert regions I was familiar with, and the first time working on country where the displacements of Indigenous people and culture had happened many generations earlier. I was a long way out of my comfort zone, in a space crowded with competing agendas. Had I known how tough the job would prove to be, I might not have taken it on, but I didn't, and I did.

By the late 1800s, most of the viable farming and grazing land in western New South Wales had been taken up by white settlers, and Aboriginal people occupied marginal niches at the edges of the pastoral enterprises, or had fallen under the control of the missions and government resettlement programs. The completion of the railway line between Condobolin and Broken Hill in 1919 made it a simple process to relocate people from Menindee Mission to a new mission at Cootamundra, often taking them far away from their traditional country.

Almost one hundred years later, I asked questions about what had happened, listened, and marked on a set of topographic maps the movements and details of families and individuals, which I then transferred to a painted map. The narratives that unfolded revealed institutional interference and control that continued down through the generations, with descendants of the first people who had been trucked off to missions showing up on the rolls of children's homes and correctional institutions. A parallel story described families who had managed to evade the intervention of the authorities through itinerant stockwork and access to land owned by white relatives or employers, and self-sustaining occupations such as fishing, kangaroo shooting, and rabbit trapping.

The people I talked with were unfailingly willing to tell their stories, but I was mapping well-travelled ground, and there were embedded grievances and politics to navigate. Some people felt a deep sense of disenfranchisement, and I had to negotiate the resulting crossfire without taking sides or breaching confidences. I was working solo, and the days spent finding my way through a world of intergenerational damage were tough. The hardest part came at the end of the day, sitting alone in a cheap motel room with Indian takeaway and a stiff gin, struggling to find the setting for the ABC on free-to-air TV, and nowhere to download the static absorbed from the energy field I had been exposed to all day.

It was a journey through wounded country, and at the same time it was like stepping into a contemporary Aboriginal world that has its own enduring viability. I'm sure I learned more in those weeks on the frontline than in the years I could have spent reading historical documents. I witnessed the damage, the courage, the resilience, the anger, the resourcefulness, the pride, the humour, and the whole complicated drama of how human actions resonate through the generations.

I was taken to the Aboriginal cemetery in Balranald, where many of the graves are embellished with the artefacts of their occupant's lives, and a chair placed beside a grave bears witness to a continuing conversation. I was shown an ochre site on a precipitous bank of the Murray River, risking life and limb to get there. A senior woman ranger took me around the shoreline of Yanga Lake, and pointed out the sites where unrecorded massacres had taken place. In the small town of Ivanhoe, I listened to the story of King Kennedy the drover, whose family camped on the town common when they weren't on the road, and whose wife raised seventeen children and lived to one hundred.

And working alone had its benefits in the moments when a confluence of place and people offered a glimpse of how things have been and could be. There was a day I spent on a stretch of the Darling River with Lottie Williams, an elderly woman who had grown up there. Her white father had protected her from government and missionary interventions when she was a child, and her marriage had given her access to station country and the means for self-sufficiency as an adult.

While her daughter, Brenda, prepared a picnic lunch, Lottie and I sat on the riverbank, and Lottie told me about her childhood and early-adult life, fishing and rabbiting, and collecting witchetty grubs to sell as bait to the local fisherman. As we talked, a disturbance in the greenish murk around a submerged tree morphed into the outlines of a giant fish. It surfaced and disappeared, circled and re-surfaced, a prehistoric visitation in a swirling displacement of water and light. I was mesmerised. The old woman told me it was a Murray Cod nesting in a fallen tree. She hadn't seen one in a long time, but when she was a girl, the great fish were part of the life and logic of the river.

After lunch, Lottie and Brenda took me to the block of land that had been purchased by Lottie's father, Charles Brodie, in the early 1900s and which Lottie still owned: an establishment made up of homebuilt sheds and a caravan, with a pump to draw water up from the river. Brenda showed me the tiny lean-to she had lived in as a child, still lined with shelves cluttered with books. 'I loved to read,' she said. The river was wide and deep, the water low and sluggish, and big gums overhung the steep bank. Grazing and drought had reduced the surrounding country to gravel and sand, but the homestead on the river was potent with living memories.

I left Lottie and her daughter to spend the remains of the day revisiting those memories, and drove back to the tiny township of Pooncarie to talk to a family with a history that was the antithesis of Lottie's. They were related to Lottie, but the random intervention of fate had sent their forbears to Cootamundra and the mission of Murrin Bridge, and had set their lives on a different trajectory. Their shared ancestor, Nellie Johnson, had once paddled a bark canoe along sections of the Darling, and ferried people across the river. The canoe is now in the South Australian Museum.

I visited and revisited the nodes and hubs that represented family clusters, learning the origin stories of the different clans, filling in gaps, checking and re-checking information, gaining a powerful sense of how people held onto the knowledge of where they came from and who they were. Using different colours to identify the different family groups, I mapped their movements onto the canvas, along with names and dates, vignettes, and significant events. In the early 1900s, an ancestor of the Kelly clan now associated with Balranald brought his family north from the Moonaculla mission in Victoria. The Victorian connection endured, with various family members spending time in Melbourne for education and work, and I had to attach an additional piece of canvas to the map to incorporate their southern migrations.

In the course of this work, Ann McGrath was made an Australian Laureate Fellow, and the Willandra map was absorbed into a global project called 'Deepening Histories of Place'. The future of the map became a question of some significance. As I write, it has recently been photographed and digitised by the National Library of Australia, and has been offered to the custodians of the Willandra stories to hold and circulate if they choose.

Now, when I drive across south-western New South Wales on my track to Alice Springs and the south-east Kimberley, I feel the web of the Aboriginal world that persists across place and time. I know the names and genealogies and wanderings of the people whose stories hold the web together. I know much more about the Indigenous history of the region than I know about its European story. The painted map, with its colour-coded record of mobility, adaptability, and survival, is a portal through which I step into a living reality.

Around the same time that I began working on the Willandra project, I was approached with a new mapping proposal by a friend who had witnessed the evolution of the Paruku maps. Kerrie Nelson has a long history in governance training, and works as a consultant with the Alice Springs–based non-government organisation Centrefarm Aboriginal Horticulture Ltd, whose mission is to steer the development of agricultural enterprises on Indigenous land. Centrefarm is heavily invested in a long-running project on the Alekarenge Land Trust, originally the Warrabri Mission, several hundred kilometres south of Tennant Creek in the Northern Territory. A successful commercial watermelon farm had already been established on the land trust, leased from the Kaytetye and Alyawarre landholders, and additional country was marked for farming purposes. Because the land trust had begun as a mission, the holding had not been subject to native title, and no mapping of sacred sites and restricted areas had been undertaken. Now, before making any further leasing agreements, Centrefarm needed to know more about the underlying Indigenous story.

The Alekarenge co-mapping project was based on established groundwork, pre-existing relationships, and a work-in-progress training farm. The location was a semi-desert environment, and half the population was Warlpiri, so I had a feel for the language and the country. The ground was familiar enough for me to feel confident that the mapping process would provide the Aboriginal custodians with a tool they could use to identify and communicate their priorities.

It was a luxury to be part of a team in which someone else took care of food and payments, collected people and brought them to the workshop in the morning and took them home in the afternoon, managed the complexities of the local politics, helped, observed, took photographs, and made suggestions on the work as it progressed.

Finding a way in that had traction took several days of trying and abandoning different tactics, complicated by the fact that being a small white woman over sixty made me hard to see. Kerrie, the other white woman on the team, is of a similar age and build, and also had short, dark hair, so when people did notice us they had difficulty telling us apart. One morning, a few days into the fieldwork, a tall, statuesque Kaytetye woman walked into the training centre, scanned the room, and announced, 'There's no one here.' I was working on the map, and Kerrie was in the kitchen preparing the food for the day. 'Excuse me,' I said. 'I'm here, and so is Kerrie.' The woman glanced at me and said, 'I meant there's no *people* here.' I said maybe she should stop talking before she dug the hole any deeper, and she had the grace to laugh. She meant Aboriginal people, but it was a linguistic indicator of how white people fitted into the picture.

To begin with, people wanted to talk about and visit the cattle station adjoining the Alekarenge Land Trust's eastern boundary. Fence lines and property boundaries were of little significance to them compared to the lie of the land and the reach of memory. On the ground, it was obvious why. It is a dynamic landscape, a zone between mountain ranges and semi-desert shaped by the flows of water triggered by tropical weather systems far to the north. It is rich with resources and excellent camping places. This was where the ancestors of the current occupants had lived and where the heart of their language was located.

People described most of the country that was within the land trust as 'hunting ground', and it was by following that lead, collecting medicinal plants and recording their uses, and establishing which animals were still hunted on a regular basis there, that it was possible to focus the conversation on the land in question.

Using printed topographic maps and hand-drawn diagrams, we marked the names and locations of plants, animals, and significant sites. With the help of local linguist Rosie Holmes, I did a crash course in the counter-intuitive orthography of Arrernte-based languages, and was the butt of much laughter at my attempted pronunciation and spelling. Once the details had been agreed, I marked them in chalk on the canvas map. There were several painters among the women, and they developed a gorgeous iconography that combined representational drawing with fine decorative dotting.

The painted map became an illustrated document of local plants and animals with their language names and uses, along with the routes that people walked and the places they camped during the days when traditional culture intersected with the priorities of the mission. (See colour section.) These routes crossed in and out of the boundary between the Alekarenge Land Trust and the station, following the flood-out zones that flowed from the Davenport Ranges into the sweet country of claypans and low, red-sand ridges. The site of the original mission of Warrabri, and the subsequent township of Alekarenge, were located at the edge of this well-watered country, and people showed us where they had camped on the sand dunes when the community was flooded.

Towards the end of the second stint of fieldwork, we spent half a day hunting for a soakage just north of the land trust border, on another cattle station. Only a couple of the old men knew where it was. They hadn't visited the soakage for a long time, and were keen to put it on the map. By this time, my GPS skills and my willingness to drive people anywhere they wanted to go had made me visible. My gender made me the designated driver for the senior women. Centrefarm's CEO, Vin Lange, had come out from Alice for the day, and in the absence of our multi-purpose multi-skilled project manager, Joe Clarke, Vin was roped into driving the men on our ground-truthing expedition. He was captivated, as enthusiastic as his passengers to find the soak, despite it being outside Centrefarm's jurisdiction. The mapping process had revealed a pre-existing landscape that carried its own authority, and the soak belonged to the web of knowledge that integrated people and country.

The story of collaborative map-making at Paruku provided the narrative structure for my book *Position Doubtful,* and following its publication I was invited by the Australian Institute of Landscape Architects to present at the 2018 International Festival of Landscape Architecture. The theme of the event was 'The expanded field', with the focus on new ways of thinking about how landscape and architecture intersect. As part of a panel called 'Cultivating cultural intersections', I gave an illustrated presentation of the mapping process. The panel's moderator, Greg Grabasch, was then the principal director of UDLA, a West Australian firm of landscape architects, and a few months later he asked me to join a project to tell the Noongar story of the land occupied by the University of Western Australia (UWA).

The UWA campus planning department had asked UDLA to create a plan 'integrating ancient and place-based knowledge of the Crawley area'. This plan became the UWA Cultural Heritage Mapping Project, designed to provide the basis for future planning and development within the Crawley campus precinct. For the first time, the map-making enterprise that had originated in the desert would be applied to the built environment. My vision was beginning to take shape.

The UDLA project called for a new level of professionalisation in my process, and an outcome that was quantifiable and, to some extent, predictable. A week was allocated to the creation of a painted map, and two established Noongar artists were employed to work under my direction. I had developed the map-making by going where it wanted to go, adapting it to the changing dynamics of people, place, and intention. It was fundamentally collaborative, grounded in familiarity and trust between me and the people I worked with. Working within a strict time frame with people I didn't know, on country I didn't know, brought a whole new set of factors into play. To commit to outcomes and to be paid as a professional consultant made me nervous. I had no certainties about what would or wouldn't work. My challenge was to honour the methodology developed outside established institutions — to stand by a process that had emerged from listening, adapting, collaborating, and amending. Its viability rested on results, and the results were a work in progress. I was confident that the basic method could work in all sorts of different situations, but I wasn't confident that I had the skills and authority to manage the various manifestations.

Greg's team had begun the ground-truthing work with the Noongar elders prior to my involvement, and they sent me the results of their research. Their consultations produced Indigenous maps labelled Abundance, Ceremony and Meeting, Connection, Language, Sharing, Water. I asked for and was provided with many other maps — satellite, contour, topographic, and historic maps of the campus and its location within the greater Perth area, and maps of Noongar place names and heritage sites. I studied them all and absorbed a good deal of the information they contained, but it wasn't until I walked the ground myself that I began to feel the story come alive.

The campus of the University of Western Australia is located on the site where Captain James Stirling disembarked in 1829. Once he became governor of the Swan River Colony, he parcelled out blocks of riverside acreage for farming and residential purposes. First encounters with the local Noongar people followed the familiar trajectory of wary friendliness, resistance, conflict, and violence, and the Indigenous occupants were soon driven off their traditional lands. This was one among many stories that the painted map would tell.

The Noongar artists, Barbara Bynder and Shane Hansen, were skilled painters who had come to the task assuming we would be creating an interpretive painting rather than a map. The university allotted us a vast working space in the Undercroft of Winthrop Hall. It was glass-walled and full of light, with a view to the south of the grounds and gardens, including a cluster of karri trees that predate colonisation by at least 200 years. Harnessing the skills of a couple of established artists in the service of an outcome based on information collected by someone else was new terrain for me. There was a surfeit of information on the maps, and the challenge was to select the elements that told the layers of the story without crowding and confusing it.

Conscious that we only had five days to complete the painted map, I had prepared the canvas back home in my studio. This involved stitching the edges of the two-by-two-and-a-half-metre rectangle of cotton duck, inserting eyelets for ease of hanging, priming the surface, projecting and tracing the topographic contours of Crawley Point and the river, and laying down base colours for land and water.

Working with Barb and Shane turned out to be the easiest part of the project. We all understood paint. I spread the canvas out on a drop sheet, we sorted out who would do what, and got on with it. As the painting progressed, the interest of passing observers quickened. The head gardener visited every day to see how the present lie of the land compared with the past, and noted that the seepage at the northern end of the sports oval had once been the site of a permanent spring.

'Pity they didn't know that when they laid down the oval,' he said.

As always, I found myself beguiled by what the map revealed — how the past seeped into the present, just as the old spring had seeped into the sports oval. According to Noongar tradition, the site where the modern university stands had always been a place for gathering and learning.

Once the stories of ancestral beings, ancient connections, historical displacements, ceremonial sites, language names, totems, resources, springs, swamps, groundwater, and topographic contours had been painted, I hung the canvas and projected onto it a map of the built environment, tracing the outlines of the university campus with a chalk pencil. (See colour section.) We took the canvas down, and

Barb painted over the chalk marks, the straight lines and sharp corners hovering between the ancestral tracks of two dingoes and a goanna, like hieroglyphs from a different language. Crosses indicated several sites of violent conflict between Noongar and settlers within the campus grounds. Waugal, the great snake that created the river, wove his serpentine way past the university. South of the campus crouched Yakkan Kooya the Turtle Frog, the family totem passed down from Yellagonga's clan to their contemporary descendants. Marli the Black Swan paddled in the bay, and Boodalong the Pelican perched on the point.

Indigenous co-mapping is not a new idea, and is gaining momentum all the time. *Planning for Country: cross-cultural approaches to decision-making on Aboriginal lands,* published by IAD Press in 2002 under the aegis of the Central Land Council, and edited by Fiona Walsh and Paul Mitchell, documents various methodologies developed to work with Aboriginal people on land-management projects in Central Australia. Ground drawings incorporating the placement of sticks and stones continues a long tradition of communication techniques. Hand-drawn diagrams, painting, photo-story books, and story canvases using desert iconography all contribute to the participatory planning process. Re-reading *Planning for Country*, I am struck by the depth of knowledge, expertise, and commitment that persists in this intercultural space. Twenty years on, many of the book's contributors are still working together in partnerships embedded in familiarity and trust.

As countries with a settler-colonial history are looking for ways to recognise the Indigenous present as well as the past, there are moves to re-map cultural landscapes. A rigorous process called 'Use and Occupancy Mapping' has been developed in Canada, and trialled in New Zealand and in Australia's northern Murray–Darling Basin. It involves a precise and detailed mapping of the ways in which Indigenous people utilise country. Icons are used to signify the locations of plants, animals, and practical and ceremonial activities, producing multi-layered digital maps that are compelling in their density. The forensic detail of digital technology provides tangible evidence that land use continues to be central to the livelihoods and identities of Indigenous people, regardless of whether or not they hold any kind of legal title over the land.

Winyama Digital Solutions, a West Australia–based Indigenous geospatial consultancy founded by Andrew Dowding, specialises in delivering culturally informed digital geographic information-system mapping to organisations working in the cross-cultural field. The company also holds an annual Indigenous Mapping Workshop to train other Indigenous groups in how to use the technology.

At Charles Darwin University in Darwin, Rohan Fisher produces 3D printed tiles of landscape topographies, augmented by colour projections that show how fire, water, and people move through and impact on the landscape. The tactile interactive properties of the tiles are accessible across cultures and generations, with immediate application for understanding and managing fire.

There is growing interest in my form of mapping. Recently, I began working with an Indigenous Ranger team who are developing a management plan for an Indigenous Protected Area in the Great Victoria Desert. The base map we made showed detailed country types and associated vegetation. We then transferred the annual digital data collected by the rangers, painting colour-coded dots to show mallee fowl nests and quandong recovery from camel damage, buffel grass management, the location of bush medicine, and the results of a camel cull. As the rangers took ownership of the map, using it to communicate their knowledge and ideas for managing their country, I wondered at the luck and hazard that had brought together my art practice, my love of the desert, my involvement with Aboriginal people, and my enduring interest in imaginative mapping.

Back in Mulan in 2019, we are making another map. This one is a depiction of the plant and animal resources of the country surrounding the Paruku lake system. We have jokingly titled it the Bush Supermarket and Pharmacy map, and the name has stuck. One of the reasons to focus on these resources is that the lake system has dried up for the first time in thirty years, and people are keen to flag the fact that, while the water is gone, the other resources are still here. The lakes have been dry for extended periods in the past, but everyone agrees that the recent summer is the hottest they can remember, and that the deaths of thousands of birds due to heat stress is an event no one can recall happening before.

We fall easily into our familiar roles. I do the technical stuff, projecting and tracing topographical outlines onto the canvas and listing scientific taxonomies. I also mix the paints for those who aren't confident about mixing their own colours, and make sure there's tea and biscuits and lunch supplies.

The map has taken on a life of its own. The original plan was to identify the locations of the common plants and animals, paint a symbolic representation, along with the Walmajarri name, in the appropriate location, and create an explanatory legend to show the common name, scientific name, cultural use, and practical use of each resource. Instead of which, the painters seem bent on putting every individual tree, shrub, herb, grass, tuber, bird, mammal, grub, and reptile on the map. Creeks are lined with river red gums and melaleucas. White-barked coolibahs fill the floodplains, and samphires frame the lake edges. Termite mounds sprout among the spinifex clumps, bush turkeys lurk in the grasslands, and a posse of bluetongue lizards marches westwards — 'Running away so they won't get eaten,' says the young woman who is painting them. (See colour section.)

There's a hiatus when one of the painters comes into the art centre, bellowing and swearing. She's been involved in a fight outside the store, in an eruption of a simmering inter-family power struggle. Someone has been punched, someone has been bitten, harsh words have been said, and blood has been spilt. I start to object to her language, and the person beside me puts her foot on mine under the table, nudging me to keep quiet. The angry woman storms out, and we exhale.

The map is beautiful and informative, and there's a palpable sense of pride as it takes shape. It's the making that matters, including the volatile moments that reflect the world people occupy — the sitting together, the inclusion of different generations, the absorbing of feuds and fights, the coming and going of family members, the gossiping and storytelling, the sharing and recapitulation of knowledge.

It's here that I have been inducted into the rigours of two-way thinking, and taught how to let contradictions play through each other instead of trying to resolve them. This is my point of reference, the university that has taught and honed my skills, and where I have earned my doctorate in cross-cultural map-making. I have learnt that too rigorous an attachment to outcomes disenfranchises the Aboriginal participants, and that the most important discoveries are often the things you aren't looking for. I have learnt that serendipity is essential to the success of a project, and that knowing how to leave the space for serendipity is a skill that can only be learned through long experience. I have learnt when to step in and when to step back, how to pay attention to what is happening on the fringes, how to listen to conversations in languages I don't understand, how to trust the slow days when nothing seems to happen, and how to recognise when the gods are smiling and to act fast when they do.

The old people, mostly gone now, taught me about the way things were. Their middle-aged children are teaching me how communities and culture are adapting to change. The young people lean towards the future, with its hopes and risks. The cattle have come and gone and come back. Through it all, the country endures. The lake fills and floods and recedes. Once every few decades, it dries up, and then the cycle begins again.

13

The night parrot — it's a whitefella thing

If you google the words 'night parrot', you will come up with a companion set of adjectives, the most common being 'elusive', followed by 'mysterious', 'secretive', 'enigmatic', 'mythical', and — until recently — 'thought-to-be-extinct'. Apart from anecdotal claims, there were no confirmed sightings of the night parrot between 1912, when a bird was shot in Western Australia, and 1990, when a dead and headless parrot was found by the roadside in western Queensland. Then, in 2013, a live bird was photographed by naturalist John Young, again in western Queensland. Young, otherwise known as the 'Wild Detective', had a complicated backstory, which included an uncanny ability to find rare birds, a tendency to hyperbole, and a reputation as a fabulist. His photograph of the plump green parrot electrified the birdwatching community and the Australian scientific world. Authenticated by night parrot experts such as ecologist Steve Murphy, the photograph was accepted as proof that the fugitive bird had been found.

The initial discovery brought Young into the public eye, and made much of his larger-than-life persona and his reputation. Murphy, quiet, dogged, and self-effacing, was the antithesis of the showman

Young. He convinced Young of the need for systematic research into the parrot's habitat and behaviour, and the two embarked on an uneasy but fruitful partnership, from which Young bailed out two years later. Claims he made of further discoveries were deemed fraudulent, with suggestions of photoshopped images, faked nests, and substitute eggs.

Despite controversy, compromised reputations, and the expulsion of Young from the Australian Wildlife Conservancy, the parrot prevailed. Murphy, with his partner and fellow scientist Rachel Barr, went on to consolidate the research and to push through the establishment of a night parrot conservation reserve at Pullen Pullen, the location in western Queensland where Young had taken the photograph, and where a female night parrot was subsequently trapped, tagged, and named Pedro.

In the winter of 2017, somewhere in the northern part of the Great Sandy Desert, the Paruku Indigenous rangers and a visiting scientist from the World Wildlife Fund (WWF) set up an overnight sensor camera at a location where a night parrot had reportedly been sighted by a local pastoralist forty years earlier. Returning to the base the next morning, the ranger team discovered that the camera had captured a flare of yellow-green. The WWF scientist immediately sent the image to his ornithologist brother, who identified it as *Pezoporus occidentalis*, the night parrot.

I happened to be staying at the ranger base at the time, and accompanied the rangers back to the location the following day, where they set up the camera for a second attempt to photograph the parrot in the hope of getting a clearer image. By all accounts, the night parrot is a punctual bird, setting out an hour after dusk to graze and seek water, and returning to its nest before dawn. So, nightfall found us wandering among the spinifex and samphire-edged claypans in ones and twos, armed with mobile phones installed with the night parrot's call. Across the still night, we followed the 'ding ding' that might have signalled the presence of the parrot, but each time it was only a ranger holding his phone aloft and making his way towards another dinging phone. I imagined a baffled night parrot crouching under a clump of spinifex, wondering what horrid transformation had overtaken its parrot mates.

That night, the camera recorded wild camels, bulls, cats, and dingoes, whose grunts, howls, and bellows kept us all awake. Another photo taken a few months later, accompanied by audio identification of its call, confirmed that the night parrot was successfully sharing its habitat with multiple predators and ferals.

The Paruku ranger program was established in 2004 to help the custodians of the Paruku Indigenous Protected Area manage the unique, little-known desert lake ecosystem located at the southernmost reaches of the Kimberley cattle country and the northern end of the Canning Stock Route. Accustomed to being overlooked and under-serviced because of their remoteness, the rangers were suddenly the recipients of media attention, funding offers, and expert advice. The night parrot had been doing fine, flying under the radar during the four decades since its last sighting; but rare, elusive birds produce a strange fever in certain strata of the human population, and this low-flying, ground-dwelling, seed-eating, dumpy, nocturnal green bird, sometimes described as 'a fat budgie', was the gold standard of mythical Australian birds.

The first decision the rangers made was to keep its location secret. This was not as mean-spirited as it sounds. The twitcher fraternity among birdwatchers is renowned for the lengths it will go to in pursuit of a rare-bird sighting, and the prospect of coping with an influx of twitchers in a remote desert region managed only by an under-resourced ranger team didn't bear thinking about. Still, this was an opportunity to be grasped. If whitefellas were interested in the night parrot, and prepared to chuck money at it, it was in the interests of the blackfellas to turn it to their advantage.

In early 2019, I receive a phone call from Jamie Brown, the Paruku ranger co-ordinator, inviting me to be the master of ceremonies for a gathering at Paruku of Indigenous rangers, scientists, and other guests. Co-ordinated by the Indigenous Desert Alliance (IDA), the awkwardly named Species of the Desert Festival — whose acronym is SODF— would bring together twenty-five Indigenous ranger teams from across the Kimberley and the Central and Western Desert regions to share their knowledge and experience of desert ecology with night parrot experts and some Very Important People, including Senator Patrick Dodson, the Threatened Species commissioner, Sally Box, and *The Guardian*'s award-winning, marsupial-drawing cartoonist First Dog on the Moon.

I've never wrangled so many people, but I am curious to observe the next iteration of the night parrot story. In the two years since the parrot has been re-discovered, there have been negotiations to establish which families hold jurisdiction over the bird's territory and how the politics and benefits will play out. And such a large gathering of ranger groups would be an opportunity to see how the Indigenous ranger program was travelling.

There's a nice symmetry to the harnessing of Indigenous knowledge in the search for a bird that holds an almost mythical symbolism in the non-Indigenous imagination. The whitefella obsession with a spectral avian species could generate the money to get out on country, observe its creatures, control the impact of feral animals and weeds, support traditional management practices, and contribute to the shared endeavour to maintain the environmental and cultural integrity of the desert.

It's fortuitous that the desert Indigenous ranger groups occupy the same territory as some of our other charismatic threatened species — bilbies, marsupial moles, and great desert skinks — and so are best placed to find, monitor, and look after them. Not too long ago, the Indigenous rangers were at risk of becoming a threatened species themselves, when the federal minister for Indigenous affairs decided that the ranger program should be relegated to the Work for the Dole scheme from which it originated. This triggered a *What the fuck? You must be joking!* reaction from everyone who had spent decades working on Indigenous programs. *This is one of the few initiatives that has produced real outcomes!* The minister backed down, and since then the no-longer-threatened Indigenous rangers are discovering that some of the threatened species may not be as threatened as was previously thought. The marsupial mole is turning up all over its natural habitat, burrowing about under the sand dunes, and the greater bilby *Macrotis lagotis* (my favourite scientific name for an Australian creature) is reportedly doing well. There are lots of bilbies in the desert, possibly because the Indigenous human inhabitants of the desert have long enjoyed eating the feral cats that prey on them.

I accept the invitation, and by the middle of May am settling into my Mulan quarters, the two-roomed demountable that has served me well for many years. The festival is six weeks away, and the IDA co-ordinator of the event, Sam, has co-opted my local knowledge to help with the planning. The Mulan locals are full of excitement and anticipation. Nothing on this scale has been hosted before, and the preparations are significant.

The gathering is to be held at the Handover campsite, so named because it is the place where native title was handed back to the Walmajarri traditional owners of Paruku in 2001. Jamie and the rangers have extended the campsite to three times its original size, and are grappling with the task of building toilets for 250 visitors. The fifteen kilometres of heavily corrugated road from the community to the campsite are graded, and a water bore is drilled for camper comfort and dust management. A catering team has been booked to feed the visitors, and Sam and her sidekick, Connie, are enmeshed in the logistics of sourcing freezers, fridges, eco-friendly disposable eating equipment, toilet paper, drinking water, and hand sanitiser — the banal essentials without which nothing would function.

One of the Mulan men mentions to me that the men from the neighbouring community of Balgo have suggested they should be invited to accompany the dancing at the festival. Organising ceremonial dancing is outside the scope of my responsibilities, but I file the remark as something I need to know.

The newly established Paruku women's ranger team wants to host a stall at the festival to demonstrate how certain plants are used for healing and ceremony, so we go hunting and gathering, to locate bush food and medicine resources that we later document on a painted map. We also film the preparation and uses of the various plants. Having gathered a large quantity of the three main plants used for ceremonial smoking — conkerberry, called *marnukuji* in Walmajarri, the eremophila *wakila*, and *malarn*, the river red gum — the senior women hold a smoking and healing session for the school, to protect and strengthen the community children. Two recent teenage suicides in Balgo have reignited fears for the mental health of the local young people.

The women wash the schoolkids and their teachers with a brew of native herbs, and get them to kneel over the aromatic smoke generated by the smouldering leaves. The kids behave impeccably, submitting to having their arms, legs, bellies, and heads drenched in the tea-coloured brew, crouching in the smoke with heads bowed like penitents. As word of the washing and smoking circulates, more people arrive; some bringing babies to be smoked, and others presenting themselves to be washed and healed. An old woman has to be restrained from removing her clothes and throwing herself into the smoke. Once the kids have gone back to school, the younger women take it in turns to swab each other's bellies and backs and hair, and the rest of us are treated with whatever is deemed appropriate. Namangarli makes me kneel and, taking my head between her hands, blows smoke into each ear, murmuring, 'This is so nothing bad can get inside your head.' *What does she know that I don't?* I wonder.

Rebecca tells me that the dancing is planned for the beginning of the festival, and the Mulan mob want all the kids to participate. I suggest that she pass this information on to the school.

In the art centre, we work on the bush supermarket and pharmacy map, and I draw up a new map that encompasses the ten deserts represented by the IDA, marking the areas held under various forms of Indigenous land tenure. The plan is for the ranger teams to indicate where they know or think night parrots may live, and where they want to look for them.

A couple of men's ranger teams arrive a few days early to help build the toilets and to weld stands onto the 100-litre drums that will be used to heat water for the camp. There are two restricted women's sites close to the campground, so the women rangers paint and erect signs warning people to stay clear of these locations. This precipitates a request from the visiting men to be formally welcomed and smoked to keep them safe while on strange country. The man recognised as having the requisite cultural authority to do this is LB, son of my friend and skin-sister Evelyn, who has recently died. He is the only member of his family living in Mulan at present. LB is also involved in organising the dancing for the men and boys, overseeing a group visit to the archaeological site that is on his family ground, and facilitating one of the main field trips. He formally welcomes the men already at the site, and then takes over the smoking and welcoming of new groups as they arrive.

A senior couple from Balgo drop into the art centre and ask me when the dancing is going to happen. 'At the opening of the festival, as far as I know,' I tell them. 'Ask Rebecca or LB.' Given how long it takes to paint people up for dancing, and that the event is supposed to kick off at eight o'clock the next morning, this plan doesn't sound feasible to me. I check with Rebecca, and she confirms that this is still the intention, and asks me if I've told the school yet. Rebecca's sister, Julianne, asks me what I plan to wear as MC of the festival. When I indicate the cropped cargo pants and cotton shirt I usually wear, she's not impressed.

'You're representing Mulan,' she says. 'You need to wear high heels and a dress so we can be proud.' I remind her that the sand at the campsite is ankle deep, and that the stage is a steel LandCruiser tray sourced from the local car graveyard and mounted on stacked wheel rims. Also, I didn't bring high heels or a dress to Mulan, and she has appropriated my most presentable sandals to wear to a council meeting in Halls Creek. She offers to lend the sandals back to me for the festival.

On the eve of the event, the rest of the ranger teams arrive, checking in at the ranger base and heading down to Handover to set up camp. *Marnukuji, wakila,* and *malarn* are piled beside a fire drum in preparation for the ritual smoking ceremony with which the festival is to begin. In the late afternoon, excited by the energy of the arrivals, senior custodian Bessie initiates an impromptu smoking ceremony and welcome. The aromatic blue smoke, the glowing trunks of the white coolibahs, the red earth, and the sunset throwing pink light across the empty lake basin cast a thrall of desert magic over the gathering.

At seven the next morning, as I'm preparing for my first outing as an MC and wondering what I've let myself in for, Jamie knocks on my door. He tells me that LB is offended that the smoking ceremony took place without him, and is refusing to take any further part in the festival.

I drive around to LB's house and hammer on the door, supervised by half a dozen of LB's dogs. My dog, Pirate, watches from the safety of the ute.

'LB,' I call, 'it's Kim. I want to talk to you.'

LB tells me to fuck off. One of the dogs takes an experimental nip at my backside. I kick it in the ribs, and yell back.

'LB, open the door and talk to me. And tell your dogs to stop biting me on the bum!'

LB opens the door, hunts the dogs away, and invites me into his house. His wife, Katie, sits on a mattress on the floor, holding their young son, Lennie. LB's role in the festival is crucial. I tell him this, and that his absence will cause me a great deal of embarrassment. I offer to drive him and Katie and Lennie to the campground for breakfast before the formal opening begins, and promise to be his personal driver for the next few days, so there's no chance of him being left out of any of the important events.

LB agrees, and the family climbs into my car. I drive fast on the newly graded road to the campsite, and deliver my passengers to the breakfast queue. The visiting ranger teams and VIPs are already seated under the marquee, waiting for the MC to get the festival under way.

The proceedings begin with an extended welcome from the Walmajarri elders and the men's and women's ranger teams. The schoolkids sit proudly in the front rows of the assembled crowd. There is no dancing. The teachers, who have gone to great trouble to get the kids to the site in time for the necessary preparations, seem to think this is my fault.

The various groups deliver updates on managing the threatened species on their country. The bilby story is progressing well, and a short video of a marsupial mole charms everyone. One of the ranger teams describes the frenzy caused by the reported sighting of a princess parrot, posted online by some travellers passing through one of the land trusts, resulting in an inundation of visitors who camped where they pleased and left their rubbish behind.

While the presentations and discussions are taking place in the marquee, LB marshals a group of teenage boys to prepare the dancing ground. Hessian screens are erected to conceal the dancers while they paint up for the performance. The space is marked out by termite mounds that have been chopped off at the base and relocated. A contingent of people from Balgo set up camp under one of the coolibahs in the centre of the campground, make a fire, and cook kangaroo tails. During the morning tea break, one of the ladies calls me over and asks me when the dancing is going to happen. At lunchtime, LB tells me that the Balgo men didn't bring the boomerangs and clapping sticks required to accompany the singing, and we don't have anything suitable in Mulan. There will be no dancing that night.

On the second day, we get down to the business of the night parrot. The two scientists who have been invited to bring everyone up to speed on night parrot behaviour deliver their presentations. Nick Leseberg, who has just completed his doctorate on the parrot, plays recordings of the various calls attributed to the parrot, and Steve Murphy shows images of the Pullen Pullen reserve as examples of night parrot habitat. According to the evidence so far, the bird's optimum habitat consists of widely spaced old-growth spinifex not susceptible to wildfire, on run-off or flood-out country that supports samphire and quick-response seed-bearing plants. Murphy's images of the western Queensland reserve show country remarkably like the flat-topped sandstone breakaway country between Mulan and Balgo. One of the purposes of the Species of the Desert Festival is to identify possible habitats and to establish the groundwork for a night parrot recovery plan, with the initial input coming from Aboriginal rangers and elders who have chosen what information they want to share and how they want it used. Indigenous knowledge will provide the template to develop the recovery plan.

During a break, I find First Dog on the Moon bonding with Pirate, who has been relegated to the back of my ute. We chat for a while, and First Dog asks me when the dancing is programmed to happen. I tell him there are no guarantees, but there's a good chance it will be in the evening.

As darkness falls, the dancers assemble and the painting-up begins. This part of the event is as important as the performance, invoking the traditions and social bonds that hold people together. For an hour or so, there's activity behind the hessian screens, before the singing starts and the dancers emerge onto the floodlit dancing ground. Amplified by the professional sound system installed for the daily events, the voice of a solitary singer penetrates the night with ancient authority. The boys come out first, led by a senior man. Some of the kids are tiny three- or four-year-olds. Many have never danced before, but this is about participation rather than spectacle. The boys advance and retreat, stamping and striking the ground with makeshift spears to the accompaniment of the clapping of the boomerangs, which have finally arrived. Despite the inexperience of most of the dancers, there is something very compelling about the painted bodies and pounding feet. The kids are unselfconscious and proud to be performing in front of their families and visitors.

The girls are older, with several senior women leading them in the knee-shaking gait that is impossible to replicate if you haven't grown up doing it. They dance in an inward-facing circle, backs turned to the audience. Wearing mismatched skirts and in the rising dust, they are a slowly turning vortex of multi-coloured wraiths. When the dancing is finished, someone lets off fireworks behind the screens, and I bolt for my ute to make sure Pirate hasn't taken off in panic. As the audience disperses, two of the boys come looking for me.

'Kim, Kim, did you see us? Did you see us dancing?'

'Yes, I saw you,' I say. 'You were wonderful.'

They spin about me, sweaty and proud, before dashing off to find someone else to admire them.

The final morning begins with wind and dust, and we pile swags along the eastern side of the marquee to keep the wind from whipping underneath it. The first-aid tent has already blown away, but so far there's been no call for medical intervention, and the on-site medic is happy to take shelter in the marquee and to minister from there if required. No one wants to leave their own camps, and it takes a lot of yelling through the microphone to get people assembled.

Despite the initial reluctance, the discussion on managing feral species proves to be the most popular session of the festival. The first presentation is on the brumby problem at Paruku and on the difficulties associated with culling because of the emotional attachment people feel for horses, and the timidity of governments to authorise culls. A discussion of camels comes next, and then we move onto feral cats, which are the biggest threat to native birds, mammals, and reptiles. There's a presentation on the latest development in feral cat control — a sensor device that recognises a cat by its shape and proportions, and then releases a poison spray. Being a self-grooming animal, the cat licks the poison off its fur and dies. A young woman ranger takes us through an alternative method of cat control, using images of tracking, catching, killing, and eating a cat that had staked out a bilby burrow and killed and eaten its resident.

Someone suggests that the night parrot's habit of making its nest deep inside a large clump of old-growth spinifex might be a recent development to escape from cats. Since dingoes have been around for 5,000 years longer than cats, it seems more likely to me that the adaptation evolved to avoid dingoes, and possibly hawks, which are also efficient predators. On the other hand, maybe the hawks' practice of picking up burning twigs from bushfires and dropping them into clumps of spinifex evolved to flush out night parrots.

The various groups are asked to consider whether they have the kind of country that may suit night parrots, at which point the recently painted map is brought out, and people mark areas where they would like to look for night parrots, where there is a likelihood of finding night parrots, and where night parrots are known to be. There's a hungry light in the eyes of the visiting scientists as the map is rolled up and stashed away in its cylinder of PVC pipe, but for the time being it's up to the Indigenous ranger teams to decide where to look and what to reveal.

During the final session of the conference — 'Where to next?' — things get heated when a young woman ranger challenges the Threatened Species commissioner to explain why ranger teams have to look for night parrots in order to be funded to manage vast tracts of desert, and why the government can't just give them the money anyway. It's a fair question, but tough on the commissioner, who doesn't control the money. Someone else wants to know what's so special about a fat nocturnal budgie that can't even fly properly, and one of the scientists says defensively that they have been known to fly up to forty kilometres in a night.

People are starting to peel away and head back to their camps to pack up and prepare for the long drives ahead. One of the Balgo ladies approaches me.

'Kim,' she says, 'when will we be paid for the dancing?'

'See that Kimberley Land Council guy with the dreadlocks?' I say.

'Go and ask him.' I watch as she makes her way over to the person I've pointed out and asks her question. His affable expression changes to deer-in-the-headlights.

LB, Katie, and little Lennie get into my car, and I drive them home, the recently graded track now a washboard of corrugations from the passing traffic.

15

It is not our place to find the bird

'It is not our place to find the bird.' So says one of the ancestral beings who have gathered to discuss the attempt by two of their fellows to flush out a night parrot. A single glimpse of the mysterious green bird has triggered in the two beings a passionate desire to see it again, and they pursue the parrot until one of the beings collapses from stress and exhaustion. They set fire to the spinifex in which they believe the parrot is hiding, and when it refuses to reveal itself, they create a storm that turns on them, dousing the fire and flattening the surrounding country:

> Lightning and hail fell on the two beings
> who had made the storm to find the bird
> and their storm picked them up and threw them
> to the water ... over there.
> and the fire was extinguished. Finished.

Frustrated and exhausted, the two beings commiserate with each other:

'If you are just here, the bird will be over there.'
Hugging and crying they still could not find the bird.

They seek out the locations where the bird has been seen:

'... Fly here. No there. Lost ...'

More ancestral beings assemble, and discuss the conundrum:

All of them confused ... for the bird could not be seen.
and one said, 'It is not our place to find the bird.'
and they never saw it again.
So its mad story is finished ... finished I tell you.
at that place beyond the water.
and the bird was banished to the darkness.

This ancient tale of ancestral twitchers, told by senior Martu man Geoffrey Stewart to filmmaker Rob Nugent for Nugent's 2016 film, *Night Parrot Stories*, and interpreted by Ngaanyatjatjarra linguist Lizzie Ellis, prefigures non-Indigenous night parrot obsessions. It seems that the night parrot was always a cryptic bird, long before colonisation shrank its habitat and feral predators threatened it with extinction. Smitten with the desire to find the spectral creature, the ancestral beings harness the powers available to them to flush it out, as if its very elusiveness is the thing that makes the bird desirable.

Little did I know, when I embarked on my own venture to understand the enthralment cast by the night parrot, that I was entering the forcefield of a grail bird — a creature of science and metaphor, fraud and fabrication, obsession and redemption. My quest became an enquiry into the nature of quests.

Night Parrot Stories is an elliptical search for the thing that eludes meaning, a haunting and haunted narrative of absences and extinctions. In a quest both comic and melancholy, the filmmaker tracks rumours and traces of the night parrot from the deserts of Australia to the museums of Europe, using the bird as a device to pursue his own preoccupations. It is an excuse to embark on a journey doomed to failure, to make a film about a bird that can't be photographed.

Nugent says of the Martu Dreaming story he filmed, 'The night parrot is their antagonist ... an unnamed escape artist who refuses to participate in a wider understanding of its place in the scheme of things.' He acknowledges the difficulties in attempting to translate meanings across cultures, and that filming creates its own theatrical dynamic, in which the storyteller performs the story for the filmmaker:

> Geoffrey possibly makes transpositions, for in my mind I thought Geoffrey related the story out of sympathy for me. The frustrations of the search for the night parrot seemed to mirror my own. A good oral history teller can gauge their audience. Geoffrey's story is part of a much greater story, and perhaps he was excising this particular bit, just for me.

The story as told to Nugent suggests that the glimpse of the night parrot afflicted the ancestral beings with the same fanatical ardour it unleashes in non-Indigenous bird people, and that certain behaviours are embedded in the proto-human consciousness. In flagging it as 'an unnamed escape artist', Nugent aligns the night parrot with the trickster archetypes of multiple mythologies — the joker, the fool, the creature whose behaviour resists the logic of morality. Indigenous dreaming stories are full of such beings, as are the Greek myths and other pre-Christian cosmologies. A flash of green in the spinifex, the fleeting glimpse of an idea — here, there, lost ... The trickster bird lights the spark of curiosity and desire in the ancestral beings, and the traces of an ancient story manifesting across cultures lights the spark of curiosity and desire in me.

'The most spectacular thing about him is he isn't there,' says an elderly Queenslander with a profile eerily like once-upon-a-time premier Joh Bjelke-Petersen. When, perversely, the real night parrot shows up during the making of the film, the filmmaker says, 'The night parrot that was found is not the night parrot I ended up searching for.'

What he does end up searching for is as elusive and intangible as messages from space — the music of comets recorded by the Rosetta spacecraft as it surfs the solar winds, the insomniac whisperings of inner space. The references in Nugent's film are cryptic and fugitive, like the bird itself, flying low through the lands of myth and metaphor. An old woman speaks the Pitta Pitta language to a pet cockatoo, and when she dies, the cockatoo is the last speaker of the language. A man searches for the Duck Egg Sandhill, a site recorded in a song his people sang sixty years earlier. The country is no longer recognisable. 'Fifty years, sixty years since I been here,' he says. 'You can lose it. They reckon you can't lose it, but you *can* lose it.'

During the filming of *Night Parrot Stories*, one of the Martu women remarks, 'We really did forget him, this little bird.'

For anyone on a quest for information about the night parrot, the place to look is Penny Olsen's forensically researched 2018 history of everything so far known about the bird. For her book *Night Parrot*, Olsen has unearthed and researched every known detail about the parrot and the people who have pursued it, excavating mentions in science, history, literature, art, and anecdote; reports of sightings and shootings, and hunting and collecting; and examples of hubris and humility. Because the night parrot is mostly absent, the book focuses on the character and circumstances of the men who have looked for it, where they went, and the ways in which their endeavours have affected their lives. In her methodical compiling of fact, fiction, and apocrypha, the uber-quester Olsen plants the flag for women in the story of the night parrot, although her work reinforces what is predominately a story of men chasing myths and rumours in remote places. I have drawn on Olsen's research for most of the factual material included in this essay.

The night parrot of Martu tradition is a trickster that refuses to be classified. It slips between etymologies and taxonomies.

In an Arrernte story, it stands as a sentinel for ancestral red kangaroos, warning of the approach of predators. In Xavier Herbert's *Poor Fellow My Country*, the night parrot watches out near a waterhole for the rainbow serpent, reporting to a gecko lizard before dawn, when the flock comes to drink. This bird is probably confused with Bourke's parrot, which is also nocturnal but travels in flocks, which the night parrot doesn't.

The anthropologist Norman Tindale recorded the Pintupi name for the night parrot as *tjerawiljawilja*, but linguists now believe this refers to the splendid fairy-wren.

In the margins of his account of his time at Hermannsburg Mission, some time before his death in 1922, the Reverend Carl Strehlow pencilled a reference to the night parrot, *nacht-lichter papagei*, and a possible spelling for what he believed to be its Arrernte name, *tnokkapaltara*, with alternative spellings *tnukutulbara* and *tnaljurbura*.

In 1923, Frederick Whitlock visited Hermannsburg. Whitlock, who had shed a criminal past in England and reinvented himself as an ornithologist on his arrival in Australia, noticed Strehlow's marginalia, for which he offered his own alternative spellings, *tnokkatoolpata* and *trrukutulbara*.

Strehlow's Arrernte-speaking son, Theodore, transcribed it from an Arrernte song as *ynaltjirpela* or *tnaltjirperala*.

Tindale wrote the Arrernte name as *nokodulbara*.

The prominent Australian field linguist David Nash says that these names, however they are spelled, refer to Bourke's parrot.

Ornithologist John Gould created a new genus, *Geopsittacus*, to identify the night parrot, but later consensus relocated it to the existing genus *Pezoporus*, which also contains the ground parrot. When I searched for the meaning of *geopsittacus*, I found nothing but a circular loop back to the night parrot.

Down the rabbit hole I go in pursuit of it, a flicker of green at the Mad Hatter's tea party, a flutter of wings behind the Cheshire Cat's disappearing grin.

'What's his name, that kardiya? Robert? Rabbit?' asks a Warlpiri woman during the filming of *Night Parrot Stories* in Central Australia.

'Rabbit,' agrees another woman, while Nugent's voice can be heard off-camera saying 'Robert.'

'We shoot rabbits,' says the first woman, and they cackle with laughter.

The early explorers and collectors used to shoot night parrots. John McDouall Stuart shot a night parrot during the 1845 expedition with Charles Sturt to find the inland sea, but the bird was misclassified as a ground parrot and was not correctly identified until 1928.

In 1854, seventeen-year-old Kenneth Brown shot the holotype, the night parrot specimen first identified and classified by Gould. Brown was part of an expedition to look for gold-bearing country north of the

Gascoyne River in Western Australia. He went on to marry twice, have six children, develop a drinking and gambling habit, shoot his second wife, and be hanged for her murder at the age of thirty-eight.

Frederick Andrews, chief collector for the South Australian Institute Museum between 1864 and 1884, shot most of the night parrots in the Gawler Ranges. By 1880, he noted that the area was overgrazed and drought-stricken, and that the night parrot habitat was gone, along with the Aboriginal people of the area.

The night parrot flickers in and out of accounts of early exploration — a premonition in the search for the inland sea, a footnote in the search for gold, the feathered remnants of feral cat predation. In 1894, when the ornithologist George Keartland served with the Horn scientific expedition led by Baldwin Spencer to collect new mammal species in Central Australia, he noticed night parrot feathers decorating picture frames at the Alice Springs Telegraph Station. Keartland, an exceptionally conscientious collector, went on to serve with the 1896 Calvert expedition into the Great Sandy Desert, an enterprise dedicated to mapping unexplored country, collecting scientific specimens, and searching for Leichhardt's remains. Keartland sighted but did not capture a night parrot, and had to discard most of the bird skins he had collected when two members of the party were lost and the expedition abandoned.

The nineteenth century was the heyday of collecting, and the nineteenth-century night parrots collected by Andrews and others were bartered and exchanged with collectors in England and Europe. Museums back then were not constrained by the ethics of ownership or the politics of representation. Darwin's *The Origin of Species* had been published in 1859, and British colonies took the principle of natural selection to mean 'survival of the fittest', which explained and justified the displacement and destruction of native flora, fauna, and people. The collecting policy of the board of the South Australian Institute

Museum in 1860 unashamedly reflects the understanding that white colonisation heralded the destruction of the land as it had been. Its stated aim was:

> ... to preserve for posterity the forms and semblance of the various singular and beautiful animals, birds, reptiles and insects now inhabiting Australia, ere they shall have finally disappeared before the footsteps of the white man.

In 1912, at Nichol Springs in the Meekatharra region of Western Australia, bushman and drover Martin Bourgoin mistakenly shot a night parrot, thinking it was a pigeon. Identified by an Aboriginal member of Bourgoin's team, it proved to be the last authenticated sighting of the bird until 1990. Bourgoin, whose work frequently took him into night parrot country, continued to observe the bird's habitat and behaviour. Instead of shooting them to provide evidence of their existence, he preferred to leave the mating pairs to produce eggs and young, and thus was unable to prove his observations.

For much of the twentieth century, the night parrot was thought to be extinct, but unauthenticated sightings persisted, and the search for the cryptic bird became the paramount quest of birdwatchers and bird scientists in Australia. The discovery in 1990 of a decapitated and desiccated corpse caught on a roadside fence in western Queensland confirmed that the bird was not extinct. By the early twenty-first century, it was being called 'the Holy Grail of world birdwatching', taking on religious overtones and redemptive implications.

The search for the Holy Grail is the animating force of *Le Morte d'Arthur*, Thomas Malory's definitive interpretation of the legend of King Arthur and the Knights of the Round Table, first published in

1485. The grail was reputed to be the cup Jesus drank from during the Last Supper, and the vessel in which Joseph of Arimathea collected Christ's blood at the Crucifixion. In the medieval legend, the Fisher King, keeper of the grail, presides over a blighted land and lies dying of a wound in the groin that renders him impotent and will not heal. The recovery of both the maimed king and his lands depends on a celibate and perfect knight reaching the domain of the Fisher King and asking the right question, *Whom does the grail serve?* This pursuit becomes the task of King Arthur's knights, to distract them from the infighting and plotting and general misbehaviour they have fallen into. Along with the regeneration of the Fisher King and his fields, reaching the grail confers self-realisation and spiritual awareness on the successful knight.

The legend of the Fisher King and the Holy Grail has many iterations, its Celtic origins absorbing Christian themes and iconography, inspiring poets, writers, and filmmakers into the present day. 'I see him cloaked in cold mist, the Fisher King, a desolate figure in a wasteland of his own making,' writes Jay Griffiths in an essay for *Orion* magazine. The earliest legends, Griffiths says, portray the king as suffering a moral wounding, caused by his own behaviour, the impacts of which pollute and destroy everything around him. She draws out the legend as a metaphor for our contemporary destruction of the environment. Collectively, we have taken on the character of the Fisher King, and healing the wound and the damaged lands is our shared responsibility. The notion of a moral solution persists, a grail that will transform the future, if only the finder remembers to pose the right question.

The grail and the quest usually belong to the realm of poets and storytellers. Science is based on evidence and observation, and you can't accumulate data about a bird that isn't there, so what is the redemption offered to science by the discovery of the night parrot? According to

Steve Murphy, an ecologist dedicated to the study of the night parrot and the preservation of its environment, the bird represents the harm that Europeans have done to Australian fauna. By extrapolation, to study its behaviour and protect its environment is in some symbolic way to halt and possibly reverse some of that harm.

And what about the grace bestowed on those who find the grail bird? The story of John Young, Steve Murphy, and the night parrot reads like a morality play: the showman, seduced by the attention that follows his discovery, destroys his own reputation in pursuit of further accolades, while the scientist who puts the welfare of the bird first is rewarded with sightings of more night parrots, the establishment of a reserve, and the discovery deep in Martu country of the trickster bird that had been banished to the darkness.

The night parrot's reappearance signifies its capacity to live under the radar. The bird, though rare and fugitive, survives in remote parts of Australia, in country with specific characteristics. In an alliance between scientists and the custodians, mostly Indigenous, of those regions, working partnerships are being forged that offer a model for environmental management in the future. It reflects a pattern of Indigenous participation, partnerships, and caring for country that is being replicated across the continent. The story of the night parrot is shifting from the redemptive imaginary to the pragmatics of management.

In *Night Parrot Stories*, the existential hauntings of the Australian desert are married to the northern hemisphere hauntings of T.S. Eliot's great modernist poem *The Waste Land,* with its reconfiguring of the grail legend and its undercarriage of pre-Christian fertility rituals.

Nugent prowls the museums of Europe in search of the night parrots in their collections. Through the camera lens, the museums become anterooms to the underworld: modernist catacombs of vaults and drawers; labyrinthine mausoleums of locked cabinets and abandoned taxidermies.

A middle-aged Ariadne in jeans and puffer vest leads Nugent through the bowels of the Strasbourg Museum, along passages lined with horned skulls, past rooms where the bones of leviathans wait to be reassembled, and where chimerae lurk beneath plastic sheets. Multi-headed Cerberus guards an empty room. A closer look reveals the monster to be a pair of swans in an abandoned tableau of wings and necks and shadows. When the guide opens a cabinet of primate skulls, I half expect to see the head of Orpheus, arrested in the gaze that sent Eurydice back to the underworld.

The filmmaker emerges from the Underground, a dazed Everyman trying to get his bearings, and time-travels by train through a European landscape of wind turbines and overpasses and monster chimneys belching smoke. In Budapest, the night parrot is missing, along with the museum that acquired it, both destroyed by Russian tanks in the Second World War. In the Natural History Museum at Tring in Hertfordshire, the senior curator of birds slides open a drawer and lifts out a red cardboard box that once held Oxo cubes.

'The Guam flycatcher,' he says. 'The last male became extinct on the fifteenth of May in 1984, when I was just about to turn twelve.' He gestures at the ranks of drawers, containing labelled boxes of nests and eggs. 'These are remnants of behaviour. This is something that will never happen again. That nest will never be created again.' The corridors of sliding drawers turn into halls of mirrors, multiplying evidence of the things that will never happen again.

'The images I made became remnants of my own behaviour', the filmmaker says.

The name 'night parrot' is contradictory, for parrots are supposedly daytime birds, charismatic and sociable, not reclusive and nocturnal. Parrots talk, says Paul Carter in his book *Parrot,* but only in captivity. 'In the unexpectedness of their utterances, they are unconscious consciences.' What mysteries might the night parrot be able to tell us about ourselves, if only it could be induced to speak? As far back as the Martu Dreaming story, the night parrot was seen once, and then refused to be found. It became a creature of hearsay and rumour, and its desert habitat enhanced its glamour. Like the search for Lasseter's lost gold reef, the search for the night parrot joined the narratives of quest and heroic failure that continue to haunt the white Australian psyche. The poet John Kinsella mines this mythic material in his 1989 collection, *Night Parrots.* In a poem sequence laced with arcane and inscrutable symbolism, he imagines night parrots as the spectral witnesses of encounters between Lasseter and the Babylonian king Nebuchadnezzar.

A more accessible interpretation of the redemptive quest into the desert is Dal Stivens' novel *A Horse of Air*, published in 1969 and the winner of the 1970 Miles Franklin Award, which tells the story of an expedition to search for the night parrot. Its narrator, Harry Craddock, is a grand fool of a man, in the genre of rambunctious, vulnerable, narcissistic, self-questioning male protagonists that dominated the mid-twentieth century American literary landscape in the writings of Saul Bellow, Philip Roth, and Norman Mailer, among others.

But Harry Craddock is Australian, and, while he shares certain characteristics with his American counterparts, he is undone and remade by landscape in a very Australian way. Harry is a wealthy ornithologist, a manic depressive inclined to rants and vendettas and obsessions he can afford to indulge. In 1965, when the novel is set, he is also troubled by the threat of foreign wars, the greenhouse effect, and the environmental damage humans are inflicting on the planet.

'There are strange hells in the mind the desert makes,' says Harry, but he has already created his own 'hells in the mind', and his expedition into the heart of the Gibson Desert in search of the night parrot is a quest to assuage his hungry soul. The desert promises existential revelations, and the night parrot is the embodiment of those revelations.

Constructed on the conceit of an autobiography written post-expedition while Harry is incarcerated in a mental hospital, the novel includes commentary by the psychiatrist who is treating Harry, excerpts from the diary of Harry's wife, Joanna, and comments by the manuscript's editor.

'At my centre is a despair and a passion for the something that I seek,' Harry writes in the half-invented document he concocts to excite and mislead his psychiatrist. Unable to settle for the calm, intelligent companionship of Joanna, Harry instead pursues a girl who will elude him, embarks on a scientific partnership with a colleague who will betray him, and sets out on an expedition that will send him mad and nearly kill him. This journey follows the route taken by the explorer Ernest Giles in 1873, when Alfred Gibson disappeared in the remote part of the Western Australian desert later named for him.

As well as being an excellent bushman, Giles was a classically educated scholar. Giles imagined Arthurian Knights riding through a 'paradaisal glen' in the Australian desert, and named his favourite mare The Fair Maid of Perth, after one of the mounts in the medieval legend. The mare, memorialised by Gibson when he rode her into the mirage and disappeared, reappears in *A Horse of Air* as the hallucinatory vehicle of Harry's resurrection.

The night parrots encountered by Harry's expedition don't fare well. Two are incinerated, and the third secretly killed and refrigerated by Harry's ambitious colleague Tom, who then absconds with the girl Harry fancies. Abandoning the search for night parrots, Harry redirects his quest to finding the remains of Gibson and the mare. He leaves the main party and almost dies, dreaming that he is carried by The Fair Maid of Perth to one of Giles' 'paradisal glens', where he is found by two members of the expedition who follow horse tracks into a narrow gorge. Although the tracks lead in one direction only, there is no sign of the horse that made them.

Back in the asylum, writing his account of what he remembers, Harry comes to terms with his insatiable, questioning nature, but a gratuitous twist at the end of the novel suggests that insight and self-acceptance are to no avail, and that redemption is an illusion — a sentiment that Nugent seems to echo in *Night Parrot Stories*.

Like the quest for the Holy Grail, the search for the Night Parrot is a *Boy's Own* adventure story. Those who fall under the spell of the bird are a cavalcade of male characters that include the humble, the ambitious, the self-serving, the eccentric, and the mad. From the first bird shot in Western Australia in 1845 to the bird photographed in Western Queensland in 2013, the only woman recorded to have participated in the story was Ethel White, wife of Samuel Albert White, a self-funded and self-promoting ornithologist and gentleman explorer, more self-important and less self-aware than his fictional counterpart Harry Craddock. From 1911 until 1917, Ethel accompanied her husband on several expeditions to look for the night parrot. According to a newspaper account in 1913, 'her bush wardrobe consisted of two short skirts and blouses of navy-blue coarse linen, two pairs of high boots with nailed soles, a broad-brimmed felt hat and a change of linen ...'

What her husband wore has not been recorded. What has been recorded is White's offer to the Advisory Council of Science and Industry 'to patrol the East Railway line at different times of the year ...' and, in the interests of collecting, to ... destroy all birds on sight ...' Fortunately for the surviving night parrots, none crossed White's crusading path.

Much of the terrain he covered had been the former hunting ground of Frederick Andrews, whose success in collecting night parrots most likely contributed to its regional extinction. Andrews seems to have been a humble fellow who spent most of his time living in straitened circumstances, camping for extended periods in remote locations and collecting birds, mammals, reptiles, fish, frogs, insects, and crustaceans, which he preserved as he went. This process is filmed in queasy detail for *Night Parrot Stories*, when a bush taxidermist with hands like bear paws stuffs a budgie, peeling back the bird's skin and scooping the eyes out of its skull with the delicacy of a surgeon. Andrews drowned facedown in a billabong, most likely drunk, the pockets of his coat full of beetles he had collected in the days before he died.

Nugent is a master at leaving us to make connections and to create meanings from the cryptic juxtapositions of sound and image. Inscrutable images of a fish and a pair of pink underpants suspended from a road sign signal the absurdist realm of the urban traveller entering the country of strangers. There are moments in the film when the textures of the human voices are as compelling as anything on the screen.

'That was the year we re-lined the kitchen ...'

'You hit plenty of birds on your windscreen out here, but it was just so ugly ...'

'I've never seen a dinosaur, but I don't think it would make me a better person if I had ...'

The pings and hisses of technology are like aural graffiti, while the visual graffiti provides a random script scrawled on the sides of water tanks, abandoned cars, and a table at a roadside stop.

A pair of demountables stand on a concrete slab on a treeless plain under a lowering sky. The demountable on the right appears to be two-dimensional, and the filmmaker enters the flat steel rectangle through a reflective glass door that closes behind him. Inside the windowless cabin, he forages for a book.

'I find myself accompanied by an imaginary fool,' he says. 'Who would bring Shakespeare for entertainment? Its lost language, its arcane prophecies ...'

A window into a different landscape reveals a pair of bustards strutting back and forth, accompanied by the rantings of the mad king from the storm scene in King Lear. *Aha*, I think, the third time I watch the film, *Lightning and hail fell on the two beings who had made the storm to find the bird.*

A wedge-tailed eagle lurches through the mulga, mad eyes glaring as it tries to fly, its broken wing flaring like a monk's cowl as it hops and runs towards the sound of trucks roaring past on a highway just beyond the trees.

And then there's the perfect simplicity of a scene in which the elderly linguist Luise Hercus walks with painful slowness on a gibber plain that trembles with mirage, and a young man brings a chair and sets it down for her. The unstable light, the empty terrain, and the gesture of the young man to the old woman say things about time and contingency and aloneness and humanity that words on a page can't do.

Night Parrot Stories is constructed around the metaphor of absence and the poetics of extinction. It searches for meanings that don't exist, and asks questions that can't be answered. The making of the film becomes the answer to how to make meaning — how to take absences and enigmas and remnants of behaviour, and craft them into something that communicates the inchoate nature of human desire.

Following the masculine trajectories through night parrot county, I began to feel that something was missing. Seductive as I found the search for the unattainable, there had to be more dimensions to the story of the cryptic bird.

I found what I was looking for in a wild blast from the suburban unconscious:

> How fantastic are these
>> familiar suburbs
> when the night parrot
>> is driving my car!

They are the opening lines of 'Scenes From A Marriage 1', the first in a sequence of poems by Dorothy Porter from her 1984 collection *Night Parrot*. Here was the night parrot breaking out of the desert imaginary and bringing a febrile glamour to the urban sprawl:

> when the night parrot
>> is at the wheel
>>> the Top 40
>>>> becomes hot ice,
> and I throw these burning songs
>> from hand to hand
>>> with my pulse
>>>> ticking like a gaudy grenade;
> it's the jumping blood's answer
>> to happiness

the night parrot

    drives slowly

        to counterpoint

            my exhilarated heart's speed.

This bird was a wild card, encrypted in the poetic psyche, leaking its radioactive energy into the night streets. One of the first poems in the collection, 'The Radium Chocolates', has the night parrot suggesting 'the radium cure — green worms/to swim and click/in my blood,/each with a half life/of ten thousand years ...'

The poems are about boredom and desire, disappointment, erotic possibilities, betrayal, illness, and blocked creativity. In the poet's interior dialogue, the night parrot plays multiple parts. It is inspirational and malign, complicit and abject, evasive and accusing. It is at times explicitly male, at times androgynous, a phantom ventriloquist haunting and shadowing the life of its host. Porter's *Night Parrot* poems bring something robust and visceral to the metaphor of elusiveness. The poet doesn't seek the bird; the bird turns up when it pleases. And there's no suggestion of redemption. Instead, the attraction/repulsion the poet's protagonist feels towards the bird is more like a blood sport. The night parrot '... scorches himself/on the cheap, two-bar/radiator/ and for a cruel second/you're bloody delighted ...'

The night parrot squats in the poet's psyche, mocking her attempts to find respite from the needling and buzzing of the creative impulse, sneering at her romantic view of herself:

... I nearly shot

    the night parrot

        for sniggering

            at my image of myself

    as fire on the snow —

Like a jealous spouse, it questions her fidelity, and then compounds the insult by starving, refusing to mate and nest. In an extended analogy of the creative process, the protagonist makes a pact with the night parrot:

don't raid my nest
    he pleaded
        when I had him cornered
just listen to me

let's burn our bridges
    I replied
  let's pair-bond forever —

it's a deal, said the night parrot,
    and sank our courtship
      to the ocean floor;
like Mr Hyde in the mirror
      cordially
to Dr Jekyll in the flesh
    don't meddle, I learnt,
being overcome
    by wonder
      and titanic pressure —

now
    it's quiet and dark
    the night parrot and I
      sit huddled together
        on a secret outcrop of sandstone;
    and like the wide-awake

>   lost child
>   shivering on the silvery rock
>   I don't know
>   if I'm scared stupid
>   or thrilled to the spine
>   and never want to be found.

I already knew and admired much of Porter's work, but the *Night Parrot* poems were a revelation. They combined the apocalyptic and the banal in a voice that mocked its own self-importance and pulsed with the contradictions of its authenticity. Here was evidence of what words could do, a counterpoint to the power of the moving image. This night parrot's habitat was the mind's echo chamber, '... like Mr Hyde in the mirror/cordially/to Dr Jekyll in the flesh ...'

The poet's endeavour is not a heroic quest for redemption and grace; it's a messy wrangle with the trickster inside her head, a furious tango with a taunting, shapeshifting collaborator. I am in awe of the emotional courage it reveals.

Camping at one of the places on my annual desert itinerary, I listen for night parrots. I know they are around these parts, because a pair was found drowned in a stock tank not far away. It's the right sort of country, a semi-saline ephemeral lake surrounded by samphire and old-growth spinifex, and the right time of day, the witching hour when sunset gives way to nightfall. There's rustlings and chirrups, and the sapphire gleam of spiders' eyes when I shine my torch; but if there are night parrots around, they're not letting on. Instead, it's the silence that offers revelations. My own quest has always been a search for ways to bring together my two worlds: this place, which includes the night parrot's country, where the real bird lives, and the cultural legacy that has taught me to read the bird as a metaphor for the elusive and uncanny.

The lake where I'm camped belongs to a system that was once a long, continuous waterway, created according to Warlpiri lore by the rainbow snake's passage. The Fire Dreaming also travels through here. I imagine the dark, unholy imagery of *The Waste Land* transposed from another hemisphere: The Fire Sermon; Death by Water; What the Thunder Said. I copied several lines from 'What the Thunder Said' onto a map I made a long time ago, of an imaginary journey that turned out to be the unconscious preparation for a real journey:

> Who is the third who walks always beside you?
> When I count, there are only you and I together
> But when I look ahead up the white road
> There is always another one walking beside you ...

Maybe it's time to put aside my quest, stop perceiving the absences in each place as a lack, and accept them as spaces where something I don't yet know can happen.

There's a sound in the samphire that could be the fluttering of wings, or the footsteps of an unseen stranger. Or just the wind ruffling the dark.

15

'Napurrula is here'

I've barely arrived in Mulan, having jumped through all the hoops required to gain entry to an Indigenous community in Western Australia during the Covid pandemic, when I'm shanghaied into taking a carload of people to a funeral in Wangkajungka. The community is located on Christmas Creek Station near Fitzroy Crossing, and was the home of Butcher Wise, who has recently died. Butcher was one of the team of stockmen who worked on Mongrel Downs, my family's cattle station in the 1960s, and it's taken for granted that I will want to go to his funeral. Rebecca Johns tells me that she has organised who will be travelling in my car: Anne Ovi, whose father was the cook for the Mongrel Downs stock camp; Anthony Hall, whose father was the head stockman; Anthony's partner, Rowena; and Rebecca herself. She says we can stay in her husband Joe's house when we get there. Joe is away on business somewhere, but Rebecca knows where he keeps the key.

Stuffing the spare pillows and Minkie blankets, the swags, and multiple small bags, shoes, jackets, the boxes of emergency food supplies, and bottles of water and juice into whatever spaces I can find, I reflect on how it would once have caused me real pain to disrupt the orderly arrangement of my travelling gear, which used to be protected by a canopy with zipped canvas sides. Over the years, I've dispensed with the canopy and the rack that replaced it, reverting to a canvas cover customised to fit the drop-side utility tray. The oft-mended cover disintegrated on the drive to Alice, and I've cobbled together a makeshift replacement with a Bunnings tarp and bungee straps.

'What happened?' Rebecca asks me. 'You haven't got money to fix things properly anymore?' She wants to bring her eight-year-old granddaughter, who she insists can sit on her lap in the front seat for the seven-hour drive. I list all the reasons why that can't happen, including the likelihood that my New South Wales number plate will attract the attention of the Kimberley police. Her eyes glaze over before I've finished, but I win the point.

It's dark when we arrive in Wangkajungka. We drop Anthony and Rowena off, and drive to Joe's house. There's a problem with the key, but eventually we get inside. Remarkably, the power is still on, so we have lights and can boil the electric jug. I make tea, and Rebecca chars a chunk of meat under the stove grill. She tells me that at first she was embarrassed about having me stay in the house, but then she thought, *It's Napurrula, it will be okay.* Anne is a statuesque, multi-skilled woman who has found her vocation as the senior ranger in the Mulan women's ranger team. The three of us sit on mattresses in the middle of the living room, and chat about life in the community and how to navigate the troublemakers. We are in bed by eight-thirty.

At ten o'clock, there's hammering on the door. More family has arrived, wanting somewhere to sleep. Mattresses are dragged around and rearranged. I keep my head tucked under my swag cover. 'Napurrula is here,' Rebecca says. 'Kim is here, sleeping.' The noise abates slightly.

Funerals are gruelling events for everyone, including the whitefellas who are co-opted into the proceedings. The filters that usually insulate you from the raw stuff of Aboriginal lives are removed. You wait around, you drive around, pick people up and drop them off, and wait around some more. A formal funeral tends to start hours late and to go on for hours longer than planned. It may incorporate Christian death rituals and Indigenous death rituals, eulogies, wailing, hymns, Spotify renditions of popular music, elaborate colour-coding of mourning dress, an officiating minister from whatever faith the family espouses — generally Catholic, Baptist, Lutheran, or Assemblies of God. Presbyterians and Methodists don't seem to have gained much traction among the desert congregations. Respects must be paid to the sequestered widows, mothers, and aunts of the deceased, who remain in the sorry camp; and if you have the endurance to stay the distance after the body has been buried, there's the ceremonial distribution of blankets, flour, tea, and sugar, and possibly a ritual to identify whether sorcery is implicated in the person's death.

Butcher's family has chosen to wear red and black mourning clothes, and the coffin has a dramatic image, laminated along its sides, of silhouetted stockmen mustering long-horned cattle. Several times, people have asked me if I'm going to speak. I haven't decided, but I've written down what I will say if I do speak — how I remember Butcher as a young man, his quiet, humorous personality, his skill as a stockman and horseman. The truth is, I knew him better as a middle-aged man, when he would call in to Mulan to catch up with family.

People start to speak: restrained whitefellas, emotional blackfellas, the self-important white preacher. A late contingent from Mulan arrives, wailing, conspicuous. I feel that to step up now would be an imposition, and I miss the moment. Almost immediately, I know it's the wrong call. I've got caught up in my white identity, my personal reluctance to assert my credentials. In the two years since my last visit to the desert, I've mislaid my instinct for what is important. In this moment, it's what I represent that matters — the white woman who shared the station days with Butcher, who can bear witness to his experiences as a stockman. I understand this as I let the opportunity pass. I also know that the family won't blame me, that their disappointment will fade into their generic disappointment in whitefellas. I'm just another kardiya who didn't step up when required.

It's dusk by the time I've rounded up my passengers for the long drive home. The preacher got a second wind at the graveside, so the interment of the coffin took a long time. The traditional business will continue well into the night, but I've had enough. The others seem happy to leave, although we won't get back to Mulan until the early hours of the morning. I refuel in Halls Creek, and Rebecca persuades me to buy her a packet of tobacco. Because of the astronomical price of tobacco, it's now sold in ten-gram packets for twenty-five dollars.

'I thought you gave up smoking,' I say, as I add the tobacco to the fuel and food purchase.

'I did,' she says, 'but I started again.'

When I bite into the Mexican chicken wrap I bought as an alternative to deep-fried takeaway, it turns to soggy cardboard and sticks to the roof of my mouth. I hand it into the back seat in case someone wants it. A few moments later, there's the sound of a window opening, and the wrap is thrown out into the dark.

Around midnight, we reach the Three Ways turnoff, the access track to Mulan when the shortcut through the floodout country is too wet or too rough. Rebecca requests a *kumpu* stop, and everyone gets out and wanders off for a pee or a smoke, or both. This was the old road between Balgo and Billiluna. I remember the first time I travelled this way. It was after midnight then, too. Rebecca's father, Rex, aged about twenty, was driving while my father slept in the passenger seat of the LandCruiser. I was tucked into a pile of swags on the back, along with several stockmen and a blue heeler dog. It was the Christmas before I went to boarding school, and the stockmen were heading home to

Billiluna for the long summer break to attend to Law business and other cultural responsibilities.

Of the five people in my car, the fathers of four of us are in that vehicle, along with the child I was. The ghosts keep me company for the final dark miles to Mulan, as my passengers doze around me and the planet tilts through its slow revolution.

16

Wandering with intent

'[A]bility in an essay is multiplicity, infinite fracture, the intercrossing of opposed forces establishing any number of opposed centres of stillness.'

— William Carlos Williams

Of the three occupations — writing, visual art, and map-making — from which I make a precarious living, I find writing by far the most difficult. It's an extended process of hunting and gathering from the resources of the physical world, personal experience, and the imagination, and sifting and winnowing the words until I find meanings I didn't know I was looking for.

As a small child in the company of Aboriginal people, I learned the basics of survival, how to navigate natural hazards, and to take pleasure in the friendly familiarity of the country. When I was older, the bush became a refuge as well, a place where I could escape from the static created by other people, indulge my love of solitude, and exercise my imagination. I conjured stories from fragments of detritus — a bottle gone cloudy with age, a doll's head with a rolling eye, a decaying boot, footprints preserved in the dried mud of a claypan — which imbued the whispering, scratchy landscape with an undertow of human drama. The imaginary world of books and the physical world of the bush together created a realm in which the ordinary intersected with the uncanny. I understood very early that places shape the psyche and influence the behaviour of humans, and that the currents that flow between people are amplified or muffled by landscape.

My first sustained memory of wandering is of trailing a group of Pitjantjatjarra women and children along the top of a sand dune that is a deep orange colour intricately patterned with the activities of all kinds of creatures. I am about five years old, and already I can identify the tracks of snakes, lizards, hopping mice, centipedes, birds, dingoes, kangaroos, camels, goats. The ground is close, and dense with texture and detail — crime scenes of predator and prey, tales of encounters and escapes, a palimpsest of erasures and inscriptions. The dune is pitted with the treacherous conical sand traps of ant lions, each with its huge-jawed monster hiding at the bottom. There's piebald reptile poo, dingo scats, beetles, grasshoppers, grubs, pods and seeds, feathers, and the tiny fanged skulls of rodents.

One of the women calls me to come, points to a plant with fleshy leaves, and says, 'Pullim up!' I tug at the leaves, and a translucent root the size and shape of a carrot emerges from the sand. 'Chewim', the woman says, and I do as I'm told. The texture is fibrous and the taste nondescript, but the root is juicy with stored water.

We follow the dune around the base of stony hills and into a gully that cuts through the hills to a permanent waterhole in the Finke River. The water is tea-coloured and shallow enough for the taller kids to wade in. I dog-paddle among their flailing limbs as they churn up the silty mud, bringing to the surface a multitude of silver fish that they kick onto the bank. Someone has lit a fire of bark and twigs, and several of the larger fish, still flapping, are thrown on the coals. The rest are gathered in tins and buckets. I'm given a very small fish in a milk tin half-filled with water to carry home. Not spilling the water takes most of my attention on the walk back, but I see camels watching us from an adjacent dune, their periscope heads swivelling above the grey hummocks of spinifex as we file past.

Back home, there is some kind of stand-off between my parents. My father is angry, and my mother is unhappy. My little brother is riding his tricycle along the fly-wired verandah and howling at the top of his lungs. Things changed when he arrived. I preferred life the way it was before.

I was an early reader, and keen, but reading didn't become a refuge until I was seven, when my family moved from the tiny railway town of Finke, where I had been an integral member of the polyglot, multi-racial community, to the comparative metropolis of Alice Springs. It was my first experience of a classroom of children my own age and of the savage hierarchies of the playground, where my precocious vocabulary, homemade velvet overalls, and lack of peer-group social skills marked me as an oddity. Between the taunts of my classmates and the public humiliations administered by a punitive female teacher, I was reduced to a state of acute misery. This probably lasted no more than a few months, but my memory of that time is one of boundless desolation until I discovered the local lending library.

A yellow-rendered brick building overhung by scraggly gums and set back on a dusty quarter-acre block, the library was on the same street as the school. For some weeks, walking home at the end of the day, I had noticed children peeling off from the clusters I was excluded from, turning down a path to the little yellow house and disappearing inside. Curiosity overcame timidity, and one day I followed them and found myself in a house made of books. We had plenty of books at home, but this was a revelation. There was an entire room dedicated to children. In my excitement, I forgot my fear, asked the person behind the desk how I could get a borrower's card, and took out my quota of three books, which I swallowed in great gulps over the next few days. When I continued to consume books at this rate, the librarian doubled my quota. I read voraciously and indiscriminately, unsupervised and uncensored, and soon moved on to the adult section of the library. Reading cut me loose into a world not only of adventure and imagination, but also of psychological complexity I perceived but did not understand. This unleashed a hunger in me to discover what went on beneath the surface of things.

During the time my family lived in Alice Springs, I owned or looked after various horses. One of these was a stolid blue roan called Bluey, whose owner was away at boarding school. He was quiet but recalcitrant, and I wasn't especially fond of him, but he was preferable to the evil Shetland pony that had terrorised my earlier years. Bluey was kept on the town common, and on weekends a parent, usually my mother, would drop me off at the edge of the common and I would set out on foot, carrying an apple and a bridle, to look for him. The apple was supposed to help me catch the horse, but I had usually eaten it by the time I found him.

The common was an extensive tract of mulga, ironwood, and eucalypts bounded by the ramparts of the MacDonnell Ranges, and some days I wandered for hours, following tracks that might or might not belong to Bluey, since lots of people kept horses there. It was often when I stopped looking and became immersed in the details of the place — its textures and smells, the chink of birds, the rustle and scurry of lizards, the tracks of native — that Bluey would materialise as a dappled shadow at the edge of the mulga. He would accept the browning apple core with disdain, and hold his head just out of my reach until I wrapped the reins around his neck and dragged his head down so I could get the bridle over his ears, lead him to a stump or anthill, climb onto his bare back, and ride him home.

These days, a parent who let loose a ten-year-old into a hundred acres of scrub in the morning and didn't worry about their whereabouts until dusk would likely be reported to the authorities, but I'm grateful to have grown up at a time when benign neglect was the common form of parenting. I was allowed to wander alone on the common to find a horse, but the wandering became its own purpose. Once I had learned the art of finding the blue horse by not looking for him, I relished the escape from weekend chores and the time to daydream in solitude. If I found Bluey too quickly, I would leave him where he was, knowing that I would find him again when I was ready.

At 5.00 am, my dog begins to pace. He pads from room to room, waking me into his new way of being in the world, distanced from and dependent on me. Mostly I'm touched by his confusion and vulnerability, but sometimes when he paces around the studio, intruding on my concentration while I'm trying to work, I lose patience and shout at him, and he staggers out into the studio garden to get away from me. It's the first time I've had to see a dog through a slow decline, knowing that it will most likely be up to me to decide when it's his time to die. Some mornings when he doesn't wake early and pace, he lies so still I put my hand on his ribs to check that he's still breathing. When I feel his old heart beating under my palm, I'm full of relief that he's still alive, and sorry that he hasn't died peacefully in his sleep.

Before his decline, we used to walk morning and afternoon, several kilometres every day. Pirate would lope ahead on the end of a retractable lead that restrained him from chasing kangaroos but allowed him to sniff and dawdle and dash about, while I used the rhythm of walking to untangle the snarl of sentences in my mind. With the fading of the old dog's brain, the lead is no longer necessary. If he notices the kangaroos, the best he can manage is a token canter that soon runs out of steam. I have to slow my natural pace, and turn back often in case he's got himself turned around and is trotting in the wrong direction. If I whistle, he can't tell where the sound is coming from, which causes him to run faster, so I have to chase him down.

My intention now is for the dog to enjoy the walk and take his time to attend to whatever tickles his old canine brain into activity. The nature of the walking dictates my thoughts — the stopping to wait, the turning back to look, the reminder at every step that time passes, things change, humans outlive dogs. Our walks have become, for me, a meditation on mortality and memory, of paths not taken and work not done.

Looking for mushrooms is a respite from these gloomy pre-occupations. It's the season for field mushrooms, and this year they are so abundant that it's hardly a challenge to find them. I collect only perfect specimens, and only enough for my immediate needs. Pirate is happy to accompany me on the hunts, but he scorns the cooked mushrooms.

The pandemic has circumscribed all forms of travel, and for the first time in years I'm here in autumn, instead of on the road to somewhere in the desert. The lockdown feels like a reprieve, a chance to catch up on writing projects, to slow down and reassess my life/work balance, to complete my outstanding tax return. And it has solved the problem of what to do about my old dog, who has always travelled with me. Now his world of strange, stranded absences mirrors the disorientation that grips the human world, where time and continuity seem ruptured in some irreparable way. His impending death adds an elegiac quality to the feeling of suspended time.

At the end of 2020, in spite of Pirate's frailty, I decide to drive to Queensland for the family Christmas, having missed the previous year because of the bushfires. I have to lift the old dog into the back seat of the ute, and he seems happy and excited to be back in his familiar place. The drive north reinvigorates something of his spirit, but the humid heat, the unfamiliar houses, and the break in routine is too much for him. After a night during which he paces and cries and tries to drink, and I pace and cry alongside him, carrying the water bowl and trying to comfort him, I know the time has come. We are staying on my brother Bob's cattle property in the Numinbah Valley, and he has the usual farm equipment, including a gun. It's better for Pirate to die here, not knowing what's happening, than to take him to a veterinary clinic full of the smells and atmosphere he hates, and to have him injected by a stranger. While my brother digs a grave in the orchard with a mechanical digger, I say goodbye to my old friend and companion. When the grave has been dug, I ask Bob to pull the trigger, and I hold Pirate as he dies.

A few months into the 2020 Covid lockdown, my friend John Carty asked me to help him translate his doctoral thesis on Balgo art into a book for publication. Given the evaporation of my map-making work and the sluggishness of my own writing, I was glad to take on a new project, and the Balgo story was close to my heart. I had first met John in Balgo when he had just embarked on the thesis, and over the years I'd read excerpts from it, and had some idea of the main thrust of his argument. John had long wanted to turn the thesis into a book accessible to the general reader and to the Balgo painters he had written about.

I learned a great deal about the evolution of Balgo painting and painters in the process of wrangling the language of anthropology into the language of the lay reader, but it is the story of one artist's life that haunts me. Matthew Gill grew up in Balgo during the mission era and the transition to self-determination, when the influence of the Catholic Church continued through education, health, and spiritual husbandry. He became a catalyst and a bridge: a communicator between cultures, generations, and genders. He travelled widely, bringing back news of painting from other places, and he was a central figure in the development of the Balgo art movement. Gill was an essayist in the true sense of the word. Like many of his generation, he embraced a Catholicism that had adapted to make room for the cultural practices of the desert, and was active in seeking synergies between the different spiritual traditions.

In 1982, to mark the Easter celebrations, Matthew Gill and his contemporary Greg Mosquito instigated a giant collaborative painting that reinterpreted Christ's final journey as a desert itinerary. The young men, working alongside several senior men, represented the Stations of the Cross as campsites and waterholes, with the route to Calvary, marked by Christ's footprints, following the serpentine pattern of desert iconography. (See colour section.) The ancestral creator snake appears and reappears, inscribing the landscape with the incidents of Christ's last journey. The collaboration is an extraordinary example of integrating systems of belief, and deserves a thesis of its own, but Gill's subsequent drawings take the exploration of culture, identity, and representation into unique territory.

Over the next couple of years, Gill, who was then in his early twenties, embarked on a series of drawings of the Stations of the Cross, using the cross-hatching technique of the Arnhem Land rarrk tradition, and depicting Jesus as Gill's own totemic animal, *kipara* (bush turkey). Gill was captivated by the graphic and figurative possibilities of cross-hatching and X-ray drawing, which he had seen during his travels. The suite of drawings he produced is like nothing else in Balgo art. The bush turkey Christ carries a cross formed from opposing boomerangs and a shield. The heart of the *kipara* is red and alive in the first nine drawings; stilled and monochrome in the final three. In the thirteenth drawing, the Ascension, the body of the turkey is cross-hatched, the heart once again red, but the spread wings bear the concentric circles and tracks of the desert itinerary. (See colour section.)

In a more explicitly self-referential drawing made during the same period, Gill uses his ancestral bird to illustrate the story of the prodigal son, once again employing cross-hatching and incorporating the X-ray technique only hinted at in the Stations of the Cross. Five years later, he replicates the turkey imagery of father and son, still figuratively, but this time using desert iconography and calling the work *Bush Turkey Dreaming*, embedding the biblical narrative in the Tjukurrpa.

John Carty writes, 'Gill's art offers up a profound self-portrait of a man working through the dimensions of his post-mission, post-colonial, Aboriginal Australian self-hood, an artist exploring configurations of identity that transcend concerns with "tradition" or "Aboriginality".

But the art market of the 1980s and 1990s wanted 'traditional' desert paintings, and Matthew Gill's radical and singular exploration of personal identity through figuration, drawing, appropriation, and biblical themes did not meet the criteria for authentic desert art. He was decades ahead of his time. The art emerging from the desert in recent years is astonishingly eclectic, crossing cultures and appropriating imagery, media, and methods with panache and humour. I wonder what Matthew Gill would have made of Vincent Namatjira's ironic portraits of politicians, Kathleen Whiskey's self-portraits with Dolly Parton and Wonder Woman, the extraordinary tree sculptures of the Tjanpi Desert Weavers, and the recent works from the Warlayirti Art Centre by Patsy Mudgedell. Gill strikes me as a deeply serious man. His work is preoccupied with the intersection of the different sacred traditions that produced him, and how they illuminated each other. In a culture that revered obedience to tradition, Gill's art reflects a man thinking outside its limitations.

From his status as a leader of his generation and one of the brightest stars and most interesting artists of the early days of Balgo art, Gill became alienated from the desert-painting movement, as his work was sidelined and ignored. Eventually, he stopped drawing and painting, and left the community where he had grown up and the Kingfisher Dreaming country in which his questing intellect had sought to make sense of a changing world.

He spent time in jail, later fell ill, and died at the age of forty-two. I met Matthew Gill briefly in 2002 when he returned to Balgo for a visit. He was very sick, and at the time I knew nothing of his work or his history, but my impression of him from our short conversation was of a man wise beyond his years, philosophical and sad.

What is it about the Matthew Gill story that touches me so deeply? It's of a kind with Tim Leura's assertion of selfhood in the painting of *Spirit Dreaming through Napperby Country,* and Rusty Peters seeking to accommodate mutually incomprehensible ways of being in *Two Laws, One Big Spirit,* and the *Uti Kulintjaku* women reinterpreting the Jungian archetypes through the story of 'The man in the log'. To me, these episodes represent a spectrum of moments when a fundamentally different world view uses iconographic visual language to invite us to look into the workings of a different universe. They represent windows of missed opportunity, templates for how to step outside the ruthless trajectory of history. Matthew Gill took this a step further, bringing his cross-cultural, Catholic, aesthetically sophisticated skills to the task of examining and synthesising the spiritual traditions of the world he was born into, and exploring his own unique place in that world. I find it heartbreaking that his intellectual courage and questing spirit went unrecognised, swept aside by the behemoth of the art market. Apart from the individual tragedy of his life, his story encapsulates all the lost opportunities to make something wonderful at the interface of cultures.

Eons before, around 20,000 years ago, a group of people crossed a muddy claypan in the cluster of freshwater basins now called the Willandra Lakes. Several small children capered about a group of walking adults. A very tall man ran very fast — the size of his feet and the distance between his footprints suggest he was nearly two metres tall and running at the speed of a modern Olympian. A one-legged man hopped, also at great speed. Several hunters pursued a late-Pleistocene kangaroo. The tracks of two kangaroos and an emu chick have been identified, but most of the 700 prints uncovered near Garnpung Lake are human. It's possible that thousands more lie under the shifting sands that concealed and protected the now exposed tracks for 20,000 years. The sediment in which those Aboriginal ancestors left their trace contained minerals that hardened like concrete. The claypan did not fill again, and the footprints remained hidden until a sharp-eyed young Mutti Mutti woman named Mary Pappin noticed something on the windswept clay surface during a field trip in 2003.

When the scientist Jim Bowler showed photographs of Lake Mungo to the people of Mulan as part of a planned exchange-visit between the custodians of Paruku and Mungo, the fossilised footprints roused a tremor of anxiety among the Mulan elders. Such palpable human traces held a power that artefacts and burial sites did not. I felt it myself, seeing those images for the first time. The people who made the footprints might have walked out of the frame just as the camera shutter clicked, their voices still audible as they disappeared behind the pale hummock of the dune.

A little before the Mungo people left their footprints on the Willandra claypan, a young person picked up and set down a toddler several times while skirting Lake Otero, a playa in the Tularosa Basin in New Mexico. He or she was running, carrying the child on their left hip, apparently delivering it somewhere, since the prints returned along the same route without the accompanying toddler prints or the deeper impression of the left footprint. In the interval between the young human coming and going, several mammoths and a giant sloth crossed their path. The mammoths paid the tracks no attention, but the sloth appears to have dithered, examining the footprints before moving on. Another set of prints from the same era show a human footprint placed deliberately inside those of a giant sloth, possibly by a hunter pursuing the animal. Excavations along the shore of the now dry lake basin have revealed successive layers of footprints, made over several thousand years. The oldest prints lie beneath a layer of grass seeds that have been carbon-dated as 23,000 years old: a time when vast glaciers covered North America, and 7,000 years before humans were previously thought to have occupied the Americas.

One hundred and twenty thousand years ago, in the Nefud Desert in Saudi Arabia, several *Homo sapiens* left their footprints among the fossilised tracks of elephants, camels, wild asses, and giant buffalo. An anatomically modern human left wet footprints on the side of a steep sand dune by the shore of Langebaan Lagoon in South Africa. Dry sand filled the prints and preserved them for 117,000 years. In the mid-1970s, palaeoanthropologist Mary Leakey discovered fossil trackways at Laetoli in Tanzania. Some members of the hominin species *Australopithecus afarensis*, thought to be a likely ancestor of humans, walked through volcanic ash 3.7 million years ago. A few hundred metres away, another creature walked through the same ash at the same time, before a second eruption covered the prints and preserved them. The second set of footprints, initially thought to belong to a bear, has since been re-examined, and suggests that at least one other branch of the proto-human family may have coexisted with *Australopithecus afarensis*.

Bipedalism distinguished the ancestors of the first humans from other primates. The first hominins stood upright, freeing their hands to make tools and weapons and art. Six-million-year-old footprints discovered at a site on the coast of Crete show the characteristics of bipedalism — five toes without claws, the ball of the foot, the big toe parallel to the successively shorter side toes. The prints were made towards the end of the Miocene era, when the Mediterranean Sea dried up, allowing access between Europe and North Africa. For some European scientists, the Cretan footprints are evidence that pre-human hominins evolved in Europe rather than Africa.

The palaeontologist Loren Eiseley was haunted by the glimpse that science offered into the meaning of being human, and brought a visionary, poetic sensibility to the essays that defined his later career. Among those essays is 'The creature from the marsh', in which he describes coming upon footprints at the edge of a swamp on the drowned coast of an un-named tropical country. The prints appear to belong to some transitional human species, the foot imperfectly adapted to walking upright, the arch flat, and the toes long and splayed, the second toe noticeably longer than the first — a remnant of a tree-dwelling primate ancestor. Eiseley is transfixed, wondering if he has discovered an archaic human adaptation surviving in this liminal world in which 'nothing stays put where it began because everything is climbing in, or climbing out, of its unstable environment'. Eiseley contemplates following the creature, and then, prompted by a shadowy memory, takes off a shoe and tests his own bare foot in the print. It fits:

> I had found the missing link. He walked on misshapen feet. The stones hurt him and his belly sagged. There were dreams like Christmas ornaments in his head, intermingled with an ancient malevolent viciousness. I knew because I was the missing link, but for the first time I sensed where I was going.

On a shelf in my studio is a plastic crate of footprints. The sand that held their imprint has been scooped into ziplock bags labelled with the location, the date, and the name of the footprint's maker. Many of the footprints belong to the Walmajarri children I have watched grow up. When I explained to the kids what I wanted, they loved the idea, lining up to make their mark in the white lake sand of their ancestral country. I have collected the footprints of the senior women I have worked with, and the footprints that my nieces, nephews, and brothers made in the red Tanami sand near the limestone maze where we put my parents' ashes. One day I will return the footprints to the places where they were made. Maybe I'll ask their owners to reprint their older, bigger feet in the sand that holds the memory of their younger selves.

Some years ago, I made an artwork consisting of twenty jars of black sand containing a set of my own footprints from a place called Dark Beach on the New South Wales south coast. It's the kind of work that delights some people and baffles others, or makes them angry because they think they are being tricked. For me, it contains the conundrum of presence and absence, the haunting persistence of the ephemeral. Each jar has a word inscribed on it, and, when installed, the work spells out the sentence: 'Each print traps time Tracks the gap between step and breath Holds absence in the lost space of a foot'.

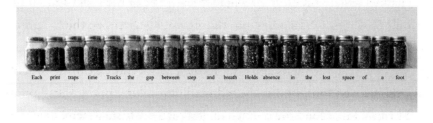

Each print traps time Tracks the gap between step and breath Holds absence in the lost space of a foot

I collected the footprints when I visited the beach with my friend the artist Pam Lofts, who died the following year.

In a remote part of the western Tanami Desert, an ancient waterway decants southwards through a series of ephemeral lakes and underground seepages, trickling from the porous limestone and gathering momentum as it joins other trickles, forming a freshwater stream that continues through limestone and sandstone soft enough to crumble in your fingers. It runs fast and narrow between ti-tree–covered banks until it reaches a bend between low cliffs and dunes, where it slows and flattens into a briny pond. Ducks clatter among the reeds, and camels and wild cattle come to drink. Beyond the pond, the stream continues for a kilometre or so between high red dunes, the sandy banks crusted with leaching salt. The depressions left by the feet of camels and the hooves of cattle contain crystallised plates of salt in the shape of the animals' tracks.

As the dunes flatten and the sand whitens, the spinifex and cassias and eremophilas give way to samphires. The stream splits, and the branches run parallel for several hundred metres before rejoining, creating a narrow island occupied by monstrous termite mounds and a solitary juvenile desert oak, hunched like a dark-cowled monk among the sentinel anthills. The channel bleeds away into the northernmost of several salt lakes, the remains of an ancient drainage system flowing into the heart of the Great Sandy Desert. I've walked the length of the channel several times, from where it leaks out of the rocky limestone hills to where it disappears into the grey sludge between the samphire flats and the white surface of the salt lake.

One year, on my second visit in the space of three months, I found a crystallised footprint in the red sand beyond the pond. Like Loren Eiseley's, my second toe is much longer than my first. When I held the foot-shaped plate of salt against my sole, it fitted.

17

Looking for mushrooms

My mother was not enthusiastic about exercise or nature, but when the right growing conditions for field mushrooms prevailed, some recessive hunter-gatherer gene would assert itself, and she would don one of the cast-off hats no one else wanted to wear, collect her favourite small sharp knife and a bucket, and head off into the bush. She liked eating mushrooms, but her real pleasure was in looking for them, a love she acquired as a child when she went on the hunt with her own mother across the paddocks near their home in the small West Australian town of York. They were the only times she recalled her mother being free of anxiety. Looking for mushrooms was an excuse to spend afternoons wandering with a legitimate purpose, away from the demands of running a boarding house, and the scrutiny and expectations of other people.

Mushrooms, like toadstools, belong to the realm of fable and hallucination. My grandmother had dreams in which she foretold the winners of local horse races, and could describe with accuracy the interiors of houses she had never visited. She developed early-onset dementia and spent her last years in an institution in Perth, where she died one night when she was in her early sixties. On the same night, my mother was woken in Alice Springs by her mother's voice calling her name, Marie, with the peremptory tone she had used when my mother was a child. My grandmother had psychic dreams and saw the future, and my mother heard voices across space and time, but I don't seem to have inherited those abilities.

My mother did pass on her love of mushrooming to me, and I have precious memories of those feelings of separate togetherness: foraging with someone nearby bent on the same task, combined with the disembodied privacy of scanning the ground. When the mushroom season comes around and I set out with my knife and bucket to scan the local hills, I pay homage to the spirits of my mother and grandmother.

Sorting through my mother's papers in the weeks after she died, I found a navy-blue plastic ring binder containing a typed manuscript with the title *I Was Listening: I just didn't hear ya*. I skimmed the chapter headings and read the first few paragraphs, inhaling my mother's distinctive voice:

> I never intended to become a teacher. If I had, in earliest childhood, made a list of possible careers, teaching would have occupied the very last place. How I despised those shining-faced, crawling little frilly girls in my grade four class who fluttered about Teacher and cleaned the blackboard, and filled the inkwells, and announced shyly that they too aspired to her noble profession.

It was the story of her accidental career as a schoolteacher. Her voice was too vivid and alive for me to bear just then, and I put the binder away in a box with the early book drafts, the hand-written rants, and other unpublished papers.

My mother taught all her grandchildren to read before they went to school, determined that no child of her bloodline would be subjected to the word-recognition method she deplored, which had replaced phonics. When she died, the grandchildren painted her coffin with images of the station life they had shared with her — brahman cattle, working dogs, four-wheeler motorbikes, brigalow scrub. A few days before the funeral, I had collected the coffin for the kids to paint and had gone in search of the celebrant who would officiate at the ceremony. My GPS took me into a retirement village with the same name as the street address I was looking for. Driving through the manicured streets, I passed some elderly residents taking a late-afternoon walk. They looked alarmed at the sight of my dark-grey hearse-like hired car with the coffin conspicuous in the back, and I could hear my mother snickering. It was just the sort of dark humour she would have appreciated.

From the age of eight, when she wrote her first novel, *Bobby. Or Jungle Terrors,* my mother's ambition was to be a writer. Her mother used the pages of that literary endeavour to light the kitchen boiler, but my mother was always resilient. On days when some or all of her children were behaving badly, she would announce that if she hadn't had kids she would have written the Great Australian Novel. Later, when she did become a writer, she gave us different names and incorporated us into the stories she wrote.

A decade after my mother's death, I dug out the blue ring binder and read the yellowing manuscript from beginning to end. The story began with how she was coerced into establishing a school at Hooker Creek, the remote Aboriginal settlement in the Northern Territory where my father was acting superintendent at the time I was born. Having given birth to me three weeks earlier in Perth, my mother made the trip to Hooker Creek via Darwin, Katherine, and Wave Hill, by plane, train, and truck, to take up her role as the Missus to my father's role as the Mulleka, or Boss. Nancy Napaltjarri, the self-appointed housekeeper, dominates the early pages of the manuscript:

Having decided that I was highly incompetent in child-care, she also took over my 'proper pretty-fella piccaninny' and bathed Kimmy, washed her nappies, fashioned a coolamon and took her for an afternoon walk, and watched me like a hawk whenever I picked up the baby. Kimmy rewarded her by gurgling 'Nan-tee' about two months before she tried 'Mum-mum' or 'Dad-dad', which stands to reason, because I only got a chance to talk to her in the evenings after Nancy went home.

Nancy was a traditional Warlpiri woman who had been born in the bush, but she had been trained by the previous superintendent's wife, and she had strong views on how a proper Missus should behave:

'Chuckim trouser, Missus. Puttim dress allasame proper lady!'
'No more eatim beer, Missus. Beer belong Mulleka, no-good bugger!'

All men were 'no-good bugger' or 'poor bugger' to Nancy.

'Chuckim cigret. Proper lady can't smokim.'

Nancy also supervised a team of house girls to do the small amount of housework my parents generated. When an eleven-year-old boy called Lindsay, who had been to school in Yuendumu, suggested my mother start a school, the entire community supported it. My mother had time on her hands, and the prospect of someone harnessing the twenty-or-so kids between six and twelve who also had time on their hands, which they generally spent making utter pests of themselves, was endorsed and acted on before my mother had a chance to say she'd think about it. Nancy's husband, Billy-poor-bugger, carved a bespoke nulla nulla that he presented on the first day of school, 'for belting cheeky-bugger students'.

The Northern Territory education department provided some basic resources for the school, but made it clear that there would be no salary. Undaunted, my mother made up a curriculum that consisted of Writing, Arithmetic, English, Reading, Drawing, Story Time, and Singing. My mother was tone deaf, so my father, who played the guitar, was responsible for the singing lessons. Each day, my mother learned several Warlpiri words from Nancy, and wrote them down so she could teach the kids to write the Warlpiri words and their English equivalents. There was no formal Warlpiri orthography at the time — in the 1950s, Warlpiri itself was spelt Walbiri or Wailbri — so, with advice from the incumbent anthropologist, Mervyn Meggit, my mother created a local standardised spelling of the language. In the process, she solved the mystery of why there were many more people recorded as residents of Hooker Creek than actually lived there. Since the northern Warlpiri had been relocated from Yuendumu, various government officials had written the Aboriginal names as they heard them, resulting in multiple versions of the same individual.

My mother also learned to speak the Kriol that people used to communicate across the cultures. Choosing *Goldilocks and the Three Bears* for her first attempt to tell the kids a story in Kriol was, in retrospect, not the best choice:

I began, 'One day three bears bin sit down longa little house.'

'Wotname bear?' asked Billy, with a puzzled frown.

'Him big animal, no more longa this country, big allasame bullock, gottim fur allasame kang'roo, nose allasame puppy dog, big mob teeth.' It was the best I could do, and I drew a bear on the board and coloured it brown.

Lindsay's hand went up.

'Missus, whichway bear go longa house? Hanimal no more gottim house.'

'This mob gottim house all right — nother country, different way. This one Daddy bear, Mummy bear, Bubba bear. Mummy bear bin makim porridge for breakfast. Him hotfella, so they bin go walkabout lettim get cool one.'

'Bear eatim porridge?' began Lindsay, still dissatisfied with the house explanation. 'Mightbe you gonna say this one bear talk-talk allasame usfella?'

Light dawned. Lindsay must have heard this story before, and he hadn't accepted it then, and was going to get to the roots of it this time.

'Lindsay', I said, 'you go find Mulleka, tellim give you lolly tin so Missus can give lolly longa good kid.' It ought to take him some time to find Joe, and maybe I could finish the story while he was away.

'Little quee-ai gottim yella hair bin come up longa house. Him bin puttim finger longa porridge belong Daddy bear — hot one. Him bin puttim finger longa porridge belong Mummy bear — cold one. Him bin puttim finger longa porridge belong Bubba bear — proper good one. Him bin eatim all up.' I decided to skip the chairs bit.

'Then him bin go longa swags belong bears.'

Fagan interrupted me. He stared at me with big brown eyes and said gently, 'Missus, you gammon, bear no more gottim swag!'

'Him gottim blanket allasame puppy dog,' I stuttered.

'Might be im stinkin one, three bear bin sleep,' contributed Gracie.

My story was getting shot to pieces, but I struggled on. 'Little quee-ai, we callim Goldilocks, bin lie down. No more likim blanket belong Daddy bear, no more likim blanket belong Mummy bear...'

'Me know!' Gracie shrieked. 'quee-ai bin go sleep longa blanket belong Bubba bear.'

'No more,' yelled Georgie, 'too much gottim flea, allasame puppy dog.'

'Three bears bin come back!' I yelled. There was a hush. Little girls sucked in their breaths and said 'Ooh-ah.' Through the window I could see Lindsay approaching with the bribe-tin.

I finished with a rush. 'Three bears bin growl-growl, Goldilocks bin wake up, jump up quickfella, bin run away. Come on in, Lindsay. One lolly each, and then all change your clothes and run home quickfella.'

I reclaimed the lolly tin and staggered up to the house for a cup of tea.

The second time my mother started a school, it was intentional, but she didn't plan to be the teacher. My father's new job as a stock inspector had brought us to the tiny railway town of Finke, and when I turned five my mother started me on correspondence lessons with the School of the Air. She soon found herself also teaching the eldest son of Lorna, the Pitjantjatjarra woman who minded my rambunctious one-year-old brother. My mother's plot to establish a school and free herself to write backfired when the territory education department agreed to support a one-teacher school as long as she agreed to teach in it. This time, they offered her a salary. The existence of a school in the town meant that the railways could employ men with families, and the population of Finke doubled in the space of a couple of months. Several of the families were assisted migrants on a two-year government work program, and along with the standard territory mix of Anglo-Celtic and Aboriginal students, my mother's classroom included a German brother and sister, a Czech girl, and the publican's extensive tribe, whose surname had its origins somewhere in east Asia.

The school supplies did not include a library. A school library, my mother discovered, was the responsibility of the Parents and Citizens Association:

Our Ps and Cs were, for the most part, poverty-stricken fettlers just surviving on the basic wage, or Pitjantjatjarra tribespeople living in humpies in the sandhills. All but four of the children were on the free-school-book list, and you had to be dirt-poor to get that.

I sat down with my clever grade five girl, Marion, and we compiled a list of 250 story books. Joe and I were regular clients of Angus and Robertson Bookshop in Sydney. I sent them the list with instructions to forward the books to Finke, and the bill to the Education Department in Darwin. They did. The cartons of books arrived on the Ghan. Two fathers erected bookshelves. Kids covered, I indexed, and we were in business. Then the blister arrived. '... unorthodox ... unprecedented ... prior permission ... requisition forms ... proper channels ... responsibility of the Ps and Cs ... how do you plan to raise the money ...?'

I didn't. Possession was nine-tenths of the law, and I had twenty-two elated little scrubbers prepared to do battle for the other tenth. I sat down at the typewriter, drew on all my powers of evocative prose to describe our embattled school hall — boys with shanghais stationed at every window, girls filing Lassie's teeth for the rear-guard ankle-nip, Teacher and Bubs chained to the books in question. Besides, I said, what would you do with the books if you did get them back, already covered, indexed, laughed and cried over?

My mother's teaching stint in Finke ended two years later with the arrival of my sister, who was born at the same time as Lorna's youngest son. Like Nancy at Hooker Creek, Lorna belonged to the lineage of powerful, charismatic Aboriginal women who influenced and enriched the life of my family. The chapter in my mother's manuscript that heralds our next move — to Alice Springs — begins:

I was sitting on the verandah nursing baby Tracey with baby Johnny lying in his coolamon at my feet. I was minding Johnny for Lorna because it was Trackers' pay day. I always minded Johnny on Trackers' pay day. The police trackers were paid twenty pounds once a month, and on that day Lorna foregathered with the rest of the Aboriginal population to play cards. She brought the baby over and borrowed ten bob from me. At sundown she would return, peel a ten-bob note from her roll, return the stake, and collect the baby.

Five years on, when my father had given up his job as a stock inspector and taken on the project of establishing a cattle station in the Tanami, Lorna contacted my mother. By this time, she was a widow subsisting on a pension, struggling to hold onto her money under the pressure of kinship demands. So when she got news that the family were moving out bush, she asked if she could bring her two youngest boys and join us. My mother set up a classroom on the homestead verandah, sent away for the appropriate correspondence lesson sets, and enrolled my younger siblings and Lorna's boys in School of the Air. She and Lorna re-established the pattern they had developed in Finke, with my mother teaching the whitefella skills of reading and writing and arithmetic, and Lorna teaching the blackfella skills of reading the country.

Before we moved to the Tanami, we spent the intervening years in Alice Springs, my father having applied for a transfer from Finke. A government house was available in Alice, but it was for a schoolteacher. There was a vacancy for a French teacher at the town's only high school. If my mother was willing to take on the job, my father's transfer was a certainty.

Like most of her generation, my mother had studied French at school, and had a sound working knowledge of the language. The high school only taught classes to third-year level, after which students who wanted to complete their secondary education went to boarding school in the south. My mother's French was more than adequate to requirements. Teaching it to Alice Springs teenagers turned out to be one of the highlights of her teaching life:

> I would have taught the French classes for no pay at all, I enjoyed them so much. I had a permanent classroom, with a small bookcase and a table with a gramophone and French records and comics. The kids were unsophisticated, and TV was a thing of the future, and to learn a foreign language was to take a step into a mysterious new world.
>
> I was warned about the terrible trio in the Junior French class. Gene (for genius), Brains, and Prof. They were inseparable, very bright young gentlemen of fifteen, who added a dimension to their school careers by searching out teachers' weaknesses and exploiting them in fiendishly clever ways. The headmaster didn't seem to have much time for them; he said they were far too smart for their own good. What had they done to him, I wondered?
>
> If I hadn't been forewarned I would have come a cropper the first day. The lesson they were working on required a composition in French — 'A day in the life of a pirate'. I asked them to do it for homework. Gene's two pages of perfect French related the most lurid, debauched 24 hours, and implied with Gallic subtlety incidents which no fifteen-year-old should even suspect. Briefly, the pirates captured a ship carrying a company of ballet dancers, who were no better than they should be, abducted the damsels, sailed away and made merry, consuming vast quantities of food and beer. In later years it occurred to me that he might have copied it from a spicy French novel. If the Head hadn't made that remark in the staff room I might have marched the brat to the office and sealed my fate. Instead, I thought a bit, marked the essay ten out of ten, and wrote in French — 'Excellent French, but your pirates are a bit sissy. In my day they drank rum.'

During the time in Alice, my mother taught French, English, and geography, with a short break when my youngest brother was born. She briefly filled the position of head of the school, on a female teacher's pay-rate, which in the 1960s was lower than that of a first-year male teacher. I still encounter people in Alice Springs, a little older than I am, who tell me that my mother was the best teacher they had, the person who saw their individual qualities, scholastic and otherwise, and taught them to believe in themselves.

The narrative in the blue binder glosses over the difficulties of the Tanami years, telling instead a story of adventure and discovery and wonder. My mother presents her teaching role as a minor part of the education provided by the desert world and station life; but without the focus on kids and teaching, I doubt she would have stayed. There's no hint of this in the pages of the manuscript. She belonged to a generation that didn't talk about the darker aspects of life and family, and in any case she was by temperament an incurable optimist. It was one of the things that infuriated me when I was a teenager. My double life of shifting between worlds began back then, and it's a legacy I still carry today. I lost sight of my mother during those years; I was at boarding school, or university, or working in the stock camp, or making solitary sorties into the bush. It was only in the rare moments when I thought she might leave that I saw her properly and understood that without her everything would come apart.

By the time we left the Tanami to take up 26,000 acres of box gum, ironbark, and brigalow scrub in the cattle country of Central Queensland, my mother had spent almost a decade outside the formal education system. It was the early 1970s, and within a year of moving to Queensland, the market for beef collapsed. My mother got a teaching job at the high school in a nearby mining town. She stayed in town during the week, and spent weekends and holidays on the station. Her wages kept the family afloat, and by the time the market recovered, she had become attached to her independent parallel life. She didn't like the changes in education that had taken place since she'd last taught in a proper classroom, but her single teacher's accommodation and a routine with spare time that didn't involve other people gave her the space to write. And she was writing — not the Great Australian Novel of her dreams, but a weekly column for a rural newspaper, *The National Farmer*, about the trials and triumphs of life on the land. *The National Farmer* shut down a long time ago, but my mother's columns were collected into two books, *Bleating About the Bush* and *Back at Sundown*. The best of those pieces still make me laugh aloud.

Fourteen years of teaching are telescoped into the last thirty pages in the blue binder. There's none of the humour, the delight in detail, the self-deprecation, and the finely honed language of the early chapters. My mother's ability to send up the absurdities of bureaucracy, her joy in the achievements of her pupils, her levity, and her inventiveness are gone. The story has become a tirade against the failures of the education system and a rant against changes she finds intolerable. For my mother, teaching has become a straitjacket of performance indicators and bell curves and stand-offs against teachers with different political positions. She has turned into a seething intransigent whose determination to see things through reads like bloody-mindedness rather than steadfast commitment.

The final paragraph tells me when the manuscript was completed:

When I retire next year I shall miss them all. Coaching? Tutoring? Oh, I think not. For some time now I've been thinking of continuing my career. It is, after all, just over fifty years since I penned my first novel, and I really think it's time I began the second one.

Salut, kids. It was nice knowing you.

My mother retired from teaching in 1988. She was sixty-two years old. Two years later, my father was killed in a helicopter-mustering accident on the station. In the nineteen years between my father's death and my mother's, she wrote memoir, history, novels, and children's books. All of them drew on the experiences of the life she had shared with my father.

In the days leading up to her death, my mother entered a feedback loop with the novel she was reading, thinking she was both a character in the story and the narrative's creator, writing her life to the last. I'm sure she didn't anticipate that the story would end with her dying. Her last meal before she died was mushroom soup, which she pronounced the best she'd ever eaten.

When I finished reading, I put the blue ring binder containing my mother's manuscript into the plastic crate with her other unpublished writings. I had resisted my mother's influence when I was growing up, for reasons that seemed important at the time. Now I could feel that influence in every aspect of my life, and was glad of it.

Acknowledgements

As always, many thanks to my editors, Margot Rosenbloom and Tamsin Wagner, for their commitment to making my writing the best it can be. To work with them is to participate in a conversation that challenges, amplifies, and clarifies what I want to say and how to say it. I'm deeply grateful to them for their willingness to travel with me through the minefields I traverse.

Thanks also to my publisher, Henry Rosenbloom, for his faith in my work, and his forensic attention to commas.

While the essays in this collection reflect my own ideas and observations, many of those ideas and observations have been teased out and honed through conversations with friends and colleagues. They know who they are, and I am endlessly grateful to them for hearing out my rants and ruminations.

Sources

Abraham, Nicolas and Torok, Maria. 1994. *The Shell and the Kernel*. Chicago: The University of Chicago Press.

Bardon, Geoffrey. 2004. *Papunya: a place made after the story*. Melbourne: Miegunyah Press.

Carter, Paul. 2006. *Parrot*. London: Reaktion Books.

Carty, John. 2021. *Balgo: Creating Country*. Crawley, WA: UWA Publishing.

Chatwin, Bruce. 1980. *The Songlines*. London: Jonathan Cape.

Darwin, Charles. 1859. *The Origin of Species*. London: John Murray.

Davenport, Sue, Johnson, Peter and Yuwali. 2005. *Cleared Out: First contact in the Western Desert. Canberra: Aboriginal Studies Press*.

Davidson, Robyn. 1980. *Tracks*. London: Jonathan Cape.

Dean, Bentley and Butler, Martin. 2009. *Contact*. Sydney: Contact Films.

Dillon, Brian. 2018. *Essaying: On form, feeling and non-fiction*. New York: New York Review Books.

Eiseley, Loren. 1971. 'The creature from the marsh' in *The Night Country*. New York: Scribner.

Eliot, T.S. 1922. *The Waste Land*. New York: Boni & Liveright.

Gibson, Ross. 2015. *Changescapes: complexity, mutability, aesthetics*. Crawley, WA: UWA Publishing.

Griffiths, Jay. 2012. 'The Fisher King'. *Orion Magazine*.

Herbert, Xavier. 1975. *Poor Fellow My Country*. Sydney & London: William Collins Publisher.

James, Diana. 2015. 'Tjukurpa time', in *Long History, Deep Time: deepening histories of place*, McGrath, Ann and Mary Anne Jebb, Mary Anne (eds.). Canberra: ANU Press and Aboriginal History Inc.

Jones, Philip. 2007. *Ochre and Rust*. Adelaide: Wakefield Press.

Kinsella, John. 1989. *Night Parrots*. Fremantle, WA: Fremantle Arts Centre Press.

Kowal, Emma. 2015. *Trapped in the Gap: doing good in Indigenous Australia*. New York: Berghahn Books.

Lawrence, D.H. 1913. *Sons and Lovers*. London: Gerald Duckworth and Company.

Lawrence, D.H. 1920. *The Lost Girl*. London: Martin Secker.

Lawrence, D.H. 1923. *Kangaroo*. London: Martin Secker.

Malory, Thomas. 1956. *Le Morte d'Arthur*. New York: Everyman's Library.

Neale, Margo (ed.). 2017. *Songlines: tracking the Seven Sisters*. Canberra, ACT: National Museum of Australia Press.

Ngaanyatjarra, Pitjantjatjara, Yankunjtjatjara Women's Council. 2020. *Tjanimaku Tjukurpa: how one young man came good*. Alice Springs, NT: Ngaanyatjarra Pitjantatjara Yankunytjatjara Women's Council.

Ngaanyatjarra, Pitjantjatjara, Yankunjtjatjara Women's Council. 2022. *Tjulpunya munu Walpanya Tjitji Kutjara, Iwara Kutjara: two children, two roads*. Alice Springs, NT: Ngaanyatjarra Pitjantatjara Yankunytjatjara Women's Council.

Nugent, Robert. 2016. *Night Parrot Stories*. Mitchell, ACT: Ronin Films.

Olsen, Penny. 2018. *Night Parrot: Australia's most elusive bird*. Clayton South: CSIRO Publishing.

Pike, Andrew and McGrath, Ann. 2014. *Message from Mungo*. Mitchell, ACT: Ronin Films.

Porter, Dorothy Featherstone. 1984. *The Night Parrot*. Wentworth Falls, NSW: Black Lightning Press.

Rothwell, Nicholas. 2013. *Belomor*. Melbourne: Text Publishing.

Stivens, Dal. 1970. *A Horse of Air*. Sydney: Angus & Roberston.

Stow, Randolph. 1958. *To the Islands*. London: MacDonald and Co.

Stow, Randolph. 1965. *Tourmaline*. London: MacDonald and Co.

Stow, Randolph. 1965. *The Merry-go-round in the Sea*. London: MacDonald and Co.

Stow, Randolph. 1967. *Midnite*. Melbourne: Cheshire.

Stow, Randolph. 1979. *Visitants*. London: Secker & Warburg.

Virilio, Paul. 1991. *The Aesthetics of Disappearance*. New York: Semiotext(e).

Walsh, Fiona and Mitchell, Paul. 2002. *Planning for Country: cross-cultural approaches to decision-making on Aboriginal lands*. Alice Springs, NT: IAD Press.

White, Patrick. 1957. *Voss*. London: Eyre & Spottiswoode.